ADDRESSING TENSIONS AND DILEMMAS IN INCLUSIVE EDUCATION

Based on extensive research, *Addressing Tensions and Dilemmas in Inclusive Education* presents a contemporary and critical analysis of the interaction between different perspectives and positions in the field of inclusive education.

Referring to existing attitudes on the education of children and young people with learning difficulties and disabilities, Professor Norwich argues that despite the appeal of inclusion as a single powerful position, its practical realisation involves tensions and dilemmas that have to be addressed and resolved. This core analysis is illustrated by a review of relevant national and international concepts, principles, research and practices drawing on literature in areas of current interest and concern, such as:

- identification and classification;
- current national and international conceptions;
- pedagogic and curriculum issues;
- organisation of schooling;
- parental and student perspectives;
- the contribution of research to policy and practice.

Engaging with the fundamental issues in the field and providing a coherent perspective that recognises and justifies the interconnection between specialised and general school provision, this accessible and timely book will be of interest to all researchers and students of inclusive education.

Brahm Norwich is Professor of Educational Psychology and Special Educational Needs at the University of Exeter, UK.

ADDRESSING TENSIONS AND DILEMMAS IN INCLUSIVE EDUCATION

Living with uncertainty

Brahm Norwich

Routledge
Taylor & Francis Group
LONDON AND NEW YORK

First published 2013
by Routledge
2 Park Square, Milton Park, Abingdon, Oxon OX14 4RN

Simultaneously published in the USA and Canada
by Routledge
711 Third Avenue, New York, NY 10017

Routledge is an imprint of the Taylor & Francis Group, an informa business

© 2013 Brahm Norwich

The right of Brahm Norwich to be identified as author of this work has been asserted by him in accordance with sections 77 and 78 of the Copyright, Designs and Patents Act 1988.

All rights reserved. No part of this book may be reprinted or reproduced or utilised in any form or by any electronic, mechanical, or other means, now known or hereafter invented, including photocopying and recording, or in any information storage or retrieval system, without permission in writing from the publishers.

Trademark notice: Product or corporate names may be trademarks or registered trademarks, and are used only for identification and explanation without intent to infringe.

British Library Cataloguing in Publication Data
A catalogue record for this book is available from the British Library

Library of Congress Cataloging in Publication Data
Norwich, Brahm.
Addressing tensions and dilemmas in inclusive education : living with uncertainty / Authored by Brahm Norwich.
pages cm
Includes bibliographical references and index.
1. Inclusive education. I. Title.
LC1200.N67 2013
371.9'046--dc23
2012051066

ISBN: 978-0-415-52847-4 (hbk)
ISBN: 978-0-415-52848-1 (pbk)
ISBN: 978-0-203-11843-6 (ebk)

Typeset in Bembo
by Saxon Graphics Ltd, Derby

Printed and bound in Great Britain by
TJ International Ltd, Padstow, Cornwall

CONTENTS

Acknowledgements   *vi*

1 Setting the agenda   1

2 Special educational needs, barriers and disability   13

3 Classification and identification of special educational needs or disability in education   31

4 Inclusive curriculum issues   54

5 Inclusive pedagogy   73

6 Inclusive schooling   92

7 Parents and children: participation, partnerships and preferences   113

8 Philosophical and research issues   130

9 Conclusions   154

References   *165*
Index   *182*

ACKNOWLEDGEMENTS

I appreciate the comments of colleagues and students who read draft chapters of this book: Rupert Wegerif, Sam Carr, Margie Tunbridge, Hazel Lawson, Alison Black, Andrew Richards and George Koutsouris. Many thanks also to my colleagues and students for engaging in discussion and debate over the issues examined in this book.

1
SETTING THE AGENDA

Introduction and context of the book

The field of inclusive education has developed internationally into a very influential position on the education of children and young people with difficulties and disabilities. The aim of this book is to present a broad contemporary and critical analysis of the field. Though inclusive education has a strong intuitive ethical appeal, and has been called a 'passionate intuition' (Pirrie and Head, 2007), it involves tensions and dilemmas that have to be addressed and resolved. However, this is not a book about inclusion in its most general sense of going beyond disability and being about education for all (UNESCO, 2001; Ainscow et al., 2006). It is specifically about how such generalised ideas about inclusive education deal with issues in the education of children with disabilities and difficulties, what has come in recent decades to be called in some countries special needs education. The outcome of this analysis will then reflect back on the coherence and usefulness of more generalised ideas about inclusive education. The book will therefore analyse some of the key areas: models of disability, identification and classification of disability, curriculum, pedagogy, organisation of provision/placement, philosophical issues (about rights, needs, knowledge and research) and pupil participation and parental choice. The analysis will draw on literature from across different disciplinary perspectives, including sociological, psychological, philosophical, health and educational theory. Although grounded on policy and practice in England, the book refers to and draws on the Scottish and international literature about other countries as well as the international United Nations-based system.

The approach that I take has several features. First, the analysis draws on the different disciplinary traditions in the field in an open and even-handed way. Second, the analysis will question some distinctions, while making other important ones and reflecting on core basic issues. For instance, there is often a tendency to assume uncritically certain distinctions as oppositions (medical versus social model, integration versus inclusion); I aim to examine such distinctions and consider more nuanced and refined assumptions. Third, the analysis highlights the links between diverse and sometimes opposing perspectives and argues for the value of recognising these links. But, the primary feature of the book is its recognition of several key values and philosophical tensions that permeate the education of those with disabilities and difficulties, as part of wider tensions about values within education, and the importance of addressing these tensions. More will be said about these tensions later in this chapter. The book examines theoretical rather than practical matters in the field, but it does so in the expectation that the conclusions will frame how practical issues are approached and decisions made.

There has been a considerable growth of interest in inclusive education since the 1990s (UNESCO, 1994; UNESCO, 2001; Armstrong et al., 2010). In many countries the use of 'inclusive' language has followed the UN conventions and declarations, though some Scandinavian ones, who were pioneers in provision for children with disabilities and difficulties, have tended to use other terms. For example, Sweden has used the term 'school for all' and Denmark 'differentiation' (EADSEN, 2011). In Chapter 6 there is a brief examination of how the term 'inclusion' came to be used, but it is important to note that its use is fairly recent. For example, the terms 'inclusion' and 'inclusive education' came into use in the UK following the UNESCO Salamanca Statement (UNESCO, 1994). This is shown by the lack of any entries for the terms 'social inclusion' or 'inclusive education' in the title or abstract of academic papers and entries between 1977 and 1991 in the British Education Index (BEI; a leading UK database of academic and research publications in education). After the Salamanca Statement in 1994 there was a gradual growth of publications about social inclusion and inclusive education, with 90 per cent of the BEI publications published after 2000. However, though the use of inclusion/inclusive is recent, it is based on old and established values. Inclusion can be seen to represent a contemporary mixture of the values of equal opportunity, social respect and solidarity. Along similar lines, Ameson et al. (2010) identified the values associated with inclusion in a European context as: 1) access and quality, 2) equity and social justice, 3) democratic values and participation and 4) the balance between unity and diversity. It is this mix of values that can lead to significant ambiguities in its meaning and use (Barton, 2003) and to the tensions that will be examined in this book.

Theoretical concerns about inclusive education

Not only has inclusive education become internationally pervasive (e.g. United Nations Conventions of the Rights of Persons with Disability: Article 24: United Nations, 2006), but it has also come to be seen as self-evidently a 'good thing' in a similar way that democracy or human rights have come to be self-evidently good (Fagan, 2005). Its adoption has occurred despite the ambiguity that can be seen in the analysis below of the key themes in various definitions or characterisations of inclusive education (Clarke et al., 1995; Thomas, 1997; Rouse and Florian, 1996; Farrell, 2000; Barton, 1997; Sebba and Sachdav, 1997; Barton, 2003; Mittler 2000):

- accepting/valuing/extending scope to all;
- not leaving anyone out;
- school reorganisation/problem-solving organisation;
- promoting fraternity;
- enhancing equal opportunity;
- listening to unfamiliar voice/empowering;
- active participation in school life;
- a road without end;
- not an end in itself but a means to inclusive society.

It is often unclear which combination of themes defines what is inclusive education and whether some themes are inconsistent with other ones. Some inclusion theorists have recognised this ambiguity and suggested that we talk about various inclusions rather than inclusion (Dyson, 1999). Ainscow et al. (2006) in their discussion of inclusive education also recognise tensions over the definition: whether to keep an open mind about the meaning of inclusion and how we can know what it is and support it without a clear definition. But though admitting that 'we faced this tension directly as we began our work in schools' (p. 22), these authors had no more to say about this tension.

Nevertheless, these authors have developed a useful typology that shows the progression from defining inclusion in terms of narrower learner characteristics (SEN/disability and behaviour) to more inclusive characteristics (groups that are vulnerable to exclusion) and then by reference to 'all' and finally to value principles (see Chapter 6 for more details). The effect of defining inclusion, as they do, as about everybody's learning guided by abstract values, is that it distances inclusive education from the specific circumstances of disability and difficulties. Disability becomes one amongst various facets of diversity, such as ethnicity, gender, second language learning and socio-economic disadvantage. This can have the effect of oversimplifying the differences between the various facets of diversity (Shakespeare, 2006); what has been seen as a homogenising effect on differences (Cigman, 2007b).

This is where a gap also develops between ideals and practices. The prescriptive definition of inclusive education (for instance, UNESCO, 2009 guidelines on inclusive education) departs from the common usage of inclusive education as predominantly associated with SEN/disability. Some inclusion theorists have noted and regretted this (Slee, 2010). It was also evident in an analysis I conducted for this book of the proportion of all papers and entries about 'inclusion' in English language education databases that are about SEN/disability, gender or ethnicity. In an analysis of the UK BEI, Australian education index and US (ERIC) databases between 3 and 15 times as many papers on inclusive education or inclusion were about SEN/disability as about gender or ethnicity. Though this shows that gender and ethnic issues are studied much less in terms of the language of inclusive education or inclusion than disability/SEN, it does not imply that inclusion cannot be used in this wider 'for all' sense. However, doing so carries the risks of not recognising that different education approaches and considerations may apply across these areas of difference. There is also the risk that the interests of those with disabilities might be secondary to or overlooked when pursuing other less minority interests; for example, gender and socio-economic class interests (Miles and Singal, 2010).

The move away from learner characteristics in definitions of inclusive education is partly about avoiding the definition of differences in terms of challenge or 'difficulties', what is often presented as the rejection of the 'deficit model'. For example, Slikwa (2010) presents the progression of ideas about difference as going from homogeneity to heterogeneity to diversity. In homogeneity, learners are seen as similar and treated as such; in heterogeneity, adjustments are made for 'difficulties'; in diversity (the inclusive notion), difference is seen as a resource and opportunity. So, the language of diversity deliberately turns away from 'difficulties' even though some research shows that for some people disability is experienced as 'difficult differences' (e.g. Rogers, 2007). This reflects a tendency in some versions of inclusive education to deny the challenges and difficulties associated with disability, as will be examined further in Chapters 2 and 3.

Inclusive education has its basis in the social model of disability (Barton, 1997; Thomas and Loxley, 2001). This has been defined in opposition to the medical or deficit model and as having educational implications for the transformation of the school system. In this position, inclusivity comes to be seen as opposed to providing special provision, defined as additional provision to what is generally provided (Florian, 2010). This is the assumed opposition between inclusivity, which relates to a social level of analysis, and additionality, which relates to an individual level of analysis. Here is an example of the point made above about how from an inclusive education position there are different and opposing perspectives: inclusivity versus additionality. What follows is an argument to show how links between perspectives can be made, an example of a more general position developed in this book. What counts as additional provision (for children with disabilities/difficulties) is relative to what is generally provided. As will be discussed in Chapter 5, if generally provided teaching for most children already involves what a child with a disability requires, then there is no need for additionality. From this it follows that the more a school or class has inclusive provision, the less additionality is required. This is one way in which additionality links to inclusivity. But inclusivity also links to additionality in another way. Inclusivity is a principle of adapting the general system to the diversity of learners. If designing education for diversity means design for the range of differences in a group of learners, this also has to take account of the individuality of learners. This implies that inclusivity requires a response to individuality. In this way, inclusivity requires extending general provision which some may call adding to or adapting provision. This is an example of the kind of links between social and individual levels of analysis to be discussed further in Chapter 7.

Another feature of inclusive education is its rejection of specialisation in the use of categories of disorder or difficulties, in curricula, teaching approaches and educational provision settings. This raises questions about when specialised or differentiated aspects of the system are excluding and humiliating and when they are not; when they serve the interests and requirements of people with disabilities and difficulties as seen from their own perspectives. This is one of the central issues and tensions addressed in this book, what has been called dilemmas of difference (Minow, 1990; Norwich, 2008). To resolve this dilemma in its various forms, as will be discussed in several chapters, is to combine, integrate or connect elements of the common and differentiated or generic and specialised elements of the system, what has been called a principle of connective specialisation (Norwich, 1996).

Some inclusive theorists have also expressed concerns about how inclusive education has become assimilated and neutralised by its policy adoption by national government and by international organisations. Allen and Slee (2008) describe inclusive education as 'troubled and troubling': 'troubled because it has found respectability in policy and practice, while troubling because it is meant to be an intentionally bothersome ethical project' (p. 99). Slee (2008) laments the resilience of the special educational needs system, while trying to renew his commitment to 'critical confrontation' by portraying inclusive education as part of a broader reform of regular schooling. To this end he presents the idea of an irregular school as a provocation to retrieve the adoption of the language of inclusion into a system that he sees as having lost touch with inclusive values. Armstrong et al. (2011) also identify a failure of inclusive education in an increasingly globalised world where inclusion is contested in both developed (North) and developing countries (South). For these authors the weakness of inclusive education has a theoretical and practical aspect. Theoretically inclusion is seen to have become weakened by the 'pragmatic watering down of the underlying idealism of inclusion' (Armstrong et al., 2011: 37) associated with the 'escapism' of postmodern thinking about inclusion. Practically, inclusion is seen as not engaging with the realities of education and schooling. These authors also recommend going back to the big picture of inclusion and to the radical beginnings of the movement. These perspectives represent a particular emancipatory stance that regards inclusion as a political and ethical movement. The issues arising from this stance are also addressed in various chapters of this book.

Practical concerns about inclusive education

Not only are there theoretical issues about inclusive education, but also the practical experiences of inclusion have presented many practical challenges. Progress towards inclusive education is often portrayed as a matter of identifying and removing barriers to participation and learning (Booth and Ainscow, 2011). The term 'barrier' has come to replace the language of special educational needs or difficulties in line with the social model of disability. But, as will be argued in several chapters, this is to oversimplify matters in terms of what 'removal' and 'barriers' mean. Attribution theory identifies several dimensions of judgements about the causes of specific events or circumstances (Weiner, 1985). Two of these dimensions are about the stability or alterability of causal factors (low–high) and about the location of factors (internal–external to the person). In much inclusive thinking it is assumed that barriers to participation and learning are external and alterable; for example, steps (external) that impede wheelchair access can be changed into ramps or lifts (alterable). In this kind of thinking it is also assumed that internal factors (e.g. impairments) are a given and not alterable; this might relate to why impairments in social model terms are not to be called barriers. However, it is possible that some internal factors (or 'barriers') are to some extent alterable or even compensatable; for example, a visual impairment by wearing glasses. Also, external factors may not be easily alterable – for example, basic written language literacy standards – because although they may not be accessible to some children with profound intellectual impairments, removing these standards would incur social costs and personal costs for the majority who can access them (Wolff, 2009a).

There have been many reports and studies of barriers to inclusion that need to be informed by the above analysis of the location of barriers, their interaction and whether they can be removed and if so, the consequences of doing so. Evans and Lunt (2002) found in a UK context that a range of professionals involved in the school system believed that there were limits to inclusion, implying that some barriers are not that easily removable. Hodkinson (2010), also based on an analysis of the UK (English) system, identifies barriers to inclusion as not only at a class teaching level, but also at teacher, teacher education/training, school, local authority and government levels. One of the main criticisms of the policy implementation of inclusion has been the distortion of inclusive principles to fit a 'standards'-driven accountability system of schooling driven by neo-liberal policy principles (Allan, 2008a). But, when it is argued that a 'standards agenda' is a barrier to participation and inclusion (Benjamin, 2002: 56), it is unclear whether this means specific performance-based standards or any educational standards and what removal might imply. These are curriculum design questions about what is worth learning and what might be common–differentiated about curriculum goals – issues that will be examined in Chapter 4.

Book rationale and core ideas

There are two basic reasons for writing this book. The first is to further develop ideas about a range of tensions and dilemmas in inclusive education that include but go beyond my earlier work on dilemmas of difference arising from disabilities and difficulties. The other reason is to engage in dialogue with others who responded to my earlier work and who have related ideas.

I summarised in a previous book (Norwich, 2008) thinking about dilemmas of difference that brought together ideas from legal studies (Minow, 1990), political studies (Dahl, 1982) and political philosophy (Berlin, 1990) and integrated them with parallel ideas from education and special needs education. The idea of dilemmas of difference is best expressed in the words of Martha Minow who first used this term:

> When does treating people differently emphasise their differences and stigmatise or hinder them on that basis? And when does treating people the same become insensitive to their difference and likely to stigmatise or hinder them on that basis?
>
> *(Minow, 1990: 20)*

Artiles (1998) has examined the disproportional representation of ethnic minorities in US special education in terms of the dilemma of difference. Though he suggests that these dilemmas can be transcended, by questioning underlying assumptions about difference and norms, there is no specific explanation about how this will work. I have identified previously three aspects of schooling where educational differentiation relevant to children with disabilities and difficulties could be stigmatising and individually enabling: 1) the identification–non-identification of some children as having special educational needs or disability in educational terms; 2) curriculum commonality–differentiation; and 3) common–separate teaching and learning settings. These ideas were examined empirically in terms of professional, administrators and policy-makers' perspectives about these kinds of differentiation across three countries: UK (England), USA and Netherlands. The findings are discussed in the various chapters of this book in the wider context of other tensions and dilemmas relevant to inclusive education.

Where this book is distinctive and goes beyond my previous writing is in broadening the analysis of inclusive education to cover a range of related tensions that can lead to dilemmas. In addition to the tension between difference as individually enabling–stigmatising, I will address the following tensions that arise in connection with inclusive education:

1. participation–protection
2. choice–equity
3. generic–specialist
4. what exists as real–relative
5. knowledge as investigation–emancipation.

This will give a broader analysis of the underlying tensions in inclusive education than the previous work that focused just on dilemmas of difference. The first two tensions are about values associated with plural and liberal democracies and lead to what Dahl (1982) called dilemmas of plural democracy. The second tension is specifically about the relationship between states and markets, which has become a key educational issue with the introduction of market principles in the school system. The third tension between the generic and specialist is linked to dilemmas of difference, but relates more to maintaining coherence and unity in specialist organisations. The last two tensions are about the philosophical questions associated with ontology (whether disability exists and are rights and needs real?) and the purpose and nature of knowledge in the field (epistemology: knowledge for understanding and explanation–emancipation). How these tensions emerge will become clear within and across the following chapters of this book.

8 Setting the agenda

The other basic reason for writing this book was to engage with the arguments of those who responded to my earlier work and who have related ideas. Two inclusion theorists have responded in different but related ways to my call for a dilemmatic approach to addressing issues in pursuing inclusion in the area of disability and difficulties. Slee (2010) suggests that a dilemmatic approach embodies the 'inevitability of compromise' and that 'this is a conservative option that will not change the relations of inequality' (p. 109). He does recognise that the approach provides some useful ways of promoting change, but says no more than this. For Slee compromise is a questionable response to dilemmas especially if it 'evacuates principle' (p. 14). The style of this criticism of a dilemmatic approach is cursory. It also overlooks that these dilemmas arise from value tensions, not mere convenience or self-interest, ones which are experienced by those involved in the education system, as will be discussed in this book. His approach resembles one associated with Karl Kraus, quoted by Bourdieu (1992), that 'between two evils I refuse to choose the lesser'. This raises some questions. Is this deep reluctance to resolve dilemmas an escape from confronting the plural values that characterise our humanity and that lead to value tensions? Or does this reluctance represent an heroic attempt to transform society in terms of a singular bold, coherent vision? These questions will be addressed directly and indirectly in the chapters of this book.

Florian (2007) identifies dilemmas of difference as one of two problems that are faced in special education; the other is the concept of the normal as usual and good. While recognising that there is a need to confront the paradoxical nature of special education, Florian asks whether it should be acceptable that dilemmas of difference be seen as a 'necessary evil that must be endured' (p. 12) to provide education. Though she does not answer this question, treating it as rhetorical, her next question implies that she does not find it acceptable. She then asks whether it is time 'to reimagine the work of educating children ... as an integral part of school's response when students experience difficulties?' (p. 12). Florian's finding of dilemmas as unacceptable parallels Slee's rejection of compromise. She suggests that reimagining the field along certain lines will be transformatory: through clearer fulfilment of rights to education, challenging deterministic beliefs about abilities and shifting the focus from differences between learners to learning for all. These ideas will be addressed too in the chapters that follow.

There are similarities between the above rejection of compromise and the criticism of closure and decideability in Derrida's (1992) ideas about and use of deconstruction. Allan (2008a) believes that deconstruction can be a practical tool for playing with some of the certainties and closures which trouble inclusion and education more generally and which recreate exclusion. Deconstruction is not seen as serving a reconstruction but a re-description of existing concepts. Nor is deconstruction about destroying well-intentioned products, but about some of the 'impossible choices we face in trying to be inclusive' (p. 82). What deconstruction produces are aporias, the term Derrida (1992) used to describe double contradictory imperatives. Allan suggests that schooling is full of aporias, such as the requirement to raise attainment and to promote inclusion. She also identifies them in other areas, such as teacher education in the imperative to operate autonomously while collaborating with others.

The key feature of aporias seems to be that they create tensions that are assumed to be resolvable or reduced to one choice. But, following Derrida, Allan sees decision and closure as creating injustice and as irresponsible. For her, resolving aporias in inclusive education reintroduces exclusion. Allan's suggestion is to present the findings of deconstruction to policy makers as a series of aporias rather than recommendations. They are therefore faced with contradictory double imperatives and the 'discussion with policy makers about how they respond effectively to both demands would be productive' (p. 83). What policy makers might make of these double imperatives when it comes to policy making is left unaddressed. Nevertheless, it is clear that what I have called a dilemmatic approach and Allen's use of aporias in the context of deconstruction have a common focus on tensions. The difference between them is that aporias are about conflicting imperatives, while dilemmas are about hard choices between options with negative consequences. But the key difference between them is that dilemmas are to be resolved even if with some loss or compromise as they are about decisions, whereas aporias 'must not be reduced to singular choices' (p. 82). This shows how aporias within a Derridean context of deconstruction can be seen to represent a philosophy of hesitation (Critchley 1999). It is also unclear whether aporias represent a critical outsider perspective on tensions where decisions are suspended to avoid injustice or whether undecidability demands urgency and activity (Reynolds, 2010).

Basic stance taken in this book

What the above analysis shows is a basic stance that helps to clarify the distinctive stance in this book about value and philosophical tensions. While Slee, Florian and Allan reject 'compromise' and/or hesitate about decisions and closure because of the risk of injustice or exclusion, the stance taken in this book is to accept that this critical outside position may stay 'pure' in some ethical sense, but will not engage and change the world. I interpret Slee's (2008) position that inclusive education is an ethical provocation as purity maintaining, as providing a stimulus to thought and action, but not engaging in formulating any feasible ways forward. This difference can be seen to be one between ideological purity and impurity (Norwich, 2002a). This distinction has parallels with one used by Isaiah Berlin in his distinction between the hedgehog and the fox (Berlin, 1978). From the Greek poet Archilochus's statement that the fox knows many things while the hedgehog knows one big thing, Berlin distinguished a deep difference between thinkers, writers and people overall:

> those who relate everything to a central single vision ... in which they think and feel about a single universal organising principle in terms of which alone all they are and say has significance – and on the other side, those who

> pursue many ends, often unrelated and even contradictory, connected if at all ... The first kind of ... personality belongs to the hedgehogs, the second to the foxes.
>
> *(p. 3)*

Berlin's use of these styles is not rigid as shown by his portrayal of Tolstoy's view of history, suggesting that he was by nature a fox but believed in being a hedgehog. My contention is that inclusive education or inclusion in education, especially in its radical version is a hedgehog position, representing one big value and idea that provides security and purpose. For others, inclusion, or at least the long-standing values underpinning it, is one among many values that can come into conflict and present dilemmas; this is a fox position with which I align the argument in this book.

Berlin suggests that the fox stance does not try to fit varied experiences and values into an unchanging, all-encompassing unitary vision, as does the hedgehog stance. The fox stance goes beyond critique and seeks resolutions to tensions, realising that this will not be in the form of a pure coherent position. It is also suspicious of a style of thinking that sets up over-simplified dichotomies and favours one element to the exclusion of others in order to fit the single principle or position. Examples of this style of thinking will be examined in various chapters; for example, social versus medical models of disability, pedagogy for children with disabilities and difficulties being specialist or not. I extend Berlin's hedgehog–fox distinction by identifying two typical approaches to value and philosophical tensions. In the hedgehog approach, the two elements or principles in tension are split from each other with one invested with negativity and rejected, while the other is invested with positivity and strongly endorsed. There is also an account of a progressive switch or turn from one perspective to the opposite; for example, from medical to social models of disability, from special needs to inclusive education. No relationship is seen between these principles and there is a silence in response to contrary views about any relationships. Nor are practical resolutions sought that might imply some less than perfect resolution. In the fox approach, by contrast, there is openness to seeing some connection between the elements or principles in tension. Positive and negative judgements are not confined to one or other element; it is not about either/or, but both/and. Resolutions are sought which combine plural values as far as possible with these resolutions open to change over time. But, because values cannot sometimes live together we are 'doomed to choose and every choice may entail an irreparable loss (Berlin, 1990: 13). This is a general outline of the fox stance that recognises tensions leading to dilemmas and hard choices; it will be applied to understanding inclusive education in what follows.

Organisation of the book

I have already used the terms 'disability and difficulties' in this introductory chapter to refer to those about whose education the book is about and will do so across the book. I have avoided using the term 'special educational needs' unless it is the object of discussion, because this tends to have a specific UK meaning and also disability, despite its ambiguities, has come more into common use. The term 'difficulties' has also been used to cover those problems in learning associated with disability but not always counted as a disability, connected with the generic use of the term 'learning difficulties' in the UK. The terms 'child/children' rather than child and young people are also mostly used for brevity purposes.

The book is organised into nine chapters. Following this introductory chapter I examine the concepts of special educational needs, barriers and disability in Chapter 2. This points out the early recognition of a dilemma about identification in the Warnock Report (1978), though not in the language used in this book. It also covers different kinds of social analyses of disability and relates them to the distinction between medical and social models. Other dichotomies such as disability as oppression or as a disadvantage are also discussed in preparation for the next chapter. Chapter 3 examines how the 'SEN' term is used in a UK and international context, which is followed by a review of the arguments against the use of the 'SEN' term. This leads into an examination of the tensions about labelling and the tension between the real or socially constructed nature of learner categories. The chapter concludes with an analysis of a dilemma of difference about identification and how this can be resolved through the development of a teaching based bio–psycho–social model of disability.

The next three chapters focus on curriculum, pedagogy and schooling in that order. Usually inclusion in education is taken to be about where children with disabilities and difficulties go to school. This gives priority to where rather than what and how questions in the education. To rebalance the importance of what and how questions, Chapters 4 and 5 focus on curriculum and pedagogy questions before placement questions in Chapter 6. Chapter 4 examines inclusive curriculum issues in the context of an overview of current curriculum issues in education. This highlights tensions and incompatibilities between different curriculum perspectives that reflect philosophical tensions about the nature of knowledge, autonomy–control and curriculum commonality–differentiation. The latter tension is discussed in the context of the moves towards universal design as an inclusive approach and the extent to which it resolves the commonality–differentiation tension. This leads to the discussion in Chapter 5 about the recent moves towards inclusive pedagogy. The concept of inclusive pedagogy is questioned in terms of whether it depends on some elements of specialist teaching. What is meant in practice by inclusive teaching is also considered and there is a discussion about whether an analysis of the idea of continua of pedagogic strategies can resolve the tension between the notions of generic and specialist teaching. Chapter 6 focuses on the complex issues and tensions in inclusive schooling. The origins of the term inclusive/inclusion are examined in this chapter followed by an overview of the UK debates about inclusive schooling. What specialisation of schooling and learner grouping means is analysed as part of multilevel and multidimensional analysis of inclusion in education. This chapter also picks up and continues the issues raised in this introductory chapter about the purity of inclusion.

12 Setting the agenda

Chapter 7 is about tensions and dilemmas from the perspectives of children and parents. It covers dilemmas of difference and dilemmas of participation and protection. The issues of parent partnership in theory and practice are analysed and then related to the wider tensions between equity and choice that have come to permeate debates about schooling in general and for children with disabilities and difficulties. Chapter 8 then moves the analysis to a philosophical level, with an analysis of different versions of inclusion and the basis for claims that inclusion is a human right. This leads to an examination of what went wrong with the concept of special education needs and whether concepts of rights and needs are interconnected. Current basic needs models also connect with the recent moves towards a capability approach to education including children with disabilities and difficulties. The philosophical analysis then moves on to how to research inclusive education and its methodological tensions and debates. The final Chapter 9 summarises the key arguments in the preceding chapters and then restates and elaborates on the process and significance of addressing a range of tensions and dilemmas in inclusive education.

2
SPECIAL EDUCATIONAL NEEDS, BARRIERS AND DISABILITY

Introduction

'Special educational needs' is a fairly recent term in the history of the education of children and young people with difficulties and disabilities. It was introduced and used in the 1970s in the UK and is attributed to Professor Ron Gulliford, who was the first professor of special education in the UK (Wedell, 2005) and taken up by the Warnock Committee (DES, 1978). It was then adopted in the landmark UK legislation to replace handicap and impairment categories that had been used in legislation since the first UK special education legislation in the late 1890s. It is revealing to go back to the terms and arguments with which the Warnock Report justified this switching of perspective and terminology in the 1970s. This is a way of introducing this discussion about the issues and tensions over concepts of special educational needs and disability. The chapter then examines the rise of sociological critiques and the growth and influence of the social model associated with the disability movement. One aspect of this sociological critique was about the expansion of the special educational needs system, a critique shared with a right-wing perspective on the SEN system as a failure of schooling. The chapter then analyses the various kinds of social model that represent different kinds of social theory. These perspectives represent different philosophical assumptions about the nature of disability and the purpose of knowledge about disability.

Special educational needs: its original purposes and ambiguity

It may seem strange to some that the term 'special educational needs' was introduced by the Warnock Committee in 1978 to move away from deficit categories; with the explicit aim to turn away from what the child or young person could not do to what was required positively to provide appropriate learning opportunities:

> to describe someone as handicapped conveys nothing of the type of educational help, and hence of provision that is required. We wish to see a more positive approach, and we have adopted the concept of SPECIAL EDUCATIONAL NEED, seen not in terms of a particular disability which a child may be judged to have, but in relation to everything about him, his abilities as well as his disabilities – indeed all the factors which have a bearing on his educational progress.
>
> *(DES, 1978: section 3.6)*

It is understandable that this would seem strange 30 years later as the term has come to be commonly used in both professional and official use to refer to and imply difficulties and deficits. This is evident in the current English government categories (DfES, 2005) where the SEN term is used interchangeably with terms such as 'disorder', 'difficulty' and 'impairment'. This use of the SEN term had already been found shortly after the legislation introducing the SEN term had been implemented. Goacher et al. (1988) reported that statements of SEN and the professional reports, on which they were based, focused largely on deficits and difficulties, with little attention to other factors such as the child's other strengths and the learning environment.

One of the key assumptions in the SEN framework, as shown in the above excerpt, was the gap between general categories of difficulties and disabilities (e.g. specific learning difficulty) and the education needed for an individual said to have this kind of difficulty. The Warnock Report accepted the interactionist model that understood the educational progress of a particular child in terms of the interaction between personal strengths and difficulties and environmental supports and obstacles (Adelman, 1971; Wedell, 1993). Another key assumption in the adoption of the SEN term was that the significant difficulties that give rise to special educational needs lie along a continuum in which human characteristics differ by degree. For this reason, the Warnock Committee was critical of the assumption that there is a clear distinction between those with difficulties and those without:

> we believe that the most important argument against categorisation is the most general one. Categorisation perpetuates the sharp distinction between two groups of children – the handicapped and the non-handicapped – and it is this distinction which we are determined, as far as possible, to eliminate.
>
> *(DES, 1978: section 3.24)*

The continuum concept was central to the assumptions of the Warnock Committee and reflected the growing influence of psychological ideas, assumptions and practices in special education. This influence of psychology goes back to the international origins of psychology in Europe, UK and the USA as a field that uses and applies scientific methods towards the end of the nineteenth century (Rose, 1985). In the UK this approach was represented by the work of Cyril Burt for the London County Council (Burt, 1937). This reflected the close interconnection between education and psychology in the measurement of ability in the context of social policies which promoted the role of meritocracy in allocating educational opportunities (Sutherland, 1984; Wooldridge, 1994). The Warnock Committee based its figure of one in five children as having special educational needs on these scientific-style epidemiological studies, such as the Isle of Wight study (Rutter et al., 1976).

The continuum concept was not the only factor relevant to the thinking of the Committee. It is possible to adopt the continuum concept while retaining categories about difficulties or disabilities, as did the Warnock Report and shown by recent changes in the special educational system in the UK (DfES, 2005), and classification practices in Europe and the USA (McClaughlan and Florian, 2008). It was the combination of the continuum concept with a position about the stigmatising effects of diagnostic categories which led the committee to adopt the concept of special educational needs, in the belief that this abandoned categories. The importance of the stigma argument is evident in this excerpt:

> Moreover, labels tend to stick, and children diagnosed as ESN(M) or maladjusted can be stigmatised unnecessarily for the whole of their school careers and beyond. More important, categorisation promotes confusion between a child's disability and the form of special education he needs. The idea is encouraged that, say, every child with epilepsy or every maladjusted child requires the same kind of educational regime.
> *(DES, 1978: section 3.23)*

This excerpt shows that the Warnock Report thinking took the critiques about categories seriously, reflecting the contemporary beliefs about medicalisation and stigma (Szasz, 1974). But, it also shows recognition of other critiques about labelling: that it can lead to stereotyping and ignoring of individual needs, on the one hand, and that a focus on difficulties and disabilities was not a focus on educational needs or requirements, on the other. It is interesting that the majority of written submissions to the committee also supported abandoning the category system. The Warnock Report then explains clearly the arguments it took into account. It refers to five points which went against categories: 1) many children had more than one disability and this made classification complex; 2) categories tend to stereotype; 3) and to stick and stigmatise; 4) that there is a gap between general categories and education provision needed by individuals; and 5) that categories can exclude some children from receiving additional provision which they need. There was one major point which did weigh in their deliberations: that categories were a 'valuable safeguard of the right of a child ... to an education suited to his needs' (DES, 1978; section 3.30). Categories were recognised as underlying local authority duties to children. The committee found itself experiencing a dilemma:

> We have found ourselves on the horns of a dilemma. On the one hand, we are aware that any kind of special resource or service for such children runs the risk of emphasising the idea of their separateness, an idea which we are anxious to dispel, and of limiting the notion of special education to the

provision made for such children. On the other hand, unless an obligation is clearly placed on local education authorities to provide for the special needs of such children, there is a danger that their requirement for specialist resources will be inadequately met.

(DES, 1978: section 3.30)

The report then explains how it tried to resolve this by avoiding the disadvantages of categories while preserving its advantages in these terms:

We recommend that there should be a system of recording as in need of special educational provision those children who, on the basis of a detailed profile of their needs prepared by a multi-professional team, are judged by their local education authority to require special educational provision not generally available in ordinary schools.

(DES, 1978: section 3.31)

The committee considered that by recording a detailed profile of needed provision for individual children judged to require special provision that the dilemma could be resolved. There was no discussion of the possibility that abandoning specific disability categories, while instituting a system that judged whether some children required special education, would lead to a new category.

Special educational needs: its uses and critiques

Since the introduction of the SEN term and its legislative enactment in the Education Act 1981 in the UK, the term 'special needs' has spread to other countries. It has wide international currency as one way of talking about providing additional support and provision for some children. It is used in the USA, for example, in formal and professional contexts about students with disabilities in education, and also for those from disadvantaged backgrounds and for whom English is not their first language (for instance, State of New Jersey, 2010). This wider use is also evident in the way that the SEN term is used by international organisations such as the OECD (OECD, 2000) which will be discussed further in Chapter 3. It is important to note that in English legislation difficulties in learning associated with English as a second language were explicitly excluded from the definition of SEN in the 1981 Education Act; this definition still applies. The English approach is also distinctive from other national systems in having a formal role for special educational needs in legislation, a legacy of the Warnock Report. Despite the use of special needs language in the USA, the US Individual with Disabilities in Education Act stipulates that for a student to receive special education provision s/he has to meet two conditions:

1. have one of several recognised disabilities that
2. requires special education or related services (IDEA, 2004).

By contrast, in English legislation, the term 'special educational needs' was and is defined in terms of a 'learning difficulty that calls for special educational provision' (Education Act, 1996: section 312). Although the term 'learning difficulty' was recommended by the Warnock Committee, when calling for the abandoning of categories, its legal definition still involves the language of difficulty and disability. A learning difficulty has been defined as a significantly greater difficulty in learning than the majority of children of the same age or a disability preventing or hindering the use of educational facilities (Education Act, 1996: section 312). It is evident that the term 'learning difficulty' acts legislatively in a very similar way to the US legislative term 'disability', even though special educational needs could be interpreted to go beyond difficulties and disabilities. That SEN was tied to difficulties and disabilities is clear from its legislative definition and the brief of the Warnock Committee. The committee was not required to consider learning difficulties associated with social disadvantage (Warnock, 2005) and the 1981 and subsequent legislation has excluded second language factors as defining a learning difficulty (Education Act, 1981: section 1.4). That SEN and its associated term 'learning difficulties' did not go beyond difficulties and disabilities is also clear from the research studies used to justify the expansion of the field to one in five children. These studies were epidemiological ones (Rutter et al., 1976) based on contemporary public health ideas about childhood disorders and disabilities.

Though the term 'SEN' was meant to replace difficulty and disability categories through the use of detailed descriptions of individual educational needs, the system still required some judgement about what learning difficulties and what degree of difficulties called for special provision. The 1981 education legislation, which has remained unchanged for 30 years, and its associated regulations have overlooked these operational matters, in the spirit of abandoning categories. The consequence was that previous disability categories were used informally in practice with decisions about who required special provision being based mainly on children's functional difficulties. Though an interactionist model, implicit in the SEN framework, has been represented in government policy over many years (DfES, 2004), it has not been consistently enacted (Goacher et al., 1988; Frederickson and Cline, 1995).

The effect has been that using the term 'special educational needs' was not an abandoning of categories, but a replacing of more negative by less negative categories. Terms such as 'educational sub-normality (mild/ moderate)' were replaced, for example, by more positive-sounding terms such as 'moderate learning difficulties'. This may reduce the devaluing connotations associated with 'sub-normality'. For instance, studies have shown that college students and various professional groups evaluate the term 'learning difficulties' less negatively than other terms such as 'sub-normality' and 'handicap' (Hastings et al.,1993; Norwich, 1999). However, these studies are several years old and connotations might have changed with social and cultural changes since then. In a slightly more recent study of children and young people identified as having moderate learning difficulties, it was found that the term 'learning difficulties' was evaluated less negatively than other related terms (Kelly and Norwich, 2004).

The generic term 'special educational needs' has come to operate as a superordinate category – or a super-category – covering needs arising from the range of more specific areas of learning difficulties and disabilities (Ainscow and Muncey, 1989; Norwich, 1990). The introduction of the term 'special educational needs' has also involved an expansion of those included in special education from about 2 per cent of pupils in special schools in the early 1980s in England to the Warnock 20 per cent with special educational needs, the majority of whom had always been in ordinary schools. This expansion could be seen in different ways: positive and negative. From the Warnock Report perspective, this expansion can be seen positively as turning away from the distinction between the disabled and the non-disabled by focusing on individual education needs (the continuum assumption). This reflects what is common and shared between those in special schools and those in ordinary schools; what in current terms would be seen as an inclusive move. But there have also been those who saw SEN as acting as a devaluing and discriminating label as it marked out some pupils as different (Solity, 1991); or as expressing a language of sentimentality and prejudice (Corbett, 1996). These critical perspectives have been expressed since the origins of the SEN system by sociologists from a critical perspective in the 1980s (Barton and Tomlinson, 1984) and will be discussed in more detail in the next section.

What arises from this analysis is the complexity of the SEN concept and its function in trying to resolve the dilemma, as noted in the Warnock Report, between aiming to avoid stigmatising differences, while recognising the responsibility to provide appropriate resources to meet needs. There is an ambiguity in the meaning of SEN about representing certain differences from the norm, with the risk that this might be a negative difference, on the one hand, and as standing for a detailed profile of individual educational needs, on the other. The ambiguity of the meaning of SEN with its associations with individual requirements has also drawn the criticism that all children could be said to be 'special' in the sense that everyone has unique individual needs. The importance of clarifying the meaning of special educational needs has been recognised for many years (Norwich, 1993). It can be concluded from this analysis that so long as the term or its derivatives are used, further clarification is required.

Individual versus social perspective dichotomy

Special educational needs was introduced as abandoning medical categories in favour of a focus on individual educational needs that applied to a wider group than those found in special schools. Since the early 1980s when the ideas from the Warnock Report were translated into educational legislation and enacted in local authorities and schools across the UK, there also emerged a critical account from sociologists about the place of special education in the education system and the social interest that it served (Tomlinson, 1982). This critical stance was evident in its questioning of the assumed ideology of special education as enlightened and advanced. Tomlinson identified an ideology of 'benevolent humanitarianism' as providing a moral framework within which professionals and policy makers work. At the root of this critical perspective was a model of social relationships between more and less powerful social groups which have differing and conflicting interests. Professionals and policy makers have the power to categorise weaker groups, such as those with disabilities and difficulties, in ways that involve unequal and differential treatment. Tomlinson was emphatic that the concept of special educational needs had become:

> an ideological rationalisation for those who have power to shape and define the expanding special education system and have a vested interest in this expansion.
> *(Tomlinson, 1985: 156)*

Tomlinson's critique of special educational needs and the expansion of its scope had some force and has been seen as a landmark in the development of a social analysis or model in the field (Thomas and Vaughn, 2004). Though she recognised SEN as a more positive term than handicap or impairment, it was ambiguous and tautological, offering no clear way of deciding who had special educational needs. Problems were found with its loose definition and uncertainty about its coverage: did it cover children who were very able or talented and what about those who needed additional provision, such as those for whom English was an additional language? The expansion of the special education system was portrayed as expressing the interests of special education professionals that were underpinned by wider social interests concerned with protecting the interests of mainstream schools and teachers. From a wider macro-social perspective, the special education system catered for children who were excluded from ordinary education into what she termed the 'ultimate in non-achievement' (Tomlinson, 1982: 21).

Central to the social perspective was a critique of the individual approach to difficulties and disabilities, which was clearly at the core of the Warnock framework and the concept of special educational needs. This set a conflict-based social theory, which questioned 'positivist' and functional sociology, as opposed to a psychological approach. Even though the psychological model used in the Warnock framework was interactionist in recognising the interplay between multiple child and environmental factors, the focus was still on the child in context. From a social perspective, this did not address how these micro-contexts were embedded and influenced by significant middle-level (school) and macro-social (policy) processes. This focus on middle- and macro-level processes raises questions about whether schools can and should expand their capabilities to provide for the diversity of children and young people. From this perspective it is understandable that special educational needs would be seen to be those needs which schools cannot meet (Booth and Potts, 1983; Dyson, 1990). From this perspective special educational needs were interpreted as not about children's needs, but about how responsive schools can be: it becomes about system limitations and enhancement.

This switch in focus from the child's needs to the school's need for reform and change in the 1980s was an important one that pre-figured the development of ideas about inclusive schools in the 1990s. It is notable that those authors who adopted this interpretation of SEN were subsequently central in developing similar ideas about inclusive education (Booth and Ainscow, 2011). However, this switching perpetuated a dichotomy between the social and the individual, even though there was some reference to individual factors in interaction with system factors. If SEN is attributed to system limitations, then system change can take place to accommodate individual differences. But, what is not acknowledged is that individual factors might place some limitations on what a system can accommodate. For example, Dyson (1990) said that:

> Special needs are not the needs that arise in a child with disabilities with regard to a system that is fixed. Rather they are needs that arise between the child and the educational system as a whole when the system fails to adapt to the characteristics of the child.
>
> *(p. 59)*

The phrase 'arise in a child' sees needs as not belonging just to a child, but as relational, so they 'arise between the child and the education system'. This seems to recognise an interaction of factors, which would have been in line with the Warnock framework of SEN. However, in the above excerpt, there is an inconsistency between recognising an interaction and then referring only to systems failure: a systems limitation perspective. Adopting an interactionist framework implies that limitations can arise from both child and systems factors. Child factors need to be taken into account in practice and therefore the assumption that schools can be reorganised in principle to accommodate the full diversity of children is one perspective. But there is another perspective. In this one taking account of child factors in practice means that there is still some scope for programmes aimed at reducing the impact of these child factors as part of wider programmes of systems change.

Through the 1990s the systems limitation perspective was further developed to become the foundation of the ideas of inclusive education and schooling. The focus on systems limitation was translated into the language of 'barriers' to learning and participation (Booth et al., 2000). Barriers are treated as central to understanding educational difficulties, not just for those with difficulties and disabilities. They can be about the physical environment, the organisation, culture and policies of schooling, in relationships and in teaching and learning approaches. On one hand, barriers are seen as more or less alterable, while on the other their discovery and removal is seen as the central endeavour. Inclusion in this perspective comes to be seen as:

> a never-ending process which involves the progressive discovery and removal of limits to participation and learning.
>
> *(Booth and Ainscow, 2011: 40)*

Uncovering barriers and reducing them is seen to replace the framework about identifying special educational needs and providing for these needs. Using the language of special educational needs is represented as 'seeing the "deficiencies" or impairments of children as the main cause of their educational difficulties' (p. 40). This focus on the child's difficulties is seen to deflect from barriers in settings and systems.

There are two important points to be made about this account of special educational needs and barriers. One is that 'special educational needs' was meant to be about provision, not about just identifying difficulties or impairments. Barriers are about limitations that are external to the child, but nonetheless limitations. As external limitations they cover macro (policy), middle-level (school) and micro-level (teaching and learning) factors. They do not cover internal factors, whether these are called impairments or difficulties, that children bring to their learning and development. The language of barriers clearly avoids talking about a child's impairments as barriers, whether these are more or less alterable. For this reason the barrier approach is inconsistent with an interactionist model which takes account of internal and external factors, both strengths and limitations. This leads to the second point, that had the SEN approach been made more explicit about the kinds of provision that were required in terms of the organisation of schooling and learning opportunities at macro-, middle- and micro-levels of the system, then it would have been less easy to reduce SEN conceptually to within child factors. However, this would have required integrating elements of the individual and social perspectives, which has been difficult given the divisions between those affiliated to psychological and sociological traditions in education (see next chapter for a discussion of an integral approach).

Medical versus social models of disability

Even though the concept of SEN was a deliberate move away from medical categories to examine the interaction of child factors (that might include impairments) and contextual factors, SEN has still been seen by some as expressing a medical model because of its individual rather than social analysis. This indicates how the term 'medical' is ambiguous in its meaning. It can refer to impairments/difficulties as the main or only cause of educational difficulties. But, it can also refer to explanations of educational difficulties at the individual child level rather than at various social levels. In the second sense, the opposite of a medical model is a model which only focuses on external social processes, factors at macro-level, middle-level and micro-level – what has come to be called the social model.

The social model of disability in education has developed partly from critiques by sociologists of education, as discussed above, and also from the influence of the disability movement as a political movement and the growth of disability studies to aid this movement. At the core of the social model is a particular orientation to knowledge, understanding and social action which sees it as serving emancipatory purposes, what has been called a critical perspective (Habermas, 1978; Popkewitz, 1984). The purpose of knowledge is seen to redress oppression and domination, to eradicate injustice. Mike Oliver, a leading social model theorist, has expressed this position in his critique of 'research as investigation' as what he calls the 'dominant discourse of social research' (Oliver, 1999: 163). 'Investigatory research' using 'tourist' approaches and done by 'tarmac' professors and researchers is condemned by him as unacceptable to 'oppressed groups such as disabled people who collectively empower themselves' (p. 191). Oliver brings out starkly the difference between investigatory research and emancipatory research that serves empowerment. If the social model is seen to be part of an emancipatory position, then this works to different purposes from the technical purposes that underlie the causal explanations sought in much psychological and medical research, which has influenced the SEN framework (cf. Warnock Report, DES, 1978). This difference is at the base of tensions and dilemmas which are examined in this book.

Those who have advocated for inclusion in terms of the social model have set up a particular dichotomy between the social model and what is called the individual or medical model. This is justified in terms of the development of disability studies and portrayed as representing the experiences of disabled people. For instance, Booth and Ainscow (2011) present a social model by contrast to a medical or individual model in these terms:

> Disabilities can be seen as barriers to participation for people with impairments, chronic pain and illness ... A medical or individual model of disability views the barriers faced by people with impairments as a direct consequence of their impairments.
>
> *(p. 42)*

Thomas and Vaughn (2004) present this position in related terms:

> When thinking this way, success or failure at school is not seen as governed by complex social, cultural and intellectual interactions but rather by one-dimensional factors, such as disability. The thinking is in *a deficit or medical model wherein something is seen to have gone wrong and is to be put right.*
>
> *(p. 109)*

It is notable that complex interactions are contrasted with 'simplistic' (p. 109) explanations in terms of disability as a deficit or medical model. Yet, what is proposed, despite the recognition of this complex interaction, is a model which switches focus from impairment to society, where disability comes to be redefined as social barriers and oppression. These ideas have come to be used widely in education and training, as shown in this account from a website about 'how to make your teaching inclusive':

> In the medical model, disabled people are seen as the problem. They need to change and adapt to circumstances (if they can), and there is no suggestion that society needs to change. This model reflects the World Health Organization definition of disability.
>
> The social model has been developed by disabled people. In their view disability is caused by the barriers that exist within society and the way society

is organised, which discriminates against people with impairments and excludes them from involvement and participation. This model reflects the Union of Physically Impaired Against Segregation (UPIAS) definition of disability.

(Open University, 2006)

Whether the so-called 'medical model' suggests that disabled people are the problem and that society does not need to change is a position that needs to be questioned. Also, there may be more to disability than its causation by social barriers. Attributing this model to a group within the disability movement also suggests that there is a single position about the social perspective on disability.

Individual and social models of learning

There is an important connection between models of disability, as discussed in the above section, and models of learning and abilities. The medical model has been criticised in terms of also being an individual deficit model, which uses the 'language of buckets and other instruments of capacity measurement' (Thomas and Loxley, 2001: 56). These authors argue that this language involves metaphor and despite the use of psychometrics (measurement and statistics) is not useful educationally. This is a critique of the language of individual dispositions such as 'lacking intelligence' and 'poor phonological awareness', especially when it refers to difficulties and low levels of individual functioning. Thomas and Loxley suggest that this kind of language is at best analogical and operates as a myth that leads practitioners and researchers towards a dead end. I see this kind of critique of the individual *deficit model* as connected to the development of more social theories of learning which question what has been called 'acquisition metaphors' of learning (Sfard, 1998). The acquisition metaphor of learning assumes that something is taken in and owned by an individual person and that knowing is a having or possessing. The metaphor underlies most of what counts as psychological theory about learning and ability, from behavioural, Piagetian, information processing, connectionist to Vygotsky's theories of internalisation. Despite important differences between these theories, they can be seen as sharing a common acquisitional assumption that when an individual learns, they come to possess and carry something from this process and then bring and use (transfer) it in other situations.

Although environmental factors play a key role in some of these psychological theories, even in Vygotsky's original social constructionist theory of learning, the focus is on the learning and development of the individual and not learning as a social process (Lave and Wenger, 1991). These more social theories of learning – for example, learning as participation in a community of practice –can be seen to reflect a participation metaphor of learning (Sfard, 1998). In the participation metaphor, learning is about becoming a participant in a community, knowledge is an aspect of practice or an activity and knowing is about belonging, participating and communicating. So, when looking at learning difficulties or disabilities, the acquisitional approach makes it possible to see learning difficulties as gaps and lacks of something – as individual difficulties or deficits, whereas the participation approach sees process and activity. The appeal of participative approaches to learning is therefore clear for those who reject the 'medical' model and who favour what is construed as the opposite, a particular version of the social model and inclusion. This is evident in more recent thinking about socio-cultural theories of learning and teaching and developing ideas about inclusive pedagogy (see Chapter 5; Hart et al., 2004; Florian, 2009).

However, as Sfard (1998) argues, neither metaphor of learning can operate without the other, despite attempts by participation theorists to be rid of acquisition language. She does not advocate cross-breeding between the metaphors as they are different approaches, but argues that they do not have to be seen as competing. In recognising that 'there is no simple way out of the entrapment' (p. 10), she advises that if one cannot solve the dilemma, then one can at least learn to live with it. One way of reconciling these learning approaches, an individual and social ones, is similar to the way of understanding the relative contribution of the individual and social models of disability; the focus is on different levels of analysis. In the acquisitional approach, the goal of learning is thought about in terms of individual development while in the participative approach it is about community development. Both can be recognised as important as argued by other authors (Eraut, 2007) and as will be argued more fully in Chapter 5.

Critique of the 'social model'

Having shown how the tension between medical/individual and social models of disability connects with different frameworks for understanding learning and abilities, I will now discuss the critique of the social model from within disability studies. Tom Shakespeare (2006) has argued that it is possible to question the social model of disability, as defined above, while still adopting a political approach to disability. His claim is that an examination of recent history shows that the British social model is just one of several socio-contextual accounts of disability. He puts it in these terms:

> The legend is of a polar switch: the social model replaced the medical model. Thanks to the pioneering activists of UPIAS and the academics who followed them. The truth is that there was, and always has been a plurality of social approaches, the most extreme version of which triumphed and has become orthodoxy of the British disability movement and British disability studies.
>
> *(pp. 10–11)*

He contends that disability campaigners and social researchers have approached disability internationally from a social perspective and campaigned against social exclusion and oppressive policies, but only in the UK has disability come to be defined as oppression. Characterising the social model as 'extreme' and 'rigid ideology' (p. 10) positions, Shakespeare is not sharing the same political views as others in the disabled people's movement. Some critiques of his current position see Shakespeare as 'no longer disabled, but disabling' (Koch, 2011). Koch argues that Shakespeare is not disabled by his short stature but by his rejection by the 'communities of difference' (p. 19), which not only see his views as 'simply incorrect but literally threatening to many with whom he once made common cause' (pp. 19–20). This difference between Shakespeare's and Koch's perspective is about the nature and purposes of ideas and models of disability and which better serve the interests of those with 'disabilities'. A way of understanding this difference is in terms of their different knowledge stances (as discussed in the previous section). One stance is an emancipatory one that links disability studies and concepts of disability to the priorities of organisations of disabled people. Another is an investigatory one that follows a more independent and less politically committed set of priorities.

Shakespeare gives an account of UPIAS as one of several disabled people's organisations. Another, such as the Liberation Network, is described as recognising disability as a form of oppression, but also seeing that people with disabilities experienced problems arising from their impairments. The UPIAS position made a fundamental distinction between impairment and the social situation of people with impairments, called 'disability'. Where impairment was about a defective part or mechanism of the body, disability was the disadvantage or restriction of activity caused by social organisation. So, from this position, disability was imposed on top of impairments, and so distinct and not interacting and affected by impairments. The UPIAS position which was adopted and used in training and advocacy set itself against the World Health Organisation's International Classification of Impairments, Disabilities and Handicaps (ICIDH; WHO, 1980), which was portrayed as the symbol of the medical model. In this classification, impairment was defined as deviations from biomedical norms including functional deviations; disability was defined as any restrictions or lack resulting from impairments of the abilities to perform an activity in the manner or within what is considered as normal; while handicap was the 'disadvantage for an individual resulting from impairment or disability, that limits or prevents the fulfilment of a role that is normal (depending on age, sex, and social and cultural factors) for that individual' (WHO, 1980: 14). What is interesting is that those who developed the ICIDH saw it as focusing on the consequences of health-related conditions and enabling recognition of the social disadvantages experienced by disabled people (Bury, 2000). However, as Shakespeare comments, while the ICIDH may have been useful compared to other medical approaches, it was still lacking in taking account of how the social world created the disadvantages recognised in the handicap classification (Shakespeare, 2006).

Shakespeare's conclusion was that the concepts of medical and social models have become polarised. The ICIDH came to be seen as representing all that was wrong with conventional attitudes to disability: the non-involvement of disabled people, the dominance of professionals and defining people by their impairments rather than in terms of their citizen rights. For Shakespeare:

> The opposition of the 'medical model' to the 'social model' is more about actual symbolism than actual content.
>
> (p. 18)

Though Shakespeare credits the social model with having a positive strategic impact on definitions of disability and policy change, he contends that it needs to be developed because of its questionable, dangerous and unacceptable implications. First, if disability is about social oppression, then analysis on the basis of impairment and organising on this basis is unnecessary. Second, if disability is about social arrangements and not impairment, then trying to address or cure medical problems would be unnecessary, another implication which would seem strange to many. Third, if disability is about social exclusion, then the number of people with impairments becomes less important. The priority is to remove social barriers rather than meet the needs of impaired individuals. So, knowing how many people have impairments becomes less important.

In addition, a 'disability correctness' has arisen in which the term 'disabled people' is judged to be correct from a social model perspective, because people with impairments are disabled by society, not their impairments, The term 'people with disabilities' (the people first usage) is unacceptable because it implies that disabilities belong to individuals; those using this phrase are, it is argued, adopting the 'medical model'. The counter argument to this 'correct use' of disability is that the people first usage recognises the common humanity of all, irrespective of whether they have impairments or not, so reflecting a common rights approach. Though some may see this language usage issue as a diversion from more important matters, it does reflect the differences over conceptual and value issues, discussed in this chapter.

The range of social approaches

In this section I now question the presentation of the social model in education as representing a single model. There is no one social model of disability, nor does this way of representing the social model fit with debates and positions within disability studies or medical sociology. At the root of the 'social model' is the duality between impairment and disability, which has come to be an issue within disability studies, a development that is often relatively unnoticed from an education perspective. It is also an issue that has been given a positive gloss: as showing healthy dialogue (Barton, 2003), and not as also showing a problem with the medical–social model dichotomy. Impairments have been experienced as causing discomfort and associated with pain (Corker and French, 1999), so making the distinction between impairment and disability hard to maintain. Impairment, disability and society are also seen to be interrelated. This follows from the recognition that impairments, not just disability, can be generated and affected by social arrangements (Abberley, 1987). But, this does not mean that all impairments are only socially determined, some are inherited or some dispositions to developing them may be inherited biologically. What counts as an impairment is itself influenced by social judgement;

it is a social construction in the sense that it depends on what a society expects and values and how society is arranged. So what counts as a disability can be seen to result from the interaction of impairment effects and social restrictions.

Female authors in the disability studies field have underlined the significance of impairment for concepts of disability by recognising the central role of personal experiences, that impairment can result in pain and that limitations of activity are interconnected with impairments (Morris, 1991; Crow, 1996; Thomas, 1999). For Crow (1996), a renewed model would operate at two levels, she suggested: understanding impairment and disability as social concepts and recognising individual experience in changing contexts. In advocating a revised social model, Crow examines various ways in which impairment interacts with disability; for instance, how impairment can be caused or compounded by disability, such as discrimination causing major emotional stress and putting mental health at risk. It is clear from her use of the term 'disability' and her definition above that she sees 'disability' as a restricting process on an activity. Carol Thomas (1999) also uses the term in a similar way, but makes the crucial point about the two different ways in which 'disability' is used:

> First, an unequal relationship between impaired and non-impaired people; and second, as a property of the person with impairment (restricted activity) which is attributed to social factors.
>
> *(p. 41)*

She explains how these meanings have been conflated and then uses the distinction to explain how medical sociologists, such as Bury (2000), came to reject the social model because they understand 'disability' in terms of a property of a person (restricted activity). She analyses the medical sociology logic in these terms: social model advocates are seen to say that all restrictions of activities are socially caused, but this is inconsistent with impairments that can cause restrictions, so they conclude that the social model is over-socialised. Thomas argues that this logic does not engage with the social relational definition (the first one above) which is that 'disability is the disadvantage or restrictions put on activities by social organisation', the unequal relationship referred to in the above definition. So, she develops a model of disability and impairment effects which have consequences for doing (restrictions of activity) and being (psycho-emotional well-being) (Thomas, 1999: 157).

Thomas (2004) adopts this dual interpretation of 'disability' as a social relational concept as she wants to retain it as meaning social oppression like other forms of oppression associated with race, gender and class. It is interesting that she interchanges the word 'disablism' for 'disability' at times (Thomas, 1999: 156) and it is this usage that suggests that she is not being consistent with her use of terms. 'Disablism' relates to racism and seems to be the more appropriate term for what she refers to as social oppression in the social relational approach. This is her first meaning of what she calls 'disability' (above) – as *'restrictions on activity'*. This is a very different meaning from *'restricted activity'* as a property of an individual person. I have not used the term 'restrictions of activity' as this seems to be ambiguous as to whether this is about

28 Barriers and disability

restrictions imposed socially on activity or a person's restricted or limited activity. Were Thomas to talk about disablism in reference to social oppression (restriction on activity) and disability as restricted activity, then she would agree with everyday usage of the term 'disability'. But, she does not do this, perhaps because of her commitment to the advances by 'oppressed groups' when she argues:

> The social model remains and should continue to remain in place as a powerful organising principle, a rallying cry and a practical tool.
>
> (p. 581)

In this she is true to the original UPIAS position and the emancipatory position of Oliver (2004). Yet, she recognises the crude equation of disability with restricted activity within disability studies and the limited nature of the social model of disability for academic purposes. This brings us back to the basic differences between investigatory and emancipatory positions, discussed above, that reveals tensions which are at root about fundamental differences of purposes and interests. Thomas sees the

> advances of oppressed groups are always of much greater significance than any loss of clarity of ideas along the way.
>
> (p. 581)

In this stance she departs from Shakespeare (2006), who is not willing to sacrifice clarity when he insists that disability should not be defined as social barriers or oppression, but as restricted activity or in everyday terms as 'not being able to do things'.

The social relations perspective has a materialist assumption about social processes in which disability as oppression is seen as materially produced in terms of socio-economic factors. This has been questioned by some disability theorists who doubt the binary divide between impairment and disability, seeing impairment as discursively produced (Corker and French, 1999). This perspective reflects the wider post-structuralist moves in sociology to focus on discursive productions rather than material–structural productions. This post-structural discursive turn, which has been associated with the postmodern condition, is seen to make it possible to better understand disabled people's experiences (Corker, 1999). Corker argues that to explain the experiences of impaired people requires a communicative–discursive approach, while seeing disabled people as social agents. This approach questions binary opposites, such as impairment-disability, seeing the elements of this distinction as related in terms of how they are talked about. However, Corker stresses that she sees the communicative–discursive approach as one that supplements the Marxist materialist approach. She sees it as opening up issues about attitudes and discriminating language, while also challenging an exclusive materialist position by seeing disability as also produced in the relationship between impairment and disablism.

There is another perspective within the range of social approaches that merits a brief mention in this chapter, which starts with the contested nature of the body in social theory. Williams (1999) identifies that both the 'social model' of disability and the post-structuralist approaches show an aversion to the body. They have this in common, despite doing so in different ways. The disability theorists avoid the body through their separation of impairment from disability, so taking medicine out of disability, while the postmodern social constructionists do so by construing the body as a 'discursive body; one whose matter really doesn't matter at all' (p. 804). Williams introduces a realist approach to the relationship between impairment and disability, placing it in the history of realism in social theory and suggesting that, in its current form of critical realism (Bhaskar (1989), it can bridge the divide between materialist and postmodern constructionism in social theory. Williams argues that the body can be brought back into social theory by questioning the 'epistemic fallacy': what Bhaskar calls the conflation of the ontological (what exists) with the epistemological (how we know). This is the fallacy that assumptions about the body can be reduced to what we know about the body.

Critical realism assumes that the social and natural worlds involve three domains: 1) the *empirical*, what we observe/experience; 2) the *actual*, both events and experiences; and 3) the *real*, deep underlying mechanisms, that exist whether they are observed or not and which are independent of our knowing. Their existence is inferred and evidenced through their generative effects that we can and do observe. The critical realist perspective therefore confronts the biological and does not avoid it by separation from the social or by reducing it to the social discursively. As a social theory, it also takes a position about the relation between human agency and structure which does not involve a one-way determinism such as materialist theory, nor represent structures as constructs subject to discursive negotiations. Social systems can in critical realist theory remain 'open' as people possess 'critical reflexivity and creativity' (Archer, 1995). From this perspective Williams defines disability as:

> an *emergent* property, located temporally speaking in terms of the *interplay* between the biological reality of *physiological impairment, structural conditioning* (i.e. enablement/constraints) and *socio-cultural interaction/elaboration*.
>
> *(p. 810; his italics)*

With relevance to the disability movement, this perspective assumes that structures can be reproduced or transformed by social agents. But, it also sets the dichotomy between 'personal tragedy' and 'social oppression' (associated with the medical and social models) as an over-drawn contrast between a 'dynamic dialectally unfolding process between body and society located in a temporal frame of reference' (Williams, 1999: 813).

Concluding comments

In this chapter I have discussed the origins and purposes of the concept of SEN and its ambiguities that affected how it came to be used and criticised. Some of this criticism derived from the divides between different disciplines or fields, the individual perspective versus the social perspective. This was associated with how different groups came to represent a dichotomy between the medical or individual and social models of disability. The tensions between these models were then shown to correspond to the tensions between individual and social models of learning. This led to a critique of the social model and a discussion of how there is a range or family of social approaches. Throughout the chapter the importance of the interaction or interplay between factors and domains has been recognised. Thomas (2004) suggests that there are consistencies between the positions of Shakespeare, Williams and Bury about disability and the WHO's International Classification of Functioning (ICF) position (to be discussed in the next chapter), an observation which she uses to criticise this common position. For me, the tensions identified in this chapter relate to basic differences about the purpose of ideas about disabilities. Thomas talks about the divide between those who recognise that disabled people are socially disadvantaged and those who see them as oppressed. This disadvantage–oppression distinction corresponds to different stances to the use of knowledge and understanding in the field: investigatory versus emancipatory positions respectively. These knowledge positions reflect differing values and ideologies which will be discussed further in Chapter 8. However, the conclusions of this chapter about the over-drawn dichotomy between the medical (individual) and social models will be pursued in the next chapter which addresses issues about the classification and identification of difficulties and disabilities in education.

3
CLASSIFICATION AND IDENTIFICATION OF SPECIAL EDUCATIONAL NEEDS OR DISABILITY IN EDUCATION

Introduction

In this chapter I follow up the discussion in the previous chapter about special educational needs, barriers and disabilities with an analysis of the purposes of identification and classification systems. I start by considering how the term 'special educational needs' is understood internationally and then focus in more detail on the system in England. This is followed by discussion of some examples of international differences in classifying special educational needs. The usefulness of the SEN category in England is then discussed by comparison with the move in Scotland to the concept of 'additional support needs'. The chapter then examines the purposes of identification and the tensions and dilemmas that arise in the process. A way of resolving these is examined in terms of what an educationally oriented bio–psycho–social model can contribute to a useful way forward.

Different national models

The Organisation for Economic Cooperation and Development (OECD) have attempted to construct a comprehensive model of special educational needs or special needs education in order to compare provision across different countries (OECD, 2000). The main feature of this definition is its focus on additional support through additional resources, whether this is the adaptation of curriculum, teaching or organisation and/or human and material resources. In its focus on provision, the influence of the UK SEN framework is evident. But, the way the SEN term is used in the OECD approach departs from the UK usage in distinguishing between the kinds of reasons or causes for children's/students' difficulties in learning. In the 2000 version, the three kinds of factors were:

32 Classification and identification

1. Category A: Refers to educational needs of students where there is substantial normative agreement – such as blind and partially sighted, deaf and partially hearing, severe and profound mental handicap, multiple handicaps. Typically, adequate measuring instruments and agreed criteria are available. Typically considered in medical terms to be organic disorders attributable to organic pathologies (e.g. in relation to sensory, motor or neurological defects).
2. Category B: Refers to educational needs of students who have difficulties in learning which do not appear to be directly or primarily attributable to factors which would lead to classification as A or C.
3. Category C: Refers to educational needs of students which are considered to arise primarily from socio-economic, cultural and/or linguistic factors. There is some form of disadvantaged or atypical background for which education seeks to compensate.

(OECD, 2000: 34)

In a later version, Category B comes to be refined to refer to 'behavioural or emotional disorders, or specific difficulties in learning' where the need arises from 'problems in the interaction between the student and the educational context' (OECD, 2007: 20). The three broad categories were also said to refer to 'A/disabilities', 'B/difficulties' and 'C/disadvantages' and the term 'special educational needs' was no longer used. Why there was this change from 2000 is not explained, but it may reflect the influence of the inclusion movement and its critique of 'SEN' as reflecting the medical model.

This broad classification system is used to encompass additional provision in various countries and in doing so illustrates significant differences in how they define and recognise different areas of impairment/disability and in what broad areas they make additional resources available. Table 3.1 illustrates the variations in how four countries allocate their additional provision systems using this model. I will identify several points of commonality and difference between the three countries of USA, Japan and France (as these represent an international range) and then contrast these with how the UK is represented. As regards Category A: disabilities, there are some common areas representing sensory, motor and intellectual disabilities, even if represented in different terms. But, for this category, there are some differences too; for example, in terms of whether speech and language impairments are represented (in the USA and France, but not Japan). For the broad area of emotional and behaviour difficulties, whether recognised as disturbance or disorder, the USA recognises Autism, but emotional disturbance is placed under Category B: difficulties, whereas in Japan, emotional disturbance is placed under Category A, while for France, this area is not recognised under Category A or B. For Category B, there is most divergence between these countries, with commonality only between the USA and France as regards learning difficulties, but what is meant varies between these countries. For Japan there is no provision that comes under Category B. Finally, for Category C, there are some commonalities

TABLE 3.1 Areas of additional resourcing in four countries and percentage of school population (OECD, 2003)

	A: Disabilities	B: Difficulties	C: Disadvantage
UK (England)	2.7%	14.4%	
	Children with Statements	Children with SEN without Statements	
USA	4.6%	6.6%	Title 1: Disadvantaged
	Mental retardation Speech or language impairment Visual impairments Orthopaedic impairments Other health impairments Deaf/blindness Multiple disabilities Hearing impairments Autism Traumatic brain injury Developmental delay	Emotional disturbance Specific learning disability	
Japan	1.1%		Students who require Japanese instruction
	Blind and partially sighted Deaf and hard of hearing Intellectual disabilities Physically disabled Health impaired Speech impaired Emotionally disturbed		
France	2.9%	1.7%	Non-Francophone students Disadvantaged children
	Severe, moderate, mild mental handicap Physical handicap Metabolic disorders Deaf Partially hearing Blind Partially sighted Other neuropsychological disorders Speech/language disorders Other deficiencies Multiply handicapped	Learning difficulties	

around provision for additional language learning and for disadvantage. Japan and France have provision for students who are additional language learners, and though the USA does not have such provision recorded by the OECD, as mentioned in Chapter 2, there is such provision (e.g. State of New Jersey, 2010).

The UK is represented as making a distinction between those children with statements under Category A: disability (more significant needs) and those with SEN without Statements (School Action and School Action Plus) without Statements (less significant needs and under Category B: difficulties). This implies that the categories used in other countries are not used in the UK, because definitions are based on needs and do not label children/students. However, this interpretation does not fit the evidence of what goes on in the UK. The extent of SEN was defined in the Warnock Report (DES, 1978; see Chapter 2) in terms of research using the kinds of categories of disability and difficulties used in other countries. Also, in the SEN Codes of Practice (DfE, 1994; DfES, 2001a; DfES 2001b) there is explicit reference to various areas or categories of SEN and this set of categories was reinforced with the introduction of categories for annual census recording of pupils with Statements and School Action Plus in English schools (DfES, 2005). Decisions about issuing Statements for children/students with severe and complex SEN in England do not require allocating explicitly to one of several categories. Individual children/students are assessed individually and provision decisions are based on this assessment, though categories might be used in this individualised process. Also, the English system is more fluid and less standardised compared to other countries because local authorities, who are responsible for the assessment and issuing of Statements, have been able to move the boundaries between Statement and non-Statement SENs (Pinney, 2004). Some children who have difficulties which might be biologically based – for example, visual impairment – could not have Statements, and therefore recorded as at School Action Plus, and come under the OECD Category B: difficulties.

Another feature in Table 3.1 is the wide range of incidence of Category B (difficulties) in the four countries (from 1.7% to 14.4%; with no programmes recorded for Japan) compared to Category A (disabilities) (from 1.1% to 4.6%). As discussed above, Category B is associated with most uncertainty about causation and originally was defined as neither Categories A nor C. But, with respect to Category B, the UK incidence is very high compared to the other three countries in Table 3.1, and is second only to Finland in the wider set analysed in OECD (2003). This suggests an internationally high identification of Category B special educational needs, which can be related to specific features of the UK (England) system. Recent statistics show a large increase in the percentage of pupils identified with SEN without Statements (School Action and School Action Plus) in the UK (England) from 2003 (14%) to 2010 (18.2%) (Ofsted, 2010). This increase can be seen to reflect a system in which identification is undertaken for non-Statement SEN at school level without the more intensive and systematic methods used for identifying Statement SENs.

The above analysis represents countries that are economically more developed. Less developed countries tend to identify fewer children as requiring additional provision. Even China, which is fast becoming a major world nation economically, only recognises six areas of disability. In terms of the OECD Category A (disability), these are visual, hearing, intellectual, physical, psychiatric and multiple impairments and this represents a lower percentage of the child and young people population than OECD countries (Kritzer, 2011). Compared to the USA, China does not recognise specific learning disabilities (or learning disability, for short) which is the largest US area. Also, there are great differences between urban areas, such as Beijing and Shanghai, and rural areas, where many children with disabilities may not attend school (Worrell and Taber, 2009). In this respect, China is similar to other developing countries in identifying fewer categories of disability/impairment. Botswana, as an example of an African country, identifies four areas for special educational provision: visual impairment, hearing impairment, mental handicap and physical disability (Dart, 2007).

Most countries use some form of categorical system, identifying between four and ten types of disability (Peters, 2003). The examples of Botswana and the USA represent this range. As discussed in Chapter 2, the identification process usually consists of two parts:

1. Recognising an impairment or disability.
2. Deciding that this condition requires some additional provision.

In the USA the first part involves identifying from a set of recognised disabilities, which are established under a legislative framework (IDEA, 2004). Countries differ in terms of whether this process is undertaken within the education system or by medical or health professionals. As countries become more developed, the process tends to be done within education, and this has been associated with the development of school or educational psychology services (Hatzichristou, 2002).

The concept of 'special educational needs' in English practice

The system in the UK (England) fits this two-part model, but rather than allocating a child to a recognised kind of disability in the first part, the child's educational functioning is assessed in context and a decision made about having a 'learning difficulty' or not. The preference for the language of 'learning difficulty' is a legacy of the Warnock Report (DES, 1978), which avoided the language of impairment and disability. That the term 'learning difficulty' acts like 'disability' in other countries is evident from the way that 'learning difficulties' are defined and are said to 'call for special education provision' (Education Act, 1996: section 312). This corresponds to the second part of the process, referred to above, about a condition requiring additional provision. 'Learning difficulty' is defined in terms of a child having:

> a significantly greater *difficulty in learning* than the majority of children of his age ... [or having] a *disability* which either prevents or hinders him from

> making use of educational facilities of a kind generally provided for children of his age in schools within the area of the local education authority.
>
> *(Education Act, 1996: section 312, italics added)*

This difficulty/disability definition of SEN is confusing for several reasons. SEN is defined as 'learning difficulties' that are then said to be 'difficulties in learning' or a 'disability'. All that is said about a 'learning difficulty' is that it is a significantly greater difficulty than the majority of the same age. This leaves quite open what is to count as a significantly greater degree of difficulty that risks divergent ideas about what counts as a 'learning difficulty'. We know that a difficulty in learning which arises from learning English as an additional language will not count as a 'learning difficulty' and therefore not as a special educational need, because this is stipulated in the legislation (Education Act, 1996: section 312). But, further details and specificity have not been available. And, as argued above, the implication is that the causes of the 'learning difficulty' in SEN are to be found in impairment/disability. That the language of SEN does not really abandon the 'deficit' language of impairment and disability suggests that the Warnock legacy could be interpreted as a non-labelling strategy that is superficial (Soder, 1989). Soder argued that attempts to change negative labels will involve replacement with alternative labels, not non-labelling, and that alternative labels (e.g. SEN and 'learning difficulties') do not necessarily change the meaning of what they denote. The reason for this is that such social meanings are anchored in a system which stands as an external reality. This is not to say that these social meanings cannot change, but they do not change by simply changing labels; such change involves wider social changes.

It is clear from analysis of policy guidance – for example, in the SEN Code of Practice (DfES, 2001a) – that 'learning difficulty' is used as a generic term and that there are different kinds of learning difficulties/special educational needs. The code talks about 'categories of SEN', though it is careful to mention that these are 'not hard and fast' and that:

> each child is unique and that the questions asked by the LEA should reflect the circumstances of that child ... there is a wide spectrum of SENs that are frequently inter-related, although there are also specific needs that usually relate directly to particular kinds of impairments.
>
> *(DfES, 2001a: section 7.52)*

It then sets out four broad areas of need on the assumption that individuals might have needs across these four areas. These broad areas were set out in more detail in the classification to be used for collecting national data about pupils with Statements and at School Action Plus (DfES, 2005):

   A. Cognition and Learning Needs:
   Specific Learning Difficulty (SpLD); Moderate Learning Difficulty (MLD); Severe Learning Difficulty (SLD); Profound and Multiple Learning Difficulty (PMLD)

B. Behaviour, Emotional and Social Development Needs:
Behaviour, Emotional and Social Difficulty (BESD) including ADHD
C. Communication and Interaction Needs:
Speech, Language and Communication Needs (SLCN); Autistic Spectrum Disorder (ASD)
D. Sensory and/or Physical Needs:
Visual Impairment (VI); Hearing Impairment (HI); Multi-Sensory Impairment (MSI); Physical Disability (PD)

One of the main problems with this scheme is that there is a slippage in the use of language from the four broad areas or dimensions as 'needs' to specific categories, which are expressed in varied terms: 'difficulties', 'needs', 'disorder', 'disability' and 'impairment'. The four broad areas are called dimensions, implying a spectrum or continuum, while these consist of categories that cover a wide range of terms which have different meanings and origins. There can be a tension between dimensions and categories, but how they coexist is not discussed nor resolved. Why some areas are defined in medical classification terms (e.g. ASD and ADHD), while others, such as moderate learning difficulties (MLD) and severe learning difficulties (SLD), are defined in terms of difficulties is unexplained. A medical term, such as 'intellectual disabilities', as used by DSM IV-TR (APA, 2000), could have been used for severe learning difficulties (SLD). Also, disability is sometimes defined in medical classifications in terms of impairments (intellectual disability as an impairment in intellectual functioning), while disorders can be defined in terms of disability (e.g. ASD as developmental disability). This confusing mix of terms can be seen to represent two influences in the UK (English) SEN framework. One is the influence of voluntary organisations and parents who define their interests and identities in terms of medical-related categories; the other is the influence of the Warnock Report and wider social model critique of medical categories.

Arguments against current use of SEN term

This analysis shows that the term 'special educational needs' has come to be used in two distinct ways which causes confusion and misunderstanding. In its original formulation and in the way it is used by OECD, it has a resource focus and is about additional provision of various types that are required given various disabilities, difficulties or disadvantages. In this sense, types of special educational needs are about different types of teaching approaches and programmes, learning settings, facilities, etc. Types of SEN are not about kinds of child and student disabilities and difficulties. However, what has happened in the UK is that the meaning of SEN has become a softened and more acceptable way of talking, at least for some, about disabilities and difficulties. The related term 'learning difficulties' also produces confusion. First, it is used as a generic term to cover all areas of SEN. In this sense it is the preferred term following the Warnock Report for 'disability' or 'difficulties'. Second, it is used to describe intellectual difficulties in the cognitive and learning dimension, as in moderate learning difficulties (MLD), severe learning difficulties (SLD) or profound and multiple learning difficulties (PMLD), what in DSM IV-TR would be called 'intellectual disabilities'.

Despite the principles of the SEN framework, as discussed in Chapter 2, with its focus on needed provision (not difficulties) and on individual needs within an interactionist causal framework, we find SEN used as a hierarchy of general pupil categories of difficulties, with little reference to the child in context or individual needs or requirements. To summarise the above analysis, I will now outline the main contemporary criticism of the term 'special educational needs'.

Perpetuating negative labelling

This criticism is about SEN as a super-category with its continued focus on children's 'difficulties'. As a super-category, the use of the SEN term, it is argued, continues to label children negatively and its use is devaluing of them. The view goes back some time; for example, Solity (1991) argued that SEN had become a discriminatory concept, while Corbett (1996) wrote about the language of sentimentality and prejudice. This line of argument has been developed since then and is incorporated in the Inclusion Index (Booth and Ainscow, 2011), in which SEN is portrayed as focusing on 'deficiencies' and should be replaced by talk about 'barriers to learning and participation' (p. 40). The issues about labelling will be examined in more detail in the next section.

Separatist industry

This criticism focuses on the expansion of the SEN field by providers with a professional interest in a separatist field. This expansion has been portrayed as costly and inefficient, when what is seen to be required is improved teaching and learning in the general system (Marks, 2000). John Marks's argument was for radical reform that would introduce more traditional teaching methods for literacy while abandoning 'inclusive' policies. This was seen as necessary to reduce the numbers identified as having SEN without Statements (those with less severe SEN) so that effort could focused on those with more severe SENs, what he calls those with 'real SENs' (Marks, 2000: 36).

What is interesting is how these politically right-wing views resemble the critical social views about the growth of SEN, from a more left-wing perspective (Tomlinson, 1985). Where these viewpoints differ is that Marks is critical of the excessive cost and inefficiency of the school system which should be serving the economy in a positive way, while Tomlinson saw dominant economic and social interests as less benign and not addressing the interests of the less advantaged. Marks's analysis has been adopted and developed more recently by the Conservative Party review of SEN (Conservative Party, 2007). This was elaborated in a policy paper (Wilkins, 2008) that used statistical data to show that the recent growth in incidence of SEN was due to the rise in those at School Action (the least severe level). Wilkins argued for a reduction in the identification of non-Statement SEN by enhancing the general teaching, especially of literacy in primary schools. This line of argument was endorsed by an Ofsted national review of SEN (Ofsted, 2010) in terms of the over-identification of SEN, and became one of the main principles of the government's subsequent SEN policy and legislation (DfE, 2011).

As poorly defined super-category

In this related criticism, SEN is seen as poorly defined and vague. This can lead to uncertainty about the identification of special educational needs and results in unacceptable variability (a 'post code lottery') about needs identification and therefore provision availability. This criticism specifically points to problems in defining the coverage of the SEN term. This is evident when comparing the current English classification with the broad three-way OECD definition of SEN (as described above). The UK (English) classification (DfES, 2005) covers A and B, but there is a silence about socially based needs seen to require compensatory education, C.

Relationship between SEN and wider group of 'vulnerable' children

As part of the reorganisation of Children's Services in local authorities during the 2000s that were integrated and focused around the broad needs of children and young people, a Common Assessment Framework (CAF) was established as part of the Every Child Matters (ECM) framework (DfES, 2006a). The CAF is a standardised approach for a range of practitioners in Children's Services to conduct an assessment of a child's 'additional needs' and decide how those needs should be met. The CAF distinguished between children with:

- no 'additional needs';
- with 'additional needs';
- with 'complex needs' who are part of the broader group of those with additional needs.

'Additional needs' was introduced to cover a wider range of 'vulnerable' children that included those with SEN and disabilities, but extended to other groups, such as those showing disruptive or anti-social behaviour; lacking parental support and boundaries; involvement in or at risk of offending; poor attendance or exclusion from school; experiencing bullying; disengagement from education, training or employment post-16; poor nutrition; ill-health; substance misuse; anxiety or depression; housing issues; pregnancy and parenthood. Children with 'complex needs' in the third group were a sub-group of those with 'additional needs' who met the threshold for statutory involvement such as: children who are the subject of a child protection plan; looked after children/children in care; care leavers; children with severe and complex special educational needs; children with complex disabilities or complex health needs; children diagnosed with significant mental health problems; and young offenders involved with youth justice services (community and custodial).

It is clear that the CAF incorporated special educational needs as one amongst other statutory systems alongside child protection, social care, mental health and youth offending. Though the CAF represents a more inclusive concept of need, not that much progress was made in integrating the SEN within the CAF system. This is an issue that the House of Commons Select Committee inquiry into SEN identified as requiring government clarification (House of Commons, 2006). Yet, with the change in government in 2010 and the move to a narrower definition of SEN in the 2011 Green Paper (DfE, 2011), this issue has been put aside. Though the English concept of 'additional needs' was more inclusive than the current concept of 'special educational needs', it still focused on 'vulnerable' children and did not include those with learning support needs arising from English being an additional language. In terms of the OECD three-way classification, it included Category C: disadvantage, but only arising from socio-economic disadvantage not from linguistic factors. Additional needs also differs from the more inclusive Scottish model of 'additional support needs' (SEED, 2003), which in replacing the concept of SEN also included those who need learning support arising from English being an additional language. It is now clear that the English and Scottish models have diverged considerably, with the Scottish adopting a broad inclusive category of additional support needs and the English adopting a narrower impairment/disability concept (Cline, 2011).

Fit with disability legislation

The extension of the disability discrimination provision through the SEN and Disability legislation in 2001 also does not fit easily with the SEN framework. This is evident in the differing approaches to definition. In disability discrimination legislation, a disabled person is defined as someone with a mental or physical impairment that affects their ability to carry out normal activities (DfES/DRC, 2006). As discussed above, in the SEN legislation, 'special educational needs' is defined in terms of 'learning difficulties' and 'disability', with the latter term unspecified and the former left vague and open.

Disability in the legislative framework is about impairment having significant and adverse impact on everyday activities. This is a cross-sector definition that goes beyond the education sector; it also relates to the second and rarely used part of the SEN framework in terms of a disability preventing the child using educational facilities. The primary definition and use of SEN is in terms of 'learning difficulties' that call for 'special education provision'; terms which were given open and relative definitions leading to some of the problems discussed above. Recent research concluded along these lines that disability and SEN are not interchangeable terms. It was found, for example, that for over half the children with SEN in mainstream schools parents did not see them as meeting the disability discrimination legislation criteria. This included some children with mental health and health needs whose difficulties were unknown to schools (Porter et al., 2011).

Figure 3.1 summarises the range of different models or definitions used in the UK which have been discussed above. The most general model is the OECD one that covers disability, difficulties and disadvantage and is based on the concept of additional resourcing. However, if resource additionality is the key to special needs, then there is a question about whether additional resourcing for children with very high achievements (abilities), often called 'gifted and talented' could be said to also have a special need. Were special need so interpreted, as a concept of exceptionality or atypicality, this unites those with disadvantages and advantages. However, the broad OECD concept of special educational needs does focus onto 'vulnerability' and disadvantage. How is the resourcing of teaching and additional language learning to be conceptualised? Whether additional resources required for learning an additional language should be construed in terms of vulnerability or disadvantage is illustrated in the difference between the Scottish concept of 'additional support needs', which does include EAL, and the English concept of 'additional needs', which does not. It is within this context that the dual English system of SEN and disability is best understood. SEN is limited to disabilities and difficulties and excludes EAL, while disability in disability discrimination legislation is confined to impairments that adversely affect activities. Finally, set against these concepts is the social model, which avoids the language of personal deficiencies and needs, preferring to talk about 'barriers' that are external factors.

Labelling: positive or negative

Central to the future of the current use of SEN in UK (England) as well as derivative and broader concepts of SEN (e.g. OECD version and Scottish model) is the use of categories as labels that are attributed to individuals and to services and organisations serving these individuals. Some people regard labels, such SEN, as

SEN
(disability, difficulties, disadvantage)
Includes EAL OECD:
three causal areas

SEN
Excludes EAL
(current English model)

Disability
(impairment interfering)
admission, services, exclusion
(current UK)

Additional needs
Every Child Matters
(English model):
'vulnerable children'

Additional support needs: Scotland
includes EAL

Barriers:
Social model – avoids SEN language/categories

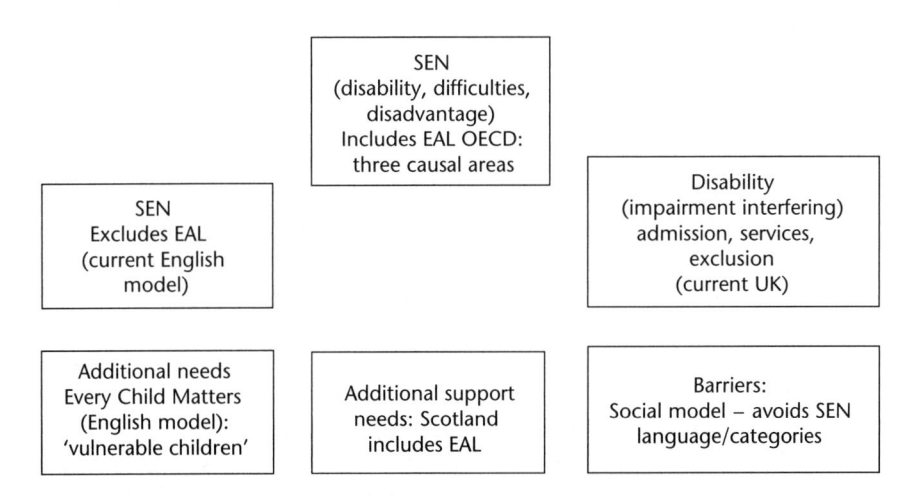

FIGURE 3.1 Different models in use

negative, as discussed above (Solity, 1991; Corbett, 1996). More recently Runswick-Cole and Hodge (2009) argued the actual use of the term SEN in schools acts to exclude pupils psychologically and socially and acts as a general term which cannot be seen as neutral or benign. However, some parents of children undergoing assessment find diagnostic categorisation useful (Brogan and Knussen, 2003). For some parents, not having a diagnosis is experienced as distressing (Dumit, 2006). Parents have been found to use difficulty/disorder categories as a shorthand concept to explain the nature of a child's difficulties to others (Farrugia, 2009; Rutter, 2011). In this sense they act as a summary of behaviours and are reductive (Jutel, 2009). The usefulness of a diagnosis for a parent, particularly a mother, may be as an explanation for a child's unacceptable behaviour or poor academic performance. It has also been argued that having a category can change attributions from holding the child responsible for being a 'problem' and so blaming her/him, to having a difficulty or impairment that can be addressed positively (Singh, 2004).

It is important to understand that an evaluation of labels depends on both the label's meaning and its context and history of use. The connotation of specific labels might change depending on the context of their use. Hastings et al. (1993) found that different kinds of labels used for adults with learning/intellectual disabilities were negatively evaluated by college students; for example, 'mental sub-normality', 'mental handicap'. Though 'learning difficulties' and 'learning disabilities' were evaluated more positively, even they were negatively evaluated; only 'exceptional' was positively evaluated. Hastings and Remington (1993) refer to a labelling cycle in which terms that start off with positive connotations accumulate negative evaluations through the negative attitudes to people with disabilities, in this case intellectual disabilities. These authors considered the option of selecting positive terms as a strategy to enhance the labels' connotation. But, they concluded that using a term where the usual usage refers to competence may not sustain a positive connotation over time. A later study of label connotation showed the variability in label connotation. Norwich (1999) found that professionals who worked with children with SEN evaluated the labels 'SEN' and 'learning difficulties' positively compared to terms such as 'disability', 'impairment' and 'abnormality'. The contrasting findings in these studies probably reflect the difference between a general college student group and professionals who are committed to working with children with disabilities and difficulties. In terms of a labelling cycle, the positive connotation associated with SEN and learning difficulties could be seen to reflect the positive Warnock strategy of focusing on educational needs which is shared by all and 'special' which has had a positive connotation. These terms may no longer have positive connotations for some people in some contexts, as argued by Runswick-Cole and Hodge (2009), but it is clear that the process of identification or using labels in the education of children with disabilities and difficulties is neither consistently positive nor negative from different perspectives.

Laughlin and Boyle (2007) consider the arguments and counter-arguments for using categories or labels in special education. They identify five kinds of arguments for how labels might be useful:

1. Labels open doors to resources and interventions.
2. Labels are awareness raising and promote understanding of particular difficulties.
3. Labels reduce ambiguities and provide a basis for clear communications.
4. Labels provide comfort to children and families by explaining their difficulties.
5. Labels provide people with a social identity and a sense of belonging to a group.

For each argument they consider the counter-argument and overall conclude that labels are more unhelpful than helpful. The negative aspects are summarised as about stigma, bullying, reduced life opportunities, reduced expectations, focus on deficits rather than other characteristics, misclassification, uncertainty about definitions of some category/labels and not necessarily leading to specific educational interventions. Yet they seem to go back on this conclusion when they recognise that a label of 'disability' is required in disability discrimination legislation, which they support, and by accepting that there might be some positive aspects in some cases and contexts. They also recognise that parents and children might have the opportunity to accept or reject a label – an approach which recognises that there is no clear-cut and definitive way of determining the value of a label. Also, their analysis does suggest that no general conclusions can be drawn, as the significance of labels depends on what specific area of disability/difficulties is involved; for example, an impairment where its presence is generally agreed (severe visual impairment) or one whose presence is more contested (dyslexia, Asperger's syndrome). The significance of labels also varies according to perspective; for example, parents and their child might see value in a label of dyslexia, but a teacher, local authority panel or education expert might not. Finally, the usefulness of labels cannot be seen out of the context of how people use the label. If it is used in a negative, excluding or demeaning way to belittle and ignore needs and requirements, then that is different from its positive use to provide opportunities and ways of participating with others.

Learner categories: real or socially constructed

Educational labels such as 'SEN' and 'learning difficulty' and medical labels such as 'dyslexia' and 'intellectual disability', as discussed above, are all seen as deficit terms and rejected from a social model. As Barnes and Sheldon (2007) argue, treating such notions as 'real phenomena in the world must be rigorously questioned' (p. 240). Clark et al. (1998) similarly questioned the assumption that differences between learners are objectively 'real' and that these differences 'take the form of deficits and difficulties' (p. 157). Now, Cigman (2007b), from a philosophical perspective, has questioned these positions about the denial of the reality of difficulties and deficits, what she sees as a metaphysical position about what exists (ontology) that is adopted to support an ethical position about inclusion. Hacking (1999) argues that the main purpose of these social constructionist positions (e.g. Barnes and Sheldon, Clarke et al.) is consciousness raising and as critical of the status quo. Hacking identifies several assumptions underlying these social perspectives:

- In the present state of affairs X is taken for granted and seen as inevitable (where X could be SEN or autism).
- X need not have existed; X is not determined by the nature of things nor is inevitable.
- X is quite bad as it is.
- Things would be better if X were abandoned or at least radically transformed.

Hacking identifies six increasing grades of commitment to a social constructionist position as:

1. Historical
2. Ironic
3. Reformist
4. Unmaking
5. Rebellious
6. Revolutionary.

The historical grade of a social constructionist position is the least demanding in seeing X as contingent (it could have been otherwise) and as an outcome of a historical process, but there is no commitment to whether X is good or bad. The ironic commitment recognises historical contingency, but there is a realisation that there is not much one can do about X in the current situation; one is ironically forced to accept X. The historical and ironic commitments accept assumptions 1 and 2 above. By contrast the reformist commitment also accepts assumption 3 (that X is bad) aiming to make changes to some aspects of X. Alongside the reformist is the unmaking commitment, which does not aim to refute ideas but to reveal the negative functions they serve. Hacking links this to a Marxian approach which aims to strip ideas of their authority by unmasking the interests served by X. An example of this approach is Tomlinson's analysis of SEN as serving professional school system interests with false rhetoric about 'benevolent humanitarianism' (Tomlinson, 1985). Unmasking is an intellectual exercise and, according to Hacking, may or may not go along with the next level of commitment to abandon X (assumption 4), being rebellious, or for radical transformation, being revolutionary, the highest level of commitment. The rejection of the 'learning difficulties' and 'SEN' from proponents of inclusion in favour of talk about 'barriers' as factors external to the child (Booth and Ainscow, 2011) can be seen as reflecting these higher levels of social constructionist commitment.

Hacking's analysis cuts through the medical–social model dichotomy and classificatory assumptions by trying to relate two lines of thinking about the kinds of things that exist: *indifferent* kinds and *interactive* kinds of things. Indifferent kinds have sometimes been called natural kinds of things, such as rocks or gold, while interactive kinds are human kinds (categories and classifications), such as psychiatric disorders or kinds of learning disabilities or difficulties. He argues that though interactive kinds may be regarded as definite categories with clear criteria, it is more credible to see them as 'moving targets' (Hacking, 2006: 2). Investigations and classifications of human beings interact with the people categorised and in so doing change them; this is what he calls the looping effect of classifications. And, this leads to him saying that in this sense the human sciences create kinds of people, what he calls 'making up people' (p. 2).

This analysis has interesting implications for classifying disabilities and difficulties in relation to education. Are categories such as dyslexia, autism or ADHD, for instance, interactive kinds and so 'made up' or are they indifferent kinds? Hacking argues that it is possible to consider a category such as autism as having features of both an indifferent and an interactive kind. If autism is at root a biological pathology, then this is what is considered a natural or what he calls an indifferent kind. This is the assumption behind the search for a biological basis of conditions such as autism and dyslexia and the increasing search for genetic and neuro-science causes. However, he also considers that autism is an interactive kind in which people categorised as autistic change through looping effects. He recognises this as setting up a dilemma (Hacking, 1999), which can be resolved, he argues, by using a semantic theory of reference, as advocated by Putnam and Kripke (Kripke, 1980). In this theory of meaning, the meaning of autism involves current ideas, descriptions and prototypes and then eventually refers to something of a natural or indifferent kind, a particular biological basis. So, it would be acceptable following this theory of meaning to say that there is probably an unknown neuropathology that is causal of examples of what we call autism, representing an indifferent kind. But, it would also be acceptable to say that 'autism' is a social construct that interacts with parents, professionals and the children involved themselves. What is socially constructed is therefore the category of autism and to some extent the children themselves and their way of being, not the neural basis which is an indifferent kind. Interestingly, for Hacking what is important is not the semantics of this resolution, but the dynamics. How would the discovery of a biological basis affect perspectives and categories of autism? Would different children be identified? Would some now identified no longer be so and how would that affect them?

Zachar (2000) argues that categories of disorder used in the DSM and similar classification systems cannot be assumed to be natural kinds. No one criteria or set of criteria are necessary and sufficient, as there are many ways of meeting the criteria for many of the categories. This implies that mental disorders and functional impairments, which are invoked in the education of children with SEN, are what he calls *practical* kinds. They are stable patterns justified by their usefulness for certain purposes such as interventions or additional resource allocations. They are not naturally occurring bounded entities defined by essential features, reflecting the world as it 'really is'. Haslam (2003) also notes that categoric judgements are endemic to psychiatry, partly from the history of such judgements in medicine. This is associated with a model of diseases as discrete entities, having an essence. This model owes its origins to the natural science approach to taxonomy; for example, the periodic table in chemistry. However, it has been pointed out that even diseases and species are not natural kinds as are chemical elements; frequently all members of a species do not share the same genetic structure (Dupre, 1981). In addition, medical categoric judgements also arise from binary decisions expected about treatment, interventions, and in special education to entitlements to additional provision.

Davis (2008) applies these philosophical considerations to learner categories, arguing that the categories of learning difficulties or disabilities cannot be given a clear, simple and unambiguous interpretation. His argument is that talk of the dysfunction of brains, with reference to, say, dyslexia, can only provide a biological basis if the function relates to biological survival. But, as he argues, how these Darwinian ideas can underpin the classifying of learners is left unclear. There are similar problems with finding a genetic basis to provide a robust essentialist basis for conditions such as dyslexia. This is because phenotypes relate to genotypes in complex ways, not one to one. Similarly, although neuro-science mapping has made considerable advances, whether this will identify discrete kinds of neural functioning corresponding to a learning disability/difficulty, such as dyslexia, is unlikely, given the brain's plasticity and its complex and integrated ways of functioning. Davis, following Hacking's analysis of mental/behavioural disorders, argues that there may be advances in identifying neurological and biological factors involved in the origin of some learning difficulties/disabilities, But, he concludes that the idea of basing learner categories *exclusively* on neuro-physiological factors – in other words, establishing categories as based only on natural or indifferent kinds – is very doubtful.

In this section I have argued that medical categories used in education can refer to phenomena that have features of natural or indifferent kinds and features of interactive kinds (socially constructed), involving looping and social interaction effects. Categories do not have crisp and objective boundaries; differentiations are made pragmatically in terms of various types of consequences, what Zacher (2000) calls *practical* kinds. This means that there is no true difference in kind across a category boundary. What is important about the above analysis is that it rejects the attributed essentialism often assumed in the use of medical categories (Slee, 2010). Contrary to critical social perspectives, as argued above, medical categories used in education do not imply essences of a natural kind. They are practical categories, and in some cases a mix of natural (or indifferent) and interactive kinds, involving a bio-social interaction.

Dilemmas in identification

The value of categories in education, whether more educationally defined ones (e.g. moderate learning difficulties (MLD), specific learning difficulties (SpLD)) or medically defined ones (e.g. autistic spectrum disorder (ASD) or attention deficit hyperactivity disorder (ADHD)) can be examined in terms of five related criteria or functions:

1. Whether there are distinctive characteristics associated with the category.
2. Whether the category provides a basis for communication and understanding of particular difficulties.
3. Whether the category has significance and is useful for teaching.

4. Providing the grounds for allocating additional resources.
5. Providing a basis for a positive social identity and solidarity of those who have the difficulty.

These functions can be seen to relate directly to the five kinds of arguments identified by Laughlin and Boyle (2007) for the usefulness of labels. It is important to understand that these criteria, though related in principle, can and do in practice operate separately. For example, a particular category (e.g. dyslexia) may provide the basis for allocating additional resources as well as a positive social identity, while not having distinct characteristics relative to other literacy difficulties, nor having significance for specific kinds of teaching. While there may be controversies about dyslexia in relation to criteria 1 (distinctive characteristics) and 3 (specific teaching) (Gibbs and Elliott, 2010), the category can provide the basis for additional resourcing (criterion 4) and the basis for social identity and solidarity (criterion 5; e.g. in category based on voluntary organisation supporting parents and their children).

One way of summarising the debates about the value of categories is to consider two basic stances to responding to learner differences:

1. Differentiation stance: in this stance significant differences are marked as 'difficulties' to focus on and ensure appropriate resources and teaching adaptations.
2. Commonality stance: in this stance significant differences are seen as requiring appropriate ordinary school and teaching adaptations.

Both stances can have risks: the differentiation stance can lead to separation, devaluation and stigma and the commonality stance can lead to overlooking individual needs and inadequate provision. This sets up a tension that can give rise to a dilemma about identification that relates to what has been called 'dilemmas of difference', a term used initially by Martha Minow (Minow, 1990). As she asks:

> When does treating people differently emphasize their differences and stigmatise or hinder them on that basis? And when does treating people the same become insensitive to their difference and likely to stigmatise or hinder them on that basis?
>
> *(p. 20)*

In an international study of policy makers', managers' and teachers' perspectives in the USA, UK and Netherlands about dilemmas of difference, the majority of those interviewed recognised to some extent a dilemma about identifying children with special educational needs/disabilities (Norwich, 2008). Most of the participants across the three countries recognised tensions over identification between *ensuring additional resources* and *avoiding devaluation and stigma*. It is notable that their recognition of tensions was despite believing that there had been recent progress in promoting positive images of disability, that stigma had been reduced and that

48 Classification and identification

many parents wanted labels (Norwich, 2008: 75). Participants in this study also suggested resolutions to the identification dilemma as involving a combination of the commonality and differentiations stances, while recognising some remaining tensions despite these resolutions. The commonality strategies involved national and local developments that promoted an improved general school system that was more 'inclusive', better staff training, improved school ethos, promotion of positive images of disability and encouraging more social mixing and peer acceptance of children with disabilities. However, differentiation strategies were still seen as necessary, but at a reduced level, what some called a 'minimal labelling' approach. When labels were recognised as necessary, the suggested resolutions involved strategies that went beyond negative labels, by focusing on individuals and needed provision and showing sensitivity about labelling.

Some attempts to reduce stigma go so far as to reject any deficit or difficulty categories; for example, disability, difficulty or disorder. For instance, instead of autistic spectrum disorder (ASD), the term 'autistic spectrum condition' is preferred because it is seen as less stigmatising (Baron-Cohen et al., 2009). Other terminological responses to stigma are to refer to 'learning differences' rather than 'learning difficulties' and neuro-diversity for categories such as dyslexia or ADHD (Developmental Adult Neuro-diversity Association, 2012). However, deficit-like terms are still used to make sense of the 'condition', 'learning differences' or 'neuro-diversity' and resource and support accessing are not abandoned. For this reason, it is possible to see these terminological responses as resolutions to dilemmas of differences, where the resolution does not fully solve the issue. Further examples of this are discussed in Chapter 7, when discussing children and young people's perspectives on their differences.

As argued in Chapter 1, though categories can be used in devaluing and discriminatory ways, they can also be used positively, and it is this latter use which is advocated here in terms of a framework that respects all learners (Cigman, 2007a). Specific categories or labels of difference (e.g. disability) can be adopted with less risk of negativity if they are set within this kind of values framework. With this value framework it is possible to derive a three-dimensions model to inform decisions about categories. Learners who experience difficulties in learning share needs or requirements with *all other children (common needs)*, while having *unique individual* needs or requirements distinct from all others. But some of these children may also share some specific general similarities in their difficulties, so becoming members of a specific category; for example, specific language impairment. So, the identification of needs or requirements can be seen from this perspective to involve these three concurrent dimensions (Lewis and Norwich, 2004):

1. Needs common to all.
2. Needs specific to sub-groups.
3. Needs unique to individuals.

This three-dimensions model provides a way of connecting the additional needs of those with disabilities, difficulties or disadvantages to the needs of all children, because all children have common and unique needs. There will be more analysis and discussion of this model in subsequent chapters. But, the key point for this chapter is that identification of subgroups is justified in terms of addressing additional needs or requirements, whatever the kind of category used.

A teaching based bio–psycho–social model

In this final section I will build on the previous analyses to make the case for a development that integrates a bio–psycho–social model of disability into an assessment for intervention approach. Picking up the argument from above, it can be seen that identifying educational needs or requirements for children with disabilities and difficulties involves balancing common–different needs; this is where the three-dimensions model is useful to recognise needs that go beyond subgroup related ones. This model provides a way to resolve conceptually the dilemma of difference as regards identification (Norwich, 2009). But, resolving the dilemma in practice, as discussed above, involves starting with and using commonality strategies as far as these can go. Where differentiating strategies begin depends on how well common or general systems of provision can be geared to individual needs; or in common usage, made more inclusive. The more inclusive the provision, the less need there is for subgroup categories and identification. This has been the basis for the three tiers and the Response to Instruction (RTI) models of identifying disability and difficulties in education (Vaughn and Fuchs, 2003), which have been influential in the USA and internationally, and been adopted in the 'Wave' model in the UK (NLS, 2003).

The tier or Wave model has its origins in public health with its framework of primary, secondary and tertiary prevention (Adelman and Taylor, 2003) which influenced US school-based mental health and psychological interventions. In school education it links general to special education through the 'three tiered' model – where primary intervention consists of high-quality general education programmes, secondary intervention involves fixed duration intensive programmes for some and tertiary intervention involves special education programmes (Vaughn and Fuchs, 2003). The UK Wave model operated at three levels:

- Wave 1: the effective inclusion of all children in high-quality differentiated literacy programme.
- Wave 2: additional small-group intervention in addition to Wave 1, for children who can be expected to catch up with their peers as a result of the intervention.
- Wave 3: specific targeted approaches for children, not responding to Wave 2, identified as requiring specialist support.

However, the relationship between Wave 3 (specialist support) and the graduated system of identifying SEN (School Action, School Action Plus or with a Statement) was not clarified in its UK use. In the USA, by contrast, RTI has been required in some states in relation to literacy and the identification of specific learning disabilities (equivalent to specific learning difficulties in the UK). In a few states the RTI is also applied for the identification or part of the identification of other disabilities in education (Zirkel and Thomas, 2010).

This three-tiered model underlies US attempts to reconceptualise specific learning disability. The idea of 'response to instruction' is to avoid what has been called the 'wait to fail' model where identification does not derive from nor is linked to teaching and learning settings. The basic principle underlying RTI is early response to signs of not progressing in literacy through an intensive fixed-duration programme. *Non-responding* is used as the criterion for identifying a learning disability that requires special educational programming.

There has been much contention about whether RTI can replace traditional child-focused psychometric assessments (Reynolds and Shaywitz, 2009; Fletcher and Vaughn, 2009). There are also conceptual and operational issues about this three-tiered model as there are with its derivative three-wave model (Vaughn and Fuchs, 2003). For instance, how much adaptation is to be made in tier/Wave 1 for those not progressing in literacy in the general classroom? Are tier/Wave 2 programmes part of general or special education programmes? How intensive do tier/Wave 1 and 2 programmes have to be for valid identification? There is also the question of whether inadequate literacy learning in response to instruction or teaching (to use the UK term) is equivalent to what is called a specific learning disability/difficulty. What about other associated difficulties, such as attentional, language and behaviour difficulties? What about inadequate literacy learning associated with consistent inadequate learning across the curriculum? And, what about children whose literacy levels and rates of literacy learning are not discrepant enough from the general school/class mean, but still below the general mean and highly discrepant from their own level and rate in other curriculum areas (so called bright students with learning disability)? In the USA, Vaughn and Fuchs (2003) recognise that these questions indicate the value of further assessment and identification procedures beyond a simple 'response to instruction' model.

Despite these issues with RTI and related technical ones that leave out socio-emotional and cultural processes in its focus on 'eliminating contextual variables' (Artiles et al., 2010), the RTI approach takes seriously that additional needs is based on an interaction between a learner and her/his environmental context. It has been characterised as an assessment for intervention or teaching, not assessment for determining categories/ labels. In this sense it is similar to the growing interest in interactive approaches and interactive models of disability (Shakespeare, 2006). Another approach, a causal modelling framework, involves the interaction between biological, cognitive and behavioural level factors in interaction with environmental factors (Morton and Frith, 1995). This framework enables analysis of the strengths and difficulties at different levels in interaction with environmental supports and barriers, and in so doing shows how similar behavioural outcomes can arise from different causal pathways, not only or exclusively of a biological basis. Frith (1999) has shown how this framework works with respect to the complexities related to dyslexia, while Frederickson and Cline (2009) illustrate the usefulness of this framework for a range of disabilities and difficulties in education. Though useful for a child-within-context framework, this framework is not a social analysis at macro-levels (policy/legislation) or mid-levels (school/class level). As such it does not address how social and cultural processes affect the child in her/his immediate context.

Another development which is also based on bio–psycho–social assumptions and has particular relevance to the issues raised in this chapter is the WHO's International Classification of Functioning for Children and Young People (ICF-CY: WHO, 2002; WHO, 2007). This classification framework represents a basic move from using medical disease and disorder categories (e.g. based on DSM and ICD) to a focus on functioning in various social contexts (Simeonsson, 2009). In this sense it represents an integration of what have been called social and medical models into a multilevel, multidisciplinary and interactive model. It also replaces the ICIDH (WHO, 1980), which was criticised for its excessive medical slant and focus on the limitations of abilities as the key factor causing disability, rather than focusing on social barriers.

The ICF model represents disability in terms of the interaction of: 1) bodily functions/structures; 2) activities (tasks and activities that can be executed); and 3) participation (what the person can do in the current environment) – see Figure 3.2. These interrelated dimensions are seen as being influenced by health conditions (disorders/diseases), on one hand, and contextual factors (environmental and personal factors), on the other. However, the ICF system has been designed to cover functions, activities and participation in general across a range of life contexts, and therefore goes well beyond those aspects that relate specifically to educational functions, needs and specific contexts. It could therefore be argued that there is a need for an ICF-type classification of function, activity and participation specifically relevant to curriculum and teaching decisions and practices.

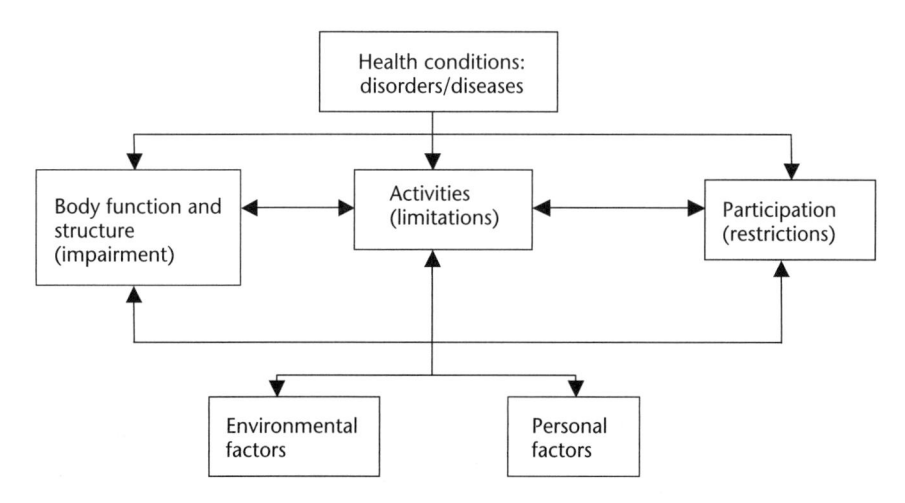

FIGURE 3.2 ICF model (reproduced with thanks to BMC Public Health)

52 Classification and identification

One of the advantages of the ICF framework is that it can break the hold that administrative and diagnostic categories have had for decisions about eligibility for special or additional provision. While eligibility decisions are made differently internationally, in terms of central versus local decisions and tight (e.g. USA) versus flexible criteria (e.g. UK), there have been concerns about how such decisions are also influenced by other factors such as ethnicity, gender and class (Florian and McClaughlin, 2008). Hollenweger (2011) suggests that the ICF provides a framework that opens up the issue of over- and under-representation, without having a fixed set of eligibility criteria, while establishing eligibility compatible with the human rights of people with disabilities. This, she argues, can be done within an ICF framework by opening up debate on thresholds for taking up access to special or additional provision. The ICF framework can also be seen to be compatible with the RTI approach, discussed above, because of its focus on assessment for intervention and programming rather than assessment for labelling.

In her extension of the ICF framework to education, Hollenweger underlines eligibility decisions as a problem-solving process that considers different professional as well as parent and child perspectives: the collecting of data from different sources. Her educational extension is based on the educational principle that eligibility is concerned not only about current participation but also future participation. This requires taking account of educational aims and goals as well as methods and practices. Figure 3.3 shows this educational expansion of the ICF framework in two ways. The first is to specific environmental factors in terms of relevant methods, services and provision, and the second is to add a dimension of educational/developmental goals that set the direction for enhancing current activity and participation levels. This extension is the basis for the development of the ICF procedures in Switzerland, which has been led by Judith Hollenweger (Hollenweger, 2011).

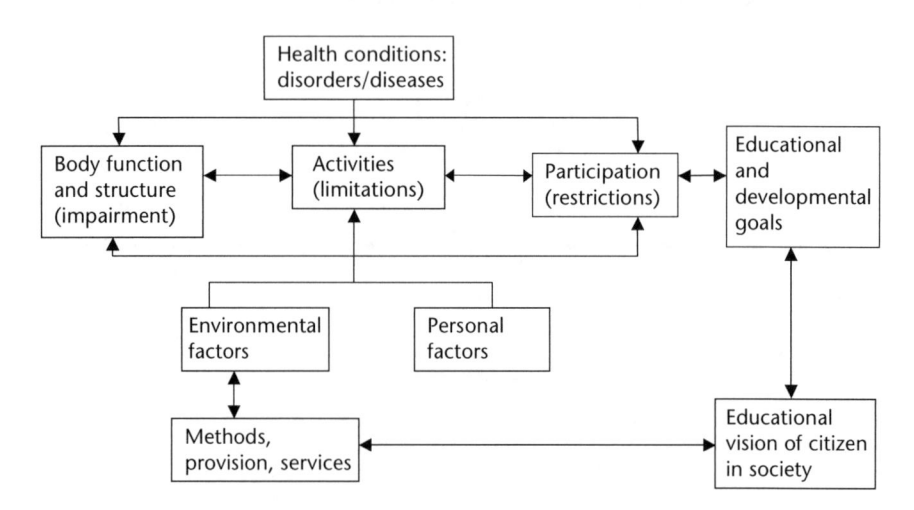

FIGURE 3.3 ICF expanded for educational use (reproduced with thanks to BMC Public Health)

Though this is early days for this kind of development and there are some issues associated with the ICF framework, the ICF is potentially a very important conceptual development with practical promise (Imre, 2004). However, Imre also considers that the ICF has failed to specify in enough detail some of the main claims about impairment and the nature of the bio–psycho–social theory. Badley (2008) also shows how there could be greater clarity about the activity and participation in the framework, while Nordenfelt (2003) identifies a confusion between capacity for action and actual performance in the ICF. However, as Shakespeare (2006) states, despite these issues, the ICF has promise as a way forward for defining and researching disability.

4
INCLUSIVE CURRICULUM ISSUES

Introduction

There is much written about inclusive teaching and inclusive curriculum where the implication is that this is for the benefit of all. Inclusive teaching often refers to teaching that recognises and accommodates all pupils or students. Sometimes this is put in terms of also meeting the individual learning needs of all, but often 'individual needs' is rejected as a phrase because it is taken to imply an individual rather than a social response to diversity and a focus on individual deficits rather than rights (Booth and Ainscow, 2011). This means that inclusive teaching acknowledges learners may be members of diverse communities, have disabilities and difficulties, have English as a second language and/or experience some specific social disadvantage. An inclusive curriculum, which is also often connected in general terms to inclusive teaching, is seen as having a key part in the role of education in society and the promotion of social policies concerned with social inclusion (UNESCO, 2009). Though concepts of inclusive curricula are opposed to a 'one size fits all' model, there is still a commitment to teaching a common curriculum by different means: by different teaching strategies and learning materials and media. This idea of diversity within a unity is one of the central issues and challenges confronted from an inclusive perspective to curriculum and teaching. These tensions between curriculum commonality and differentiation will be one of the main considerations in this chapter.

Much of the debate about inclusion, especially in relation to children with disabilities and difficulties, has been about the *location* of provision for them – whether in separate or ordinary school and class settings. Less attention has been given to the 'what' and 'how' of teaching and learning. This is why the chapter on curriculum comes before the chapters on pedagogy and schooling in this book. The focus of this chapter on curriculum also has particular significance for current debates about the nature of inclusion, whether it is a location-based concept (all in the local school: Booth et al., 2000) or a curriculum/pedagogy concept (all engaged in learning: Warnock, 2005; Cooper and Jacobs, 2011).

Current curriculum issues

Much of what has been written and done in the name of inclusive curriculum has not engaged in depth with historical and contemporary curriculum issues and tensions in school education. This may be because inclusion has its origins in the rights of those who have been socially excluded, the vulnerable and disadvantaged, to participate in local school settings. This has positioned the starting point of an inclusion perspective as outside the 'mainstream' system and the continuing issues it has confronted historically. Nor do more recent attempts to broaden inclusion as about the *education of all*, not just the 'vulnerable', engage with historical issues within curriculum (Booth and Ainscow, 2011). For instance, in the revised Inclusion Index, which re-emphasises the value basis of inclusion, five particular values are prioritised: equality, participation, community, respect for diversity and sustainability (Booth, 2011). From these and other values, a global rights-based curriculum is derived as an alternative curriculum with a strong social and functional orientation, with topics such as food, water, clothing, transport, energy, etc. However, it is said that knowledge associated with traditional curricula can be included into these functional areas; for example, biology into the areas of food and health. But, how a functional-oriented curriculum fits with a more traditional subject-based one is not discussed, nor is there any analysis of the compatibility of the various priority values underpinning inclusion.

TABLE 4.1 Typologies of educational models

Central focus	Skilbeck: Curriculum models	Lawton: Educational ideologies	Tanners: Educational vision	Egan: Ideas in education
1 Knowledge	Structure of forms and fields of knowledge	Classical humanism	Conservative	Truth about reality
2 Individual person	Pattern of learning activities	Progressivism	Romanticism	Nature's guidance
3 Society	Chart of culture	Reconstructionism	Progressivism	Socialisation
4 Effectiveness	Learning technology			

There have been deep historic differences and disagreements about the beliefs, assumptions and values that guide theorising about education. Some attempts refer to differences in theories, philosophies or ideologies. Others refer to differences in assumptions about designing the curriculum. Whatever terms are used, the differences can be understood to refer to the ends and means of education: differences in values, beliefs and assumptions about what is to be learned, society and the individual. Table 4.1 shows four different perspectives on types of educational models (Tanner and Tanner, 1980; Skilbeck, 1984; Lawton, 1989; Egan, 1998). All four authors agree on the first three types, though give them different names and emphasise different aspects of these three different orientations. Only Skilbeck identifies a fourth type: the learning technology model.

For Skilbeck, when the curriculum is approached as a *structure of forms and fields of knowledge*, it is considered as a corpus of knowledge which is to be assimilated by learners through a process of transmission from teachers. The main function of education in this approach is the growth of the mind in a variety of distinct knowledge areas. Here the main focus is knowledge-centred. Lawton refers to this orientation as *classical humanism* as it concentrates on the cultural heritage which education is to promote and reproduce. In value terms, classical humanism is conservative of what is good in literature, music and history, which links to the Tanners' description of this orientation as *conservative*. This orientation has its origins in values and beliefs associated with the ruling classes as guardians of what was good and worth preserving. As an ideology it can be traced in various forms back to the times of Plato in the fourth century BC. Egan portrays this orientation in terms of Platonic *truth about reality*. Learning these forms and fields of knowledge gives students a privileged rational view of reality so enabling them to go beyond conventional beliefs and prejudices of the time. The Tanners identify a modern version of the conservative vision, which focuses on what are seen as essential subjects that are relevant to intellectual development. This excludes subjects that focus on personal and social needs or vocational studies, and has been evident in the resurgence of the 'back to basics' moves in the UK and the USA since the 1970s.

The second orientation is person-centred, what Lawton called a *progressive* ideology that can be traced back only several hundred years to the growth of enlightenment ideas in the eighteenth century. Progressivism represents a romantic rejection of traditional values and practices, of what Lawton called classical humanism. In this approach the goal is for the child to discover for her/himself and follow her/his own impulses and inclinations. As Egan put it, the focus is on the developing child and her/his experience. If there is a planned curriculum, it would be based on experiences and topics chosen by the learner with discovery learning being the dominant style of teaching method. The Tanners describe this orientation as *romanticism* because of its thoroughgoing commitment to the individual learner's freedom to develop her or his potential without outside imposition and determination. The unfolding of natural potentials through spontaneity and the expression of felt needs is seen as central to genuine and effective learning. This emphasis on the feelings and interests of the learner has been seen historically as a reaction to authoritarian educational ideas and methods. Skilbeck refers to the model as a *pattern of learning activities*, with the curriculum defined in terms of experiences and activities rather than knowledge to be acquired. The focus in this approach is on the learner's experience and needs, treating the learner as the active subject whose growth and development is the main function of education. This expresses a progressive vision that opposes the treatment of the learner as an object to be pushed, filled or acted upon. Identified as the approach which places value on ceding power to the learner, this learner-centred approach has defined itself mainly in terms of opposing the impositions of others, whether as prescribed cognitive curriculum sequences or as patterns of social norms.

The third orientation is socially centred. Skilbeck refers to the model as a *chart or map of the culture*, in which the curriculum is a means of socially inducting people into the norms, values and belief systems of a people. In this approach, selections from the culture have to be made from a number of cultural systems, if a viable curriculum design is to be achieved. There are different perspectives on induction. It can be construed as a process of joining a pre-established culture – a form of socialising, as Egan portrays it. Or, it can be construed as projecting as yet unrealised values and aims into the future. Cultural induction does not necessarily imply a transmission process, but can be an active two-way collaborative process between teachers and learners. This is how Lawton represents this third orientation, as *reconstructionism*: a synthesis of the thesis of classical humanism and the antithesis of progressivism. Reconstructionism, in this sense, is distinct from another perspective on this socially centred orientation, which could be seen as totalitarian in its focus on socialising and homogenising children in terms of the demands of society, as Egan explains. Lawton's portrayal of this orientation as reconstructionist is influenced by democratic ideas of the US educationalist John Dewey (Dewey, 1916), which focus educational aims on improving society and promoting individual growth. This is how the Tanners come to portray this orientation as a *progressive vision*.

The fourth orientation focuses on learning effectiveness, what Skilbeck calls *learning technology*. It reflects the application of a rationalist and technical problem-solving framework that has proved successful in other spheres of activity. It adopts a single model and method across the diversity of kinds of learning and learning areas. This represents educational intentions as intended learning outcomes that are defined in specific and measurable terms. Once learning objectives are defined, then the means of achieving these learner outcomes can be selected by empirical trial and error methods. It is an approach that is associated with training pre-specified skills and has currently evoked both considerable criticism and support over its relevance to education.

Curriculum tensions and incompatibilities

It could be argued that these different orientations are not really incompatible in practice. School systems in practice can be seen to adopt and mix different aspects of these orientations – a compatibility position. There are few school systems which do not adopt aspects of a socially centred approach in seeing schools as a key social agency that accommodates changing social, economic and personal needs. Likewise, there are many people who see the cultivation of intellectual growth in terms of the breadth and balance of learning and development as a key role for schools. School education and education generally are widely seen to be knowledge-centred and to be more than just about social utility. However, there is also strong attachment to person-centred approaches reflected in the importance attached to education being about fulfilling individual potential, taking account of personal interests, social–emotional needs as well as learning how to learn. This compatibility position assumes that problems in education derive from practical management, teaching, curriculum and other factors rather than from theoretical incompatibilities and value tensions. These different orientations are compatible, it is argued, if they are adopted in general terms.

But, profound tensions and incompatibilities are evident when there is detailed examination of these orientations. For example, the contemporary interest in social and emotional literacy and well-being, representing a socially centred educational orientation (Weare, 2004; Gardner, 2006), has been criticised as demoralising and undermining education (Ecclestone, 2004; Furedi, 2009). These critiques are opposed to the image of human vulnerability associated with a therapeutic approach to education. This is seen to be distracting from a focus on intellectual challenge and growth that represents a knowledge-centred approach. These tensions reflect the historic tension between a *classical humanist* orientation which is imbued with sceptical, critical and inquiring values and a *reconstructionist* focus on addressing current social agendas.

There are also tensions between the knowledge-centred and person-centred orientations. It might seem that the classical humanist focus on forms and fields of knowledge – the ends of education – can be simply combined with a progressivist focus on means and processes. But this integration ignores that in a progressivist orientation the means are interrelated with the ends: the means are themselves part of the ends. Choice of teaching approach is not a simple strategic empirical matter: it is itself central to educational ends. These tensions are the basis for the continuing struggles between 'traditionalists' and 'progressivists' that were evident in the twentieth century and persist through to the current century.

As explained above, there are different versions of the socially centred orientation: one involves joining a pre-established culture (a socialising version), while the other is about induction into a culture that reflects projected and as yet unrealised values and aims into the future (a reconstructionist version). There is a particular tension between the former socialising version and a person-centred orientation because socialising is seen to threaten the developmental process. Though a developmental process will be shaped by social contexts, the progressive orientation aims to protect the child's development from negative social and economic pressures. As Egan (1998) argues, we cannot derive educational principles from basically different conceptions, an ideal developmental process and current social norms and values.

There are also tensions between a *learning technology* orientation and the other three discussed above. These three orientations focus on the ends and means of education, while the learning technology one is about effectiveness. The learning technology approach involves the specification of learning aims as specific definitions of learning outcomes and the sequencing of learning tasks to optimise learning progression. This generic approach, like the person-centred one, applies across areas of learning, but conflicts with the person-centred orientation in assuming that educational ends and means can be separated. Formulating well-defined learning objectives enables measurement in assessment and supports the use of feedback to alter teaching methods and/or learning objectives. As this approach requires educational ends to be defined as specific observables, it seeks to translate educational ends into specific performance terms irrespective of the nature of the end. This is where there can be a tension between these principles and classical humanism that recognises the breadth and range of educational ends, such as knowledge, understanding, dispositions or skills. A learning technology orientation has been most applicable in the teaching of basic skills, though some argue that this confines it to training rather than education. When applied to ends, such as more complex skills, its principles have been seen to degrade and undermine educational ends.

Despite opposition to the learning technology orientation, most commonly found in opposition to the objectives or targets approach, it does offer the promise of some control over achieving goals. In education it offers the promise of some control of learning outcomes, which interests politicians and policy makers who want to raise educational standards in the name of improving the quality of education. In a political climate where economic growth depends on the use of knowledge in post-industrial societies, education has come to have an increasing importance for the development of human capital in a global economy. Raising educational standards also happens within an international context and this becomes translated into national policies and procedures geared to these ends. In the UK (England), for example, though the National Curriculum introduced in 1988 had a traditional subject organisation, it was mainly driven by national attainment/performance testing purposes. Similar assessment procedures have been established in other countries, such as the No Child Left Behind legislation in the USA.

In England, pupil performance levels have been part of a more market system of schooling, on one hand, as well as the national inspection of schools and the national setting of attainment levels, on the other. This approach to the curriculum has been observed to challenge the place of conventional school subjects (e.g. history), and even undermine the core curriculum subjects such as mathematics and English. This has arisen from the challenge presented by these competency-based curriculum models. This has been evident in the focus on functional, life and work skills, where the focus has been on general competencies, such as communication, thinking and creative skills. This reflects a socially centred curriculum orientation, which has been critical of knowledge-centred approaches, based on the assumption that all the knowledge needed for the future cannot be known now and so learners need skills to access and create new knowledge. Despite the widespread international uptake of competency-based models, which focus on linearly sequenced learning outcomes and on generic skills and criteria (Priestley, 2011), there has been a significant critique of these models in terms of their superficial assumptions about the nature of knowledge (Harris and Burns, 2011). The main critique is that it is not easy to create knowledge using generic skills without understanding the discipline of what makes for distinct areas of knowledge. In History, for example, Harris and Burns (2011) suggest that this involves understanding structural concepts such as cause and consequence as well as change and continuity.

Contemporary curriculum tensions have also been identified as involving muddled talk and thinking about key concepts (Alexander, 2009), which some see as reflecting the erosion of curriculum theory (Priestley, 2011), and others attribute to a narrow economic instrumentalism (Young, 2007; Wheelahan, 2010). Alexander (2009) suggests that terms such as 'knowledge', 'subjects' and 'skills' need to be used with clarity to avoid the over-simplistic positioning that goes on in curriculum debates. 'Subjects' have been demonised in some circles as fragmenting and putting learning into boxes. This stance became caught up, according to Alexander, with poorly thought through ideas about the nature of knowledge and assumptions that subjects are 'old-fashioned' and therefore no longer relevant. Subjects are elements of the curriculum and as such may overlap with different disciplines or they may not; for example, Personal, Social and Health Education. Part of the demonising of knowledge derives from the equation of knowledge with facts or mere information. From this error follows other false assumptions about knowledge: that knowledge is inert and irrelevant and that it is associated with old-fashioned drill and practice teaching methods. However, if, as Alexander argues, domains of knowledge are not inert and obsolete collections of information, but 'distinct ways of knowing, understanding, enquiring and making sense' (2009: 16), then knowledge is essential to tackling future problems. Part of Alexander's analysis is that the rise of skills and competence models can be explained as an antidote to a degraded version of a knowledge-centred approach. The focus on generic skills is explained in terms of these being more general and enduring than vocational or job-specific skills, which could also become obsolete. But, if skills involve the capability or capacity to do something, then it is central to education, but as a complement to knowing and understanding, rather than replacing them. Alexander suggests that some skills are necessary to advance knowledge (e.g. enquiry, problem-solving), and that using skills depends on knowing and understanding and so opposes the false opposition between knowledge and skills.

Educational, social and philosophical tensions

In the previous section I have discussed different curriculum orientations and related them to more recent debates about the school curriculum in terms of the compatibility between knowledge and skills models. The compatibility between these different orientations and models can be seen to reflect deeper tensions between different epistemological positions. In a more recent work in the sociology of education, Michael Young in his *Bringing Knowledge Back* has departed from his own earlier social constructivist critiques of the school curriculum as reflecting social power (Young, 2007). He identifies the central tension between the social constructivist focus on skills and outcomes and a knowledge-centred approach as an epistemological dilemma over whether knowledge is related to social position and interests (relativist option) or is unrelated and unaffected in relation to the knower (realist option). From this analysis he identifies an educational dilemma about the curriculum:

> either the curriculum is a given or it is entirely the result of power struggles between groups with competing claims for including and legitimising their knowledge and excluding that of others.
>
> *(p. 38)*

Though he recognises the progressive possibilities in this social constructivist position to the curriculum by reminding people that matters could be otherwise, he suggests that it can be superficial, dangerous and misguided as regards emancipation. The contemporary expressions of person-centred orientations, in personalised learning, for example, are seen as not taking knowledge-centred approaches seriously. Young's resolution to this dilemma is to move away from a relativist position to a more modernist position: a social realist one. Knowledge is neither connected to specific contexts nor is context free, but is linked to a 'third world', in Popper's sense of the term (Popper, 1972). Objective knowledge, in Popper's sense, is neither a physical thing (world 1) nor a subjective experience (world 2), but a product of the human mind and autonomous of it (world 3; but in this sense not like Plato's transcendent forms). Drawing on Durkheim, Young regards the objectivity of knowledge as being grounded in its social nature, deriving from the networks and associations developed by knowledge producers. In veering away from a relativist epistemology that conflates knowledge with power, he asserts that both the sociality and the reality of knowledge are important: sociality without reality leads to relativism, while reality without sociality leads to a conservative status quo.

Underlying some of the curriculum tensions discussed above are also other basic dilemmas. Judge (1981), who identified a number of dilemmas surrounding the purposes of schooling, suggested that 'our purposes are conflicting, contradictory and largely unexamined' (p. 111). In using the term 'dilemma', he also meant not just a difficulty or an issue, but also something more specific – a situation when there is choice between alternatives when neither is favourable. Three of the dilemmas he identified are relevant to curriculum orientations:

1. Utility v. culture: individual and collective economic prosperity v. individual fulfilment and social harmony.
2. Common v. diverse school curriculum: equal provision and opportunity v. optional programmes that follow interests, providing a counter to imposed curricula.

3. Management v. autonomy: division of power between central and local government, between local government and schools and within schools between professionals and users of education services.

Writing at the same time, Berlak and Berlak (1981), who focused more on classroom teaching, identified three broad sets of dilemmas concerned with control/autonomy, curriculum commonality/differentiation and equal/additional resource allocation. What is interesting about the Berlaks' analysis is their use of Mead's symbolic interactionist theory (Mead, 1934) to account for how teachers come to experience dilemmas. In Mead's theory the 'I' represents the initiating active agent, and the 'Me' is the view of oneself as an object in the environment, which is developed from others' perspectives. Others' perspectives can become generalised into the 'generalised other' from which the person internalises generalised perspectives, values and norms. They propose that the 'generalised other' may involve shared common perspectives and values, but may also involve perspectives and values that conflict. In this way the person may internalise generalised perspectives and values that are in tension and so come to experience dilemmas.

This Meadian perspective resembles another social psychological account of everyday thinking in terms of *ideological dilemmas* (Billig et al., 1988). For Billig these dilemmas are ideological because they are about basic values: 1) relationship between the individual and society; 2) how to respond to differences between people; and 3) about conserving traditional ways from the past versus seeking change and progressive developments. Billig also rejects the sociological view that individuals are simply shaped by ideology. Individuals are not only acted on, but also think and initiate actions. They think about ideological matters that involve basic values, and this includes considering the contrary and conflicting aspects of this thinking. Billig's view is that formalised ideologies are positions that are extracted from an argumentative dialogue about education (or some other social practice). Each ideology is therefore not a separate self-contained conception, but is formulated in response and contradiction to other positions that are part of the same scheme of discourse. So, different positions – for example, 'traditional' and 'progressive' educational approaches, as part of an argumentative dialogue – are not as mutually exclusive of each other as their self-contained and purist formulations might suggest. This position can be illustrated in this way. Proponents of person-centred autonomy will rarely advise that learners be taught nothing and should not acquire some ready-made knowledge, however this is achieved. If proponents wish to pursue a radically purist line, then they find that at some point they have to own up to asserting authority, if only to set the agenda as one of learner autonomy. One finds a similar pattern with proponents of knowledge-centred education. Rarely do they see learners as only passively receiving wisdom with no change in the reproduction of traditional knowledge and understanding. Radically purist versions of transmission views also have to own up to believing that when learners receive and carry forward traditional knowledge, they have to actively own their learning. Pure passive acquisition is incompatible with a conservative transmission goal.

Curriculum design for diversity, whether it be for ethnicity or disability, has to also address two other distinct but related issues. One issue is the broadening of the curriculum offered to all pupils to reflect the diverse nature of the society. This expresses a contemporary version of the society-centred orientation to curriculum. The diversity and plural nature of society will be represented in what is taught and how different groups are represented. The second issue is about meeting the educational needs of various minority groups, whether ethnic or disabled. Though this analysis derives from an earlier UK report on the education of children from minority ethnic groups (Swann Report, 1985), it has wider application to the design of a curriculum for all. The second issue about meeting diverse needs within a common curriculum is discussed in the next section.

Common versus differentiated curriculum

In addition to historical tensions between different educational orientations, there can also be educational tensions between a common versus a diverse or differentiated curriculum, as suggested by Judge (1981) and Berlak and Berlak (1981). The common curriculum represents the values of equality and community in democratic-style countries, while differentiated curricula have been seen as relevant when learners have different interests, attainments and abilities. The contemporary separation between vocationally and academically oriented curricula is an example of this tension and has been most pronounced in the later stages of secondary schools in the UK and internationally. For instance, there has been considerable debate about moves to integrate or keep separate vocational and academic programmes in upper secondary schools in England (Hodgson and Spours, 2011). This kind of curriculum integration can be seen to reflect a commitment to design an inclusive curriculum that is appropriate for diverse learners.

Another key area where there have been tensions about curriculum commonality and differentiation has been in relation to those with disabilities and difficulties. Recent educational policy and practice in the UK and USA illustrates how these tensions are evident. In the UK (England), the 1989 National Curriculum evoked ambivalent responses from many working in the UK special educational needs field: as an entitlement for all it aroused progressive hopes, but its design and the assessment arrangements did not include practical arrangements relevant to students with disabilities and difficulties. It took 13 years to introduce national adaptations to the National Curriculum framework for those with more severe learning difficulties (QCA, 2002). In the USA, the curriculum changes introduced though the No Child Left Behind (NCLB) legislation in 2002 referred to all students (Howe and Welner, 2002; Hardman and Dawson, 2008). But, they did not include those with disabilities and with limited English proficiency (Thurlow, 2002). Subsequent federal initiatives required that students with disabilities have access to the general curriculum and participate in local assessment systems and that the Individual Education Plan (IEP) include relevant provisions for this participation. McDonell et al. (1997) noted that different students with disabilities can participate to different degrees in the common aspects of the standards-oriented reforms. Academic goals were not seen as relevant to the life goals of those with low incidence disabilities who require independent living and workplace preparation. The content and performance levels embodied in some of the academic standards might also take time away from teaching what many might regard as more valuable skills. It has been noted, more recently, that alternative or modified US standards can include up to 3 per cent of the total student population: 1 per cent for alternative standards and 2 per cent for modified standards (McClaughlin et al., 2006).

Considering the significance of the tensions over curriculum commonality/differentiation in the disability and difficulties field, it is surprising how little research has been conducted with this focus. There are some exceptions, such as a UK study of the distinctiveness of curriculum provision for students (14 to 16 years old) with significant and profound learning disabilities (Lawson et al., 2005). Several points of tension over curriculum development were identified: for example, between functional skills-based curriculum and opportunities for breadth and balance, between entitlement and individual needs, and between individual choice and organisational constraints. Grove (1998) examined English as a subject from an inclusive education perspective and found that the National Curriculum formulation overlooked social and emotional uses of language; literature was seen as a means to becoming an effective reader and effective communication was equated with the use of Standard English. Though Grove identifies imaginative routes that have been developed to access the general curriculum, she questioned the appropriateness of a common curriculum that does not start from an affective engagement and suggests that meaning be seen as inherently social and interactive. Avramidis et al. (2010) also considered the question of developing an inclusive approach to literacy and suggest that broader concepts of literacy – multi-literacies that go beyond print-based literacies – can be incorporated into the school curriculum. This can open up related forms of symbolic communication to some children and young people with severe learning difficulties. However, this inclusive resolution to the curriculum differentiation question may be suitable for some people with severe intellectual disabilities, but may still not be relevant to those people with even more significant disabilities, including those with profound and multiple disabilities.

The above discussion illustrates curriculum tensions over literacy that can be seen to reflect dilemmas of difference, as discussed earlier in this book. O'Brien (1998) has also examined curriculum design issues relevant to special educational needs and disability in terms of emphasising individuality (meeting individual needs) as well as commonality (needs that are common to all students), while addressing issues and tensions in doing so. That professionals recognise curriculum differentiation issues relevant to disability in education was illustrated in two comparative studies (Norwich, 1993; Norwich, 2010). Teachers and administrators in the Netherlands, USA and UK (England) were interviewed about whether they believed there was a dilemma in the following form and if they did whether and how they would resolve it:

- If children identified as having a disability (needing special education) are offered the same learning experiences as other children, they are likely to be denied the opportunity to have learning experiences relevant to their individual needs.
- If children identified as having a disability (needing special education) are NOT offered the same learning experiences as other children, then they are likely to be treated as a separate lower status group and be denied equal opportunities.

Findings in the more recent study showed a majority in each country recognised the dilemma about curriculum commonality/differentiation; only 12–16 per cent did not recognise such a dilemma. Comparison with the earlier study in the USA and UK showed that this had continued over a decade and that there were similarities across the countries in how the dilemma was recognised and resolved. The most frequent common recognition themes across the three countries were about:

- 'tensions' – for example, academic curriculum not meeting needs, problems in implementing differentiated programmes, some curriculum areas left out, problems in using same standards and tests;
- 'resolved tensions' – that is, tensions have been resolved to some extent, for example, meeting individual needs while experiencing a common curriculum; same curriculum areas are used but at appropriate levels, use alternative curriculum assessment to meet needs and giving a priority to what is relevant.

Curriculum resolutions

In the above sections, I have illustrated how some theorists recognise curriculum tensions, between historic orientations – knowledge, social and person-centred – as well as with the more recent effectiveness-centred orientation. There has been discussion of the parallel curriculum commonality/differentiation tension. In this section I will focus on how these tensions are addressed and resolved. Egan (1998) reminds us that few teachers and administrators adhere to only one orientation to the exclusion of others: there is a tendency to find some balance between them. He also suggests that historical orientations sometimes carry baggage that can be dispensed with to make the balance more viable. However, Egan's main point is that understanding and exposing these value tensions and issues is a vital step to overcoming them. In relation to primary education, Alexander (1992) has also suggested that any educational practice requires coming to terms with and reconciling competing values, pressures and constraints. Along similar lines Judge (1981) has argued that it is healthy to recognise tensions and contradictions. He suggests that tensions need to be addressed, not avoided, that they need to be thought through and that the form the tension takes reflects historical factors. In so doing he claims that choices cannot be absolute, and so are best seen as dilemmas to resolve. Reconciling the effectiveness-centred orientation based on a learning technology approach, discussed above, with other orientations also depends on understanding that effectiveness cannot stand alone without relating it to educational visions and values: effectiveness is only meaningful in relation to some values or goals (Hargreaves, 1996; White and Barber, 1997).

Some research also indicates that teachers are aware and feel a tension between different orientations while finding resolutions through balancing between different positions (Berlak and Berlak, 1981; Edwards and Mercer, 1987). Such resolutions draw on elements from opposing assumptions, as described in the teaching styles characterised as *cued elicitation* and *guided discovery* (Billig et al., 1988). Similarly, in the comparative research in the Netherlands, USA and UK about curriculum differentiation (Norwich, 2010), discussed above, most resolutions across the three countries were about:

- 'balancing common and different aspects' – for example, modify general curriculum to meet individual needs, change teaching/instruction, but have the same objectives and have the same general areas, but differentiated programmes;
- 'curriculum and teaching flexibility' – for example, different curriculum for severe disabilities, emphasis on life skills and collaboration between special education and regular teachers;
- 'continuing issues' – for example, dilemmas are hard to resolve and some common curriculum areas have to be left out.

What this study showed was that despite some positive resolutions to the dilemma, some participants recognised continuing issues about balancing common/different aspects. In aiming for commonality (inclusiveness, equality) and relevance (differentiation), the aim is to have it both ways as far as possible. But, sometimes this balancing can be hard and resolutions can leave residual tensions, as some participants also recognised. As Berlin (1990) has explained in relation to social value tensions in general, they can lead to some crucial losses.

This line of analysis leads to a way of examining what is meant by a common curriculum for all or an inclusive curriculum. It is useful to distinguish first between four different but related aspects of the curriculum, for conceptual purposes: 1) principles, 2) programme areas, 3) specific programmes and 4) teaching. Each aspect represents a design level that subsumes lower levels, from the higher to the lower levels as follows:

1. General principles and aims for a school curriculum (principles).
2. Areas of worthwhile learning (whether structured in terms of subjects or not) with their goals and general objectives (programme areas).
3. More specific programmes of study with their objectives (specific programmes).
4. Class teaching practices (teaching).

For each aspect, there can be either commonality (common to all) or differentiation (differentiated for some) as explained by Lewis and Norwich (2004). When these

TABLE 4.2 Model of different options for curriculum design in terms of the balance between curriculum commonality and differentiation

Design options	Principles	Programme areas	Specific programmes	Teaching
1	Common	Common	Common	Common
2	Common	Common	Common	Different
3	Common	Common	Different	Different
4	Common	Different	Different	Different
5	Different	Different	Different	Different

aspects are combined in their common–different forms (note that this dichotomy is a conceptual simplification for illustrative purposes only; commonality–differentiation is more a matter of degree along a continuum), this produces five schematic design options illustrated in Table 4.2. Options 1 and 5 represent consistent commonality and differentiation across the four curriculum aspects. Neither of these design options is used or advocated in most international debates and decisions about curriculum as either politically desirable or socially viable. Of the remaining three options, option 2 represents a tendency towards greater commonality where differentiation is only at the teaching level, while option 4 represents a tendency towards greater differentiation where commonality is at the principles level. What this model illustrates is that even when there is a predominant balance towards commonality (option 2), there is still some element of differentiation, and similarly when predominance is to differentiation (option 4), there is some commonality. This illustrates the point by Billig et al. (1988) that opposing ideological positions are often not as mutually exclusive of each other as their self-contained and purist formulations might suggest.

This model can be used to analyse curriculum design and change in different countries. Using the UK (England) as an example, the initial 1988 National Curriculum reflected more commonality elements (such as option 2 rather than options 3 and 4). Since then there were moves towards options 3 and 4. These represent a greater tendency towards differentiation at the more structural levels of the curriculum, where not only is teaching different, but also programme objectives and areas of learning differ for some students with disabilities and difficulties. On one hand, commonality was preserved at the level of general aims and principles, such as those embodied in the Inclusive Statement of the UK (English) National Curriculum 2000. The Inclusion Statement referred to: 1) setting suitable learning challenges; 2) responding to pupils' diverse learning needs; and 3) overcoming potential barriers to learning (QCA, 2000). On the other hand, differentiation was provided through curriculum modification, as found in the UK (English) national learning difficulties framework (QCA, 2002).

68 Inclusive curriculum issues

A key issue in the commonality–difference question is the nature of curriculum goals if they are going to be different for some pupils with disabilities and difficulties. This refers to design options 3 and 4 in the Table 4.2 where some specific programmes goals may be different for pupils with disabilities and difficulties. There is a tradition in special education in which what is 'special' about special education is the specialised nature of the areas of learning and the programme objectives within these areas. Specialised areas and objectives have tended to focus on the learner's difficulties either to circumvent them or reduce them to some extent or fully. These programmes might be designed as therapeutic programmes and not as educational programmes as part of a curriculum design. But, they involve teaching or instruction and learning processes. This is at the uncertain interface between teaching and therapeutic interventions that are learning based, where therapists, such as speech and language therapists or physiotherapists or occupational therapists, work with teachers in developing programmes for children with disabilities and difficulties.

TABLE 4.3 Relationships between curriculum specialisation and pedagogic adaptations

	Curriculum programme goals		
	Common to all	Specialised for some	
Pedagogic adaptations	That adapt teaching to common programme goals	That aim to accept–circumvent impairment	That aim to address–remediate functional difficulties
Examples (areas of disability/ difficulty in brackets)	1 Adapt teaching presentation and learner response modes (sensory and motor impairments)	Learn alternative communication– mobility access systems (sign systems, spatial orientation, braille, etc.)	Reduce difficulty/ disability (instrumental enrichment for cognitive disabilities; self-control programme for ADHD)
	2 Adapt level of learning objectives and mode of teaching (cognitive impairments)		Restore function (Reading Recovery for literacy difficulties)
	3 Adapt social emotional climate and relationships of teaching–learning (emotional and behaviour difficulties)		

Table 4.3 illustrates two broad kinds of specialised programmes for specific kinds of disabilities with goals which aim to: 1) accept–circumvent, or 2) address–remediate functional difficulties (the two right-hand columns in Table 4.3). Recognising this variety of possible goals and programmes does not imply any acceptance that the programmes are desirable, effective or viable. There are some key points that can be made about these two kinds of programme goals. For programmes with addressing–reducing goals there have been doubts about their effectiveness. For example, Kavale and Mostert (2004) in a US review of studies using meta-analysis distinguish between *special* education (programmes that aim to address–remediate processes assumed to cause learning difficulties; not usually used in general education) and special *education* (programmes that aim to adapt common programme goals to enhance attainment). They found that special *education* interventions (e.g. peer tutoring, computer-assisted instruction, reading comprehension strategies; adapting general education approaches) had learning outcome effects three to four times more than *special* education interventions (e.g. social skills training, perceptual-motor training, modality matched teaching; focus on special and different). Their conclusions that 'education' interventions (teaching adaptations common to all programmes) were more effective than 'special' ones calls into question some specialised programmes that aim to reduce–remediate functional difficulties.

It is these historic interventions that are the focus of certain critiques of specialist pedagogy from an inclusive perspective (Thomas and Loxley, 2001; Florian, 2010). However, though some interventions' aims to address–remediate difficulties (e.g. for children with specific or mild general learning difficulties) have been shown to be ineffective, it does not mean that other ones have not been found to be useful. More recent research about phonological awareness in literacy learning has shown that a general reading programme (e.g. phonics plus real book reading) was not as effective for those at risk of literacy difficulties as these general programmes supplemented by phoneme awareness training (Torgesen et al. 1999; Hatcher et al., 2004). An important point here is that this kind of supplementary programmes may not seem to be as specialist as the historic psycho-linguistic process training, because some elements of the phoneme awareness training resembles what is provided in the general programme. In this sense there has been a 'blurring' of specialist and general interventions (Fuchs et al., 2010) with what is considered 'specialist' at the third tier of a Response to Instruction (RTI) model compared to what is provided at tiers 1 and 2. This relativity between what is 'generally provided' and what is 'specialist' will be discussed further below.

Returning to Table 4.3, the other specialist programmes for some that aim to accept–circumvent impairment do so because unlike the address–remediate programmes the difficulties are not so readily remediated. These are traditional programmes for those with impairments, such as sensory impairments. In integrating the positions of UK specialists in different areas of special needs education, Norwich and Lewis (2007) identified different curriculum positions according to areas of disability and difficulty that fitted with the scheme in Table 4.3. For sensory impairment, curriculum design depended on the nature, severity and context of

70 Inclusive curriculum issues

impairment. For example, differences in curriculum approach for deafness depended on the severity of hearing impairment (distinctive communication routes) and the deaf culture's use of signing (Gregory, 2004). Similarly, in the visual impairment area, additional curriculum programmes about mobility, use of residual vision, maximum use of senses and special literacy routes were relevant depending on the severity of impairment (Douglas and McLinden, 2004). In some areas curriculum relevance was judged to be more important than breadth, and fewer curriculum areas were covered enabling more focus on some areas; for example, communication and choice-making in the area of profound and multiple learning difficulties (Ware, 2004a). A combination of curriculum access and remedial orientations was also recognised for children with autistic spectrum disorder (ASD) (Jordan, 2004) and for children with ADHD (Cooper, 2004).

There was also a consensus amongst the national specialists that curriculum commonality could only be defined at the broadest general level of common principles and areas (as in options 3 and 4 in Table 4.2). However, for other disabilities and difficulties areas there was no indication of the need for specialised curriculum programmes. But, in some areas, as mentioned above, there was a need for greater emphasis on certain common curriculum areas than other areas. Lewis and Norwich proposed thinking about these curriculum flexibilities in terms of a *continuum of common curriculum approaches* which assumes a balancing of curriculum breadth with curriculum relevance. For example, for profound and multiple learning difficulties the emphasis was on communication and choice making, while for those with emotional and behaviour difficulties (O'Brien, 2004) the emphasis was more towards personal and social–emotional development. For children with general moderate and severe learning difficulties (MLD and SLD; sometimes called moderate to severe intellectual disabilities), the flexibility could be about the degree of structure in the progression and sequence of the programmes.

In the Lewis and Norwich review, it was also concluded that curriculum flexibilities were not as significant a focus compared to pedagogy and knowledge in the areas of specific learning difficulties (e.g. dyslexia and dyspraxia). These areas, sometimes called 'high incidence' difficulties, are ones where teaching is adapted to common curriculum goals (left-hand column of Table 4.3). However, the term 'high incidence' is problematic as incidence is a matter of degree and does not easily map on to categories or causal models, as discussed in Chapter 3. These teaching adaptations are those in curriculum design option 2 (Table 4.2), where curriculum principles, areas of learning and programmes objectives are mainly common to all but class teaching is assumed to need adaptation–differentiation.

Universal design

Option 2, where curriculum areas and programme objectives are mainly common but where class teaching requires unusual adaptations, can be approached either by adding the adaptations to the common programme or by building in adaptations in advance. The latter approach has come to be called *universal design* (UD), which has intuitive promise as a way of extending the common curriculum to a greater diversity of learners. Universal design has US origins in the built environment associated with Robert Mace, an architect who coined the term to reflect a proactive inclusive design that minimised the need for retrofitted accommodations (McGuire et al., 2006). When applied to education, it has gone under different titles, such as UD for learning or UD for instruction and so on. In education, UD is about curriculum design to promote access, participation and progress in the general curriculum for all learners. One formulation identifies three features of UD for learning in terms of a curriculum that provides:

1. Multiple means of representation.
2. Multiple means of expression.
3. Multiple means of engagement (CAST, 2006).

Blamires (1999) interprets the first two of these (representation and expression) in terms of various input modalities (visual, auditory, etc.) including the use of multimedia. But, as Blamires notes, these different modalities are not simply interchangeable and some meaning may be lost in changing modality. The third feature about engagement is about the motivational aspects of learning and the importance of learners feeling secure and identifying with the learning activities.

It is notable that universal design has played a small part in the development of inclusive practices in the UK compared to developments in the USA. For example, a British Education Index search produced only one reference about UD in relation to special needs or inclusive education, and that is the Blamires (1999) paper. This may also be because there is no legislative basis for UD as there is in the US IDEA reauthorisation in 2004, where the term 'UD' is formally defined and linked to the Assistive Technology legislation (Edyburn, 2010). In the UK, UD may also be associated with ICT approaches (sometimes referred to as assistive technology) to education and not seen primarily as a curriculum design matter. Some US authors see assistive technology as separate but related to universal design (Messigner-Willman and Marion, 2010; Edyburn, 2010). The former authors see assistive technology as individually focused while universal design is curriculum development focused.

Much of the US literature about universal design tends to be about the promise and principles about UD, rather than practical examples or development and evaluation. It is generally recognised that there is not a well-established evidence or empirical basis to UD practices and several authors recommend that this be the way forward for translating theory into practice (McGuire, et al. 2006; King-Sears, 2009; Edyburn, 2010). However, there are examples of its use in some areas of the curriculum (e.g. in physical education; Lieberman et al., 2008) and some research into students' responses to UD practices in teaching algebra and biology in secondary schools (Kortering et al., 2008).

However, the risk with universal design is that it can be portrayed as an alternative to specialised or additional systems. A commitment to common programmes adapted to all learners may be a goal, but as argued above, there may still be a need for specialised programmes for a minority. There is a pure version of universal design that sees UD systems as an expression of the social model. For example, UD can be presented as the opposite of special or specialised education (SE) in these terms under these headings (McGuire et al., 2006):

- *disability*: impairment within individual (SE) versus an aspect of human diversity and variations (UD);
- *eligibility*: identify/label individual to give access to services (SE) versus learning needs of broad range to inform curriculum/teaching design (UD);
- *inclusion*: include students with disabilities when appropriate in general curriculum (SE), versus design curriculum/teaching for wide range of learners (UD).

As argued in other parts of this book, this sets up false dichotomies. For example, it is possible to design curriculum and teaching for a wider range of learners and still recognise that students are included in the general curriculum as appropriate. This is to recognise the curriculum commonality–differentiation dilemma discussed above. While McGuire et al. (2006) present these dichotomies, they also question whether UD is about addressing the needs of *all* students and whether UD will eliminate the need for special education services (p. 171). Ronald Mace is quoted as considering the term 'universal' as unfortunate, because of its universal implication, when that may not be feasible. This issue takes the discussion in two directions. It takes it back to Chapter 2 and the critique of the social model. Shakespeare (2006) critiqued the universality of the UD approach for similar reasons to Mace, but extends his argument to a detailed analysis of the problems of a 'barrier free utopia'. Shakespeare argued this in three ways. First, that there are limits to implementing universal design in some settings; for example, outside cities where there is less of a built environment, Second, he suggests that though barriers may be removable in a particular case, when planning a curriculum for different kinds of barriers, it may not be possible overall to have accessibility for all learners at the same time: the incompatibility argument. And third, there are practical and resourcing issues: it may be possible to have all books and texts in school designed as e-books and schools only buy these books. This may not be feasible and even if it were to become so in future, the cost may be such as to make it impractical. As with old and new buildings, where new buildings are informed by UD principles, old buildings may not be so easily adapted for financial resource reasons. This discussion of the universality of UD also takes the discussion forward to the next chapter about inclusive pedagogy.

5
INCLUSIVE PEDAGOGY

Recent moves to inclusive teaching or pedagogy

In the previous chapter, class teaching was represented within a curriculum programme context, where curriculum usually refers to the *what* of education and class teaching or pedagogy to the *how* of education. Though teaching and pedagogy are often used interchangeably, they can have different meanings. For example, in the Norwich and Lewis (2007) model of teaching, pedagogy refers to the how of classroom teaching, whereas for Alexander (2000) pedagogy is primary. He recognises four levels covering: 1) children (their characteristics and development); 2) learning (how best motivated, assessed and built on); 3) teaching (its planning, execution and evaluation); and 4) curriculum (ways of knowing etc. which are desirable to encounter). So, the context and meaning of how these terms will be used in this chapter will be clarified in what is to follow.

With the international moves towards more inclusion in education, there has been a demand for inclusive teaching practices and this has raised questions about what pedagogic approaches are useful for children with disabilities and difficulties in ordinary classes and whether there is a specialist pedagogy for children with SEN or disabilities and difficulties. This has been reflected in recent international government and other research reviews (Moore et al., 2004 in New Zealand; Davis and Florian, 2004 in the UK (England); Cook and Shirmer, 2003 in the USA). For example, a UK government-funded literature review addressed the question 'What pedagogic approaches can effectively include children with SEN in mainstream classes?' (Rix et al., 2009). The review started with 2982 papers over three successive years of reviewing – only 134 remained in the systematic map with only 28 examined in depth and of these only ten rated as medium-high for design appropriateness. Not only were most studies from the USA, but also the implications drawn from the review were fairly general as might be expected. They were about: 1) teachers' commitment and felt responsibility towards inclusion and 2) adaptations to general teaching approaches (e.g. the use of peer interaction approaches with the preparation of pupil roles). Other principles which were emphasised were constructivist in orientation, emphasising that learning activities needed to be meaningful and that basic skills are to be learned in a holist and activity-embedded way. An earlier government-funded review (Davis and Florian, 2004) had broader aims to identify effective ways to teach the range of pupils with SEN and whether there were distinctive SEN teaching approaches. These authors and their team also concluded that the research base was limited and usually involved small-scale studies. However, unlike the previous review, it was concluded that multi-method approaches were promising, that is, those that combined strategies that often related to different models of learning (e.g. direct instruction, cognitive behavioural or constructivist).

Davis and Florian (2004) also concluded that teaching approaches associated with specific areas of SEN could not be differentiated enough from those used with all children for there to be 'SEN pedagogy'. This conclusion contradicts other conclusions in their review about children with sensory and physical difficulties: that they need specialised teaching and systematic methods to access and participate in learning (p. 29). But, their conclusion also goes against a contemporary US review (Cook and Shirmer, 2003) which, though recognising that ordinary teachers could use teaching practices associated with specific areas of SEN, suggests that such approaches are unlikely to be used with all students. In relation to learning disability (specific learning difficulty in UK terms), Vaughn and Linan-Thompson (2003) identify the distinctive aspects as the 'delivery of instruction' – how teaching is organised and presented. This is a practical argument that these approaches are too time-consuming and cumbersome to be used for all students, and while most students can learn without them, this does not apply to those identified as having a specific learning disability. However, what is revealing about the UK government-funded report by Davis and Florian (2004) is that it asserts that the question of a specialist pedagogy is out of step with the government's inclusive policies, and is therefore unhelpful, and that developing a pedagogy that is inclusive of all learners is more important.

The concept of inclusive pedagogy

It is one thing to assert the need to develop inclusive teaching or pedagogy, it is another to have a clear, well-analysed and grounded concept of what inclusive teaching means. Often inclusive teaching or pedagogy is taken to be about recognising, accommodating and meeting the needs of all pupils/learners, where the emphasis is on *all*. This recognition can be about individuality, that is, meeting individual needs as well as about pupils coming from diverse communities; for example, having a disability, or learning English as additional language and/or being in the care of the local authority. Inclusive pedagogy is also about being friendly and welcoming to all and the teacher appreciating the value of a diverse classroom. Sometimes this is expressed in terms of 'inclusive learning-friendly classrooms' (UNESCO, 2004). For example, when inclusive is used in this UNESCO development toolkit, though it uses the language of participation and barriers to learning, it has a particular meaning. In this toolkit the language of 'barriers' is inconsistent with the social model of disability. 'Barriers' are seen to arise not only from social and environmental factors, but also from impairments, a position that is seen by social model advocates as reflecting a 'deficit' model. This non-social meaning of barriers can be seen to reflect the assimilation and neutralising of a radical position, which is also found in other policy documents; for example, Removing Barriers to Achievement, the 2004 UK (English) government's policy for SEN and inclusion.

Some theorists from a critical disability perspective criticise the assumed 'deficit' models associated with teaching children identified as having special educational needs in terms of 'socially just pedagogies' rather than inclusive pedagogy (Goodley, 2007). Goodley draws on Masschelein and Simons' (2005) critical analysis of inclusive schooling in the UK, a critique that identifies the student as an entrepreneur who puts her/his capital to work. The idea, as Goodly explains, is that the learner is an individual operating in a competitive neo-liberal marketised society. This entrepreneurial concept involves a model of learners as 'autonomous', which students with disabilities can be seen to disrupt. Goodley is arguing for a pedagogy that rejects this market-based concept of the learner for one influenced by postmodern thought; in this case, the concept of rhizomes as a model of communication and pedagogy. Rhizomes represent a metaphor for non-hierarchical networks in opposition to hierarchical and linear systems. So, for Goodley, the 'rhizomatic pedagogue' is interested in change, openness, movement and becoming. And, in keeping with this emancipatory stance, Goodley concludes with a call for socially just pedagogy to be open and experimental.

Goodley's deconstructivist approach is more a radical call for change than a practically and empirically grounded approach to inclusive pedagogy. But, his discussion of an entrepreneurial autonomous model of the learner has some links to Sfard's analysis of learning in terms of an acquisition model, as discussed in Chapter 2 (Sfard, 1998). The entrepreneurial autonomous learner can be seen to acquire learning as a possession, which acts as human capital. Goodley, however, does not relate his critical stance to Sfard's other model of learning, the participative one, which, as discussed in Chapter 2, represents a more socialised model of learning. Unlike Goodley, other authors have adopted a participative model of learning in basing their radical concept of inclusive pedagogy on socio-cultural theories of learning (Florian and Kershner, 2009; Florian 2010, Florian and Black-Hawkins, 2011). Their concept of inclusive pedagogy is based on the assumption that all children can learn together and that participation in learning requires a response to individual differences that does not depend on ability labelling, grouping or withdrawal from the classroom. It is clear that this concept of inclusive pedagogy is seen as opposed to a concept of specialist pedagogy for children with disabilities and difficulties, which is portrayed as segregating and stigmatising these children.

It is notable that these authors base their version of inclusive pedagogy on sociocultural theories of learning, presumably because these theories are taken to focus on the social participative rather than the individual acquisitional aspects of learning.

Though some users of socio-cultural theories present a participative theory as being opposed to individualist (acquisitional) theories, this is not how more recent versions of socio-cultural theories have been applied to disability in education. Hedegaard focuses in her socio-cultural theory on the 'person in a situation rather than towards a feature that lies within the personal alone' (Daniels and Hedegaard, 2011: 1). She presents an interaction between society, institutions, activity setting and the person. This has similarities to the principles of an interactive model discussed in Chapter 2.

Florian and Black-Hawkins (2011) have developed a concept of inclusive pedagogy both theoretically and in a grounded way in primary schools using a 'Framework for participation in classrooms' that covers access, collaboration, achievement and diversity. Their aim is:

> to focus on extending what is ordinarily available in the community of the classroom as a way of reducing the need to mark some learners as different.
> *(p. 814)*

For them pedagogic thinking therefore has to shift from planning separately for *most learners* and separately for the *some* with difficulties to providing learning opportunities that are available for *everyone* in the classroom community. The significance of what these authors suggest about 'inclusive pedagogy' will be analysed in more detail in what follows.

Does inclusive pedagogy require specialist pedagogy?

I will argue that inclusive pedagogy, so understood, is not a clear or viable concept for several key reasons. Inclusive pedagogy, as proposed by Florian and Black-Hawkins, hinges on the concept and value of inclusion that is multilevelled (used at different levels in system: national, LA, school and class) and multidimensional (covering presence, participation (social and academic), achievement and belonging). As will be argued in the next chapter, this leads to complexity and uncertainty about its meaning and to tensions between different aspects of inclusion. This version of inclusive pedagogy has clear features of what Cigman (2007b) calls 'universal inclusion': a position which is defined as antagonistic to any special or specialised schooling or classes. Cigman defines another position as 'moderate inclusion' that takes inclusion as compatible with and even requiring some special schools and classes. So, it is possible to extend this distinction from inclusive schooling to inclusive pedagogy, where inclusive teaching or pedagogy could involve or even require some specialist or specialised teaching.

Before proceeding it is useful to clarify what 'specialist' means in its practical usage. Specialist sometimes refers to what is done in separate settings by 'specialist' teachers, teachers who focus their work directly or indirectly with children identified as having disabilities and difficulties, whether in separate settings or in ordinary classes. Here specialist depends on who has teaching responsibility for children identified as having disabilities and/or difficulties, but this definition does not pick out what is different about the teaching compared to teaching those not identified as having disabilities and difficulties. For this reason, from now I will distinguish between 'specialist' teachers and 'specialised' teaching. The term 'specialist' through past usage has connotations of being about specialist roles and settings, and so will be used with this meaning. 'Specialised' will be used to refer to the teaching/pedagogy itself whether done by role specialist teachers in separate settings or general teachers in general classes.

Some have argued that what has been called specialised pedagogy is no more than teaching done with additional resources (e.g. specific equipment, staffing or available time), usually unavailable in ordinary schools and classes. If the resources were available in ordinary schools/classes, then there is nothing specialised about the pedagogy. Along similar lines, it can also be argued that what is sometimes called specialised pedagogy is just ordinary pedagogy done under exceptional circumstances; for example, a pupil with a severe learning difficulty (disability) who has to have some pain relief to be able to take part in a lesson, or a pupil with autistic spectrum disorder (ASD) who may need to be restrained for serious challenging behaviour to then engage in learning. It is possible to see these requirements (pain relief and behaviour restraint) as non-educational ones and so argue that they do not reflect on the specialisation of pedagogy. But, this is to focus on resources for access to learning and to ignore what might be specialised about the teaching per se. This is where a model of pedagogy is needed to analyse what might or might not be specialised and for what areas and severity of disabilities and difficulties.

Figure 5.1 illustrates in more detail a revised version of the model used by Norwich and Lewis (2007), which was introduced above. Pedagogy is assumed in this model to involve decisions about three interactive elements: 1) *what* is to be learned (curriculum), 2) the knowledge required to decide on 3) *how* to teach (teaching strategies). From this point I will use the term 'pedagogy' to refer to curriculum, teaching strategies and knowledge as a generic term (according to the use in Alexander (2000)) and not interchangeably with teaching. One of the

Teaching strategies: generic – specialised

Knowledge: generic – specialised

Curriculum: common/generic – differentiated/specialised

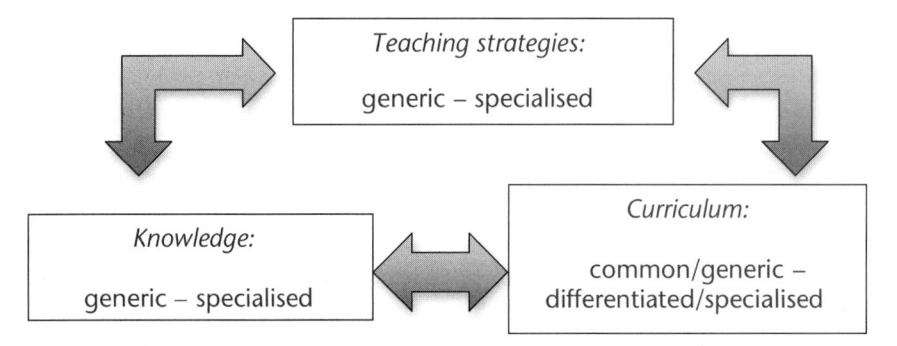

FIGURE 5.1 Model of pedagogy in terms of curriculum, knowledge and teaching strategies

benefits of this model is that it makes it possible to consider specialisation of one or more elements in the pedagogic model. For example, it may be thought that children do not require curriculum specialisation. Nevertheless, there may be some specialised knowledge about disabilities/difficulties required by teachers to support these children to learn the common curriculum. This knowledge is usually about the implications of the disability/difficulty for teaching and learning. For example, a briefing paper about autistic spectrum disorder (ASD) produced for teachers (CLDD Research Project, 2012) provides teachers with knowledge about:

1. The definition and features of ASD.
2. Implications for teaching and learning – for example, 'child's preference for highly structured environments and routines, combined with a resistance to change'.
3. General approaches to support – for example, Use of Social Stories or TEACCH-structured teaching approach.
4. Specific strategies – for example, 1) 'helping students with autism to build up relationships and develop their communication skills is as important as their academic progress, so make sure these aspects of their development are given priority', or 2) 'if students are non-verbal or have extremely limited language skills, use an alternative communication method such as the Picture Exchange Communication System (PECS)'.

The first two aspects (definition and implications) can be seen as propositional knowledge (knowing that), while the last two aspects are about procedural knowledge (knowing how). It is the characteristics of ASD and their implications for teaching and learning which are covered by the knowledge element in the curriculum-knowledge-teaching strategy model above. It is the general approach and specific strategies (3 and 4) that are covered by the curriculum and teaching strategy in the model.

There are risks in using general propositional knowledge with all children to whom the related category has been applied. Usually research-based knowledge is produced through methods which draw conclusions based on the averaging of individual variations within any category, and so may not apply to everyone allocated to a category. This is an epistemological point about general knowledge that arises from scientific-style research methods. It is important to appreciate the risks in over-generalising and to treat such knowledge not as final and definitive, but as indicative: as a working hypothesis of what might apply to particular children. Nevertheless, the key point in this argument is that this kind of knowledge is not covered by generic knowledge about teaching and learning, as it represents knowledge of atypical responses. In terms of the above model of teaching, it is specialised knowledge: knowledge based on educational implications of a category. It is interesting that Florian (2010) recognises that 'specialist knowledge' has a role in pedagogy, but thinks that this knowledge does not 'require the identification of special educational needs within individual learners' (p. 7). If specialist knowledge is, as explained above, about the learning implications of some disability/difficulty, how can it be used without identifying a child as having some specific difficulty/ disability? So, as knowledge of this kind is part of the above model of pedagogy, it follows that there is something specialised about teaching children with some disabilities and difficulties. It is also important to understand that whether such knowledge is relevant depends on whether the category (e.g. ASD or specific learning difficulty) applies to the child or children in question. However, this may be a difficult decision when there are no clear cut-off points for categories, implying a 'borderline' relevance of the category in some particular cases. This means that there may be uncertainty about the relevance of specialised knowledge in particular cases.

However, there is an important implication of this uncertainty and the gap between generalised implications in particular circumstances. Generalised teaching and learning implications require tentativeness in their use. This is relevant to the criticisms from a 'universal' inclusionist perspective that 'categorical' or 'ability' beliefs about children with special educational needs are deterministic and set false limits on learning (Hart et al., 2004; Florian, 2008). As argued above, there is a gap between propositional knowledge and its applicability in practice, and so there is no mechanical determinism. Assumptions about children's learning need to be tested in particular instances of practice, so any presumed limits need to be tested and might be rejected. Research-based evidence is moderated by professional judgement (see Pollard's (2008) concept of reflective teaching).

Returning to the question of whether inclusive pedagogy requires a specialised pedagogy, it is now possible to give a more informed response to the question. If inclusive pedagogy is understood in the universal inclusionist sense, then the answer is no, because anything separate or different threatens the common good, whether different curriculum goals, different teaching strategies or knowledge related to disability/difficulty categories. However, if inclusive pedagogy is understood with 'moderate' inclusionist assumptions, then the answer is yes, inclusive pedagogy may require some specialised teaching. What is different/ specialised is to address individual needs and avoid neglecting learners' requirements. In this concept of inclusive pedagogy, some learner differences may need to be recognised in terms of unusual or atypical functioning covered by categories of disability/difficulties. However, in affirming that inclusive pedagogy may require some specialisation, this does not mean that a separate specialist teacher is required in a separate setting, specialised teaching may be undertaken by the regular teacher alone, with a specialist teacher or teaching assistant or even by a specialist teacher in a separate class or withdrawal setting.

How useful is the concept of inclusive pedagogy or teaching?

From the above it is evident that the concept of inclusive pedagogy is problematic, especially if used without understanding different assumptions about inclusion. However, it has become widely used as a single qualifier of teaching, pedagogy, schooling and education in general. Given the multidimensional aspects of the inclusion, inclusive teaching/pedagogy can mean different things to different users. For some users it might be about children with disabilities and difficulties learning in the same classroom as other children, whether they learn together or in separate groups; for other users it may be about care, respect and a sense of belonging; while for further users it might be about seeing difficulties and challenges in teaching as requiring creative solutions rather than attributing difficulties to the learner.

An additional problem is that there are many different versions of teaching, which reflect different but related value positions to inclusion. Usually a qualifier that reflects a value position precedes the terms 'teaching', 'pedagogy' or 'education'; for example, *creative* teaching (Jeffrey, 2006), *reflective* teaching (Pollard, 2008) or *rights respecting* teaching (UNICEF, 2009). These approaches to teaching all have some similarities with the various aspects of inclusive pedagogy: children's rights and their participation in *rights respecting* teaching, teacher responsibility in *reflective* teaching and creative response to difficulties in *creative* teaching and *reflective* teaching. These overlaps raise questions about the prospect of an integrated set of values to inform teaching and what the term 'inclusive' adds distinctively to this integrated set of values.

In their perspective on inclusive pedagogy, Florian and Black-Hawkins (2011) establish their position in terms of three key assumptions which are defined in terms of what these stand opposed to. These can be summarised as follows:

1. Extending what is available in general classrooms to all *not* as additional/different teaching for some.
2. All children can learn and their capacity can change *not* teaching is based on 'types' of learner and ability that is fixed and limits learning.
3. Seeing difficulties in learning as a challenge to teachers/teaching *not* attributing difficulties in learning to deficits in learners.

In all three assumptions there is a tendency to pose false dichotomies. Extending general teaching is not different from additional teaching; extending can be construed as adding to general teaching. When Florian and Black-Hawkins use the phrase 'additional/different', they interpret this as disconnected from general teaching, perhaps because some children with identified disabilities/difficulties are sometimes separated within classes from the rest of the children. But, this disconnection is in the practice of teaching, not in the concept of extending or adding to general teaching strategies. Lewis and Norwich (2004) refer to a continuum of teaching strategies defined in terms of degrees of intensifying and adapting general teaching strategies. This idea of intensifying is very similar to the idea of extending. An example can illustrate these points. A teacher decides to add a visual mode (pictures or signs) to a written mode recording of a learning experience for some pupils on account of their disability/difficulty to enable them to participate in a common learning activity. This can be seen as extending what is available to all in the class. However, the added visual mode may also be appropriate to some other pupils with no identified disability or difficulty. When adaptations introduced for disability/difficulties have wider use, in situations such as this, it is hard to identify adaptations as only specific to particular groups of learners. However, the wider use of adaptations may not be necessary for all in the class, so a teaching decision is required about who uses which mode of recording (visual or written or both). This kind of decision will involve judgements about what is appropriate for which pupils and this will partly depend on their learning objectives and their stage of learning. If a child can develop their written skills, then the visual mode of recording will be inappropriate (if observational and written recording are objectives), whereas for a child for whom a written account is difficult, the visual mode will enable them to focus on observational skills. So, extending what is available in class teaching is not distinct from doing something additional in teaching some pupils.

The second assumption also sets up a false opposition. The assumption that all children can learn and their capacity can change is compatible with finding some categories of disability/difficulties pedagogically useful, as argued above. The critique that ability concepts imply that some children cannot learn and that ability is fixed (Hart, 1998) confuses how concepts are defined with how they may be used and abused. The contemporary educational psychology position is that neither curriculum-based nor intellectual or cognitive abilities are necessarily fixed or unalterable (Sternberg, 2005). One of the problems here is that terms are used without enough specificity and clarity. Ability is a word used to refer to being able to do something in relation to some goal and in a social context. If we assume that abilities, like disabilities, are many and are developed and learned through the interaction of genetic and environment factors, then abilities have been developed and are in principle open to further development. This implies that there is scope for further learning and development: they are alterable, but not necessarily alterable without limit or that differences in abilities between people can be removed.

When children are said to differ in learning abilities, this is more about their rate of learning and the amount of support and quality of teaching they need to progress than that they have well-defined limits (Carroll, 1989). It is clear that phrases such as 'fixed limits on abilities' and 'children's capacity to learn can change' need elaboration. That abilities and capacities can change does not mean that this is without limits or that differences in abilities can be fully reduced. However, when the use of the term 'ability' is criticised, it is often as a shorthand for intellectual abilities or intelligence and treated as the major general factor (general intelligence) determining school learning. In this critique, low intellectual abilities are represented as fixed and within-child, on one hand, and as damning or stigmatising the learner, on the other. Neither assumption is necessary nor well based, though both are widely found in practice.

The third assumption sets up a false dichotomy between seeing difficulties in learning as a challenge to teachers in their teaching versus teachers responding by attributing such difficulties to a child's learning difficulties/deficits. Some difficulties in learning may not be attributable to learners but situations and opportunities. Other difficulties, when situations and opportunities have been positive for learning, can be attributable to learners' learning difficulties/disabilities. But, even, as argued above, if there is some attribution of difficulty to the child, this does not imply indifference to or humiliating rejection of the child. Difficulties in teaching and learning, from a reflective and a creative teaching position, imply a call to rise to the teaching challenge. It could be that creative responses to teaching challenges depend on recognising disabilities and disabilities relevant to learning. Nor is this to deny or ignore that attributing disabilities and difficulties is a high-stakes matter with serious risks of negative stereotyping and false low expectations (Molloy and Vasil, 2002; Jutel, 2009). These risks relate to the dilemmas about identification examined in Chapter 3. As argued above, resolving these dilemmas depends amongst other factors on a commitment to respectful and supportive social attitudes and values. Such commitment and knowledge of capabilities and difficulties can be said to be required for teachers and learners if they are to rise to teaching challenges.

In criticising what I have called a 'universal' inclusive pedagogy, I have questioned the over-generalised analysis and use of terms by proponents of universal or full inclusion. In the quote below, for example, Ainscow represents this kind of thinking by calling for teachers to overcome limitations of 'deficit thinking':

> Teachers must overcome the dangers and limitations of deficit thinking: only in this way can we be sure that pupils who experience difficulties in learning can be treated with respect and viewed as potentially active and capable learners.
>
> *(Ainscow, 1998: 11–12)*

As I have argued above, critiques of 'deficit thinking' do not distinguish between over-generalised, dismissive and demeaning use of disability and difficulty categories or labels and a respectful and positive identification of strengths and difficulties in a social context. So, Ainscow's assertion that only by rejecting deficit thinking can pupils with disabilities and difficulties be respected and seen as capable of learning is untenable. Two questionable assumptions are often made in criticisms of 'deficit thinking': first that identifying a person's difficulties necessarily humiliates or damages self-respect, and second that differences between individuals are not 'real' but socially constructed. The first questionable assumption will be taken up in Chapter 7, while the second one relates back to the previous discussion of social construction in Chapter 2.

Practical issues in inclusive pedagogy or teaching

I have argued that a universalist concept of inclusive pedagogy is problematic in theory, but it is also problematic in practice too, as will be discussed in this section. In promoting an ideal of extending general teaching to all in a class without withdrawal, this ideal needs to be set in the practical context of contemporary schooling where there are children in special classes and schools with much more significant learning difficulties/disabilities than usually found in ordinary classes.

Were children with more significant difficulties and disabilities in ordinary primary and secondary school classes, how could general pedagogic strategies be extended without some differentiation of activities, grouping of children, learning objectives and/or teaching strategies?

For example, in Pennsylvania, USA the model of provision in ordinary schools for children with mild–moderate disabilities and difficulties is what is called 'full inclusion' with co-teaching; withdrawal to resource rooms has been largely phased out. The curriculum content derives from standards-based teaching to the general curriculum and teaching involves differentiation of activities and assignments to groups of children with special needs in diverse classrooms (Zigmond et al., 2009). Zigmond and colleagues review the US research that shows that teaching adaptations, such as advance organisers and cognitive strategy instruction, have positive effects on students with specific learning disabilities (specific learning difficulties in the UK), but are not explicitly and systematically applied by teachers (Swanson, 2008). But, there are not only research–practice gaps, the special education–general education co-teaching model hardly happens; in secondary, co-teachers usually help out but do not teach. From their review, Zigmond and colleagues provide some evidence that primary-age children with disabilities receive no additional reading teaching compared to those without disabilities. This raises questions about why some students are put through the statutory identification and assessment procedures (in the Individual with Disabilities Education Improvement Act (IDEA) system). Though these authors recognise some of the benefits of the current provision model – learning on the same curriculum content to the same high standards and not singled out for withdrawal teaching – they wonder whether children with disabilities are receiving appropriate education as mandated by US legislation – 'to meet the unique needs of the child with disability' (IDEA, 2004: sec. 1404 (a)(16)). This evaluation of current US class teaching illustrates the dilemmas of identification and curriculum, discussed above. However, the practical resolution is found to be inadequate by these authors.

A similar research base does not exist in the UK about pedagogic practice for children with disabilities and difficulties in ordinary schools. But, there have been some teacher surveys including a recent report by the national inspection agency, Ofsted (2010), that indicates some of the issues about teaching and learning in English schools. A national study by academic researchers and funded by a teaching union examined the impact of inclusion in primary, secondary and some special schools in a range of local authorities (MacBeath et al., 2007). It was found that though teachers generally welcomed the principles of inclusion (seeing academic and social exclusion as harmful and favouring the social education benefits of inclusion), they confronted many issues. These included the demand for more differentiated teaching in ordinary classes, insufficient planning and consultation about placing pupils with disabilities/difficulties in ordinary schools, perceived lack of expertise in dealing with behavioural and learning needs, the nature and quality of support available and the impact on the balance of teachers' work. These authors also set these issues within a policy context where teachers are subject to the inclusion agenda while also under pressure from the standards agenda. They conclude that increasing the diversity of needs and attainments in the ordinary classroom in the context of standards-driven accountability has had a major impact on the nature and balance of teachers' work. They based these conclusions on consistent themes arising in interviews and written comments from school staff.

When Ofsted as the national inspection agency were asked by government to review special educational needs and disability, they undertook a large-scale survey of English schools and relevant stakeholders as part of a wider survey of educational institutions including further education colleges (Ofsted, 2010). Despite not having full details about sampling and methods, in line with the usual style of Ofsted reports, this report has some conclusions about class teaching and learning. The report concluded that based on inspectors' observations, the best lessons which included pupils with SEN and disabilities were characterised by established general teaching approaches (e.g. having detailed knowledge about children, knowledge of teaching strategies and techniques), but also understanding how learning difficulties can affect children's learning. This reinforces the argument above about the importance of specialised knowledge in teaching a diversity of children. The report also identified various barriers to learning that included a lack of careful planning of lessons and poor deployment of adult support, adult support focused too much on task completion rather than on the learning and too many lessons where children with disabilities/difficulties were prevented from working with their peers. Where children were reported to learn best there was, it was concluded, flexibility in lesson structures, adaptations made without fuss, information provided in different ways and lesson pace adjusted to learners.

Despite talk about inclusive pedagogy or teaching, there is little detailed UK research relevant to it. However, it is possible to consider how Florian and Black-Hawkins (2011) use a researched episode of 'inclusive pedagogy' in a primary class to illustrate their distinction between an individualised pedagogic approach and their favoured inclusive pedagogy – an approach which is supposed to be for everybody. The strategy was called 'work choice' and involves asking children to write a poem with various available resources. The teacher consulted learning support colleagues about how to differentiate learning tasks to accommodate children with disabilities/difficulties. The intention is to provide learning opportunities for everyone so all children can participate in the activity. The main focus is on *what is* to be taught with a range of possible *hows* rather than on *who* was to learn it. Children are trusted to make good decisions about their new learning and are supported by being given the tools necessary to experience success. These authors represent the individualised approach as inclusive insofar as they are working at appropriate levels that have been pre-determined and selected to respond to individual needs. One or two students may work individually with a learning support assistant, while others may be required to complete fewer or simpler tasks. However, Florian and Black-Hawkins represent this model as also having excluding aspects: students are assumed to know who is 'smart and who is not' (p. 821); some students will be unable to work without adult help; and it is assumed that teachers by setting 'appropriate' tasks could put a ceiling on some pupils. This is contrasted with the inclusive pedagogical approach which is 'for everybody' because children choose how, where, when and with whom they learn. The principle is that teachers devise the options and create the conditions to support children to work with different groups.

Florian and Black-Hawkins's representation of the distinction between individualised inclusion and inclusive pedagogy for all is over-idealised in several ways. Trusting the children to select appropriate work is fine but it may not always work well. The teacher involved in this episode said as much herself in the interview excerpt:

> They know what's expected of them so why can't they just give it a go on their own? ... teacher directed differentiated tasks ... sometimes it's necessary but sometimes it's not necessary.
>
> *(p. 824)*

Children might select inappropriate activities, ones that are too challenging or too easy. Also, some of the possible negative aspects of the individualised approach that they criticise could apply to this 'for everybody approach' too. Children will still form ideas about what others are selecting to do and whether they need more or less assistance from others. The 'for everybody approach' may mark out some children in negative ways too. There is clearly scope to use this approach in teaching a diverse group of children, but there is also the risk of negative aspects that lead to dilemmas about how to plan teaching. These dilemmas about classroom teaching relate back to the teaching dilemmas that were studied by Berlak and Berlak (1981), as mentioned in Chapter 4.

Integrating a general difference and individual differences model of pedagogy

Ravet (2011) characterises this 'for everybody approach' to pedagogy as a rights-based perspective in its adoption of the social model, avoidance of labelling and rejection of 'special pedagogies'. A rights-based approach therefore advocates a single inclusive pedagogy for all, seeing no need for separate provision. She contrasts this with a needs-based perspective that adopts a mix of the social and medical model, seeing labelling as useful and inclusionary as well as recognising special pedagogies. A needs-based perspective therefore advocates some separate needs-adapted provision for some children. Ravet's analysis focuses on what counts as a 'special pedagogy' and whether teaching takes account of needs that are specific to a group that shares a characteristic (e.g. autistic spectrum disorder). She recognises that pedagogic approaches that are said to be specific to particular disabilities and difficulties are often also relevant to other children (Davis and Florian, 2004). Ravet calls this the 'many kids' argument and addresses it by examining an example of a difficulty with English idioms that may be shared by children with autistic spectrum disorder (ASD) and by English as additional language learners. It could be argued that taking account

86 Inclusive pedagogy

of this difficulty with idioms does not depend on the ASD category. However, her argument is that the reasons that children may have difficulties with idioms may differ and this difference has relevance to teaching. In the case of English as additional language learners, the difficulty could be due to a weak grasp of English. In time and with greater grasp of the language, idioms may become less of a difficulty. In autism, despite sophisticated use of language, there may be a difficulty with idioms because of a literal understanding of language as part of a particular conceptual style.

To give another example, a visual approach to communication may be seen as relevant not only to those with ASD. But, Ravet's point is that those with ASD may benefit from this kind of approach for longer, more intensively and across more of their learning and communicating. She argues that there should be an understanding of the reasons for difficulties, not seeing them in isolation but in their connection with other features of how a child learns. In this way she aims to turn the 'many kids' argument around and warns against the 'appearance of commonality' in teaching approach (2011: 677). In posing the rights-based against the needs-based perspectives, Ravet aligns the former with the individual differences model and the latter with the general differences models of pedagogy, a distinction introduced by Lewis and Norwich (2004) in their review of SEN pedagogies.

This distinction is understood in terms of three kinds of pedagogic needs, introduced in Chapter 3 (see Table 5.1) – two of these are about needs that are common to all and one about needs that are unique to individuals. At this stage only two are discussed, the third is raised in what follows below. These kinds of needs reflect a value position that recognises what is pedagogically common to all and what is unique to individuals. Both the individual differences and general differences model recognise these needs, but they differ over whether they recognise group-specific needs. From the rights-based perspective, difference is recognised but this is confined to an individual tuning of what is common to all; there is no place for group specific needs because of the assumed exclusionary impact of such pedagogy, which is in line with the 'many kids' argument. From the needs-based perspective there is a generality of need associated with a category such as ASD, though in this model it is assumed that these needs are attuned to what is common to all and is individually unique.

TABLE 5.1 General and individual differences models in terms of kinds of needs

		Kinds of pedagogic models	
		General differences model	*Individual differences model*
Kinds of pedagogic needs	Common needs		
	Group-specific needs		
	Individual needs		

Note: shaded area indicates the kind of need relevant to the model.

Ravet has developed an integrative model that recognises a balance of rights to similar and different pedagogy, adopting a social model informed by possible implications of a disability/difficulty. When applied to autism, as she does, it supports an autism distinct pedagogy to complement an inclusive pedagogy. So, returning to the argument above, that inclusive pedagogy may sometimes require some specialised teaching, it is clear that Ravet's integrative perspective is consistent with this 'moderate' inclusion version of inclusive pedagogy: one in which some learner differences require the recognition of unusual or atypical functioning in terms of categories of disability/difficulties. Also, as argued above in this chapter, this does not necessarily mean that a separate specialist teacher is required in a separate setting, but, as Ravet argues in regard to ASD, it requires autism (and disability) friendly schools and classroom practices. However, where I referred to specialised teaching, she prefers the term 'distinctive teaching/pedagogy' because she sees this as preserving pedagogy that is different, but is not confined to those with disabilities/difficulties.

Ravet also suggests that her integrative perspective resolves the dichotomy between the general differences and individual differences models. However, there are two reasons to doubt this. One is that even though a pedagogic approach related to some specific group can be applied to others, it does not mean that it is relevant to all other learners. Being appropriate for 'many kids', to use Ravet's phrase, may not be appropriate for all children. Why an approach may not be used for all children could be because it removes an opportunity to learn for some children where this is appropriate; for example, a visual method of recording some observations may stop a child from using a literacy mode and so develop her/his literacy. Also, as Cook and Shirmer (2003) have suggested, a method may be cumbersome and time-consuming to use with all learners. The second reason to doubt that this integrative perspective resolves a dichotomy between the individual and general differences models is that Ravet herself, following Allan (2008a), identifies a paradox, which is that both the rights-based (individual differences model) and needs-based perspectives (general differences model) can be inclusive or exclusive. She sees her integrative perspective as being in the space in-between these two polarities. This way of putting it resembles what I call a dilemma in this book, so what she calls an integrative perspective is a way of resolving a dilemma, but not a final solution.

Specialised pedagogy and continua of pedagogic strategies

The Lewis and Norwich (2004) review about whether there is a specialised pedagogy for children with disabilities and difficulties has been interpreted as indicating that there is no specialised pedagogy. However, this review was not meant to be definitive but an analysis of how leading specialists in different areas of disability/difficulties reviewed the then current international literature. A more accurate summary of this review was that a specialised pedagogy could be identified as appropriate for some areas and within some disability/difficulty areas, but not for others. This inaccurate reading of the review shows a commitment to inclusion, which has often been taken to imply that good general teaching can be inclusive teaching.

The general differences model was only supported in a few of the Lewis and Norwich review areas; for example, ASD and ADHD. The position in the case of ASD, for example, was that these children share common pedagogic needs with all others, but their individual needs can only be identified through a framework of distinctive group needs (Jordan, 2004). It is notable that the reviews in these two areas are medically defined conditions that have come more recently to parental and professional attention. General differences positions were also supported where pedagogic strategies interact with aspects of teaching access (visual impairment) and communication mode (hearing impairment). It is important to be clear that the general differences position does not imply that pedagogic decisions flow just from group membership. As shown in Table 5.1, this position also assumes that common needs inform decisions and practices and that these are attuned to individual needs. In the same way, the individual differences position is not merely about individual needs, as it is based on a framework of common needs that is attuned to individual needs.

Most of the other contributions to the Lewis and Norwich review adopted a perspective that assumed generic teaching strategies that are geared to difference by degrees of deliberateness and intensity of teaching. Many supported this position by arguing that variations of teaching strategies for their SEN area can also be useful for other children. The chapters on dyslexia, dyspraxia, moderate learning difficulties (MLD) and severe learning difficulties (SLD), for example, represent the pedagogic variations as reflecting deliberateness and intensity, in line with an earlier review by Norwich and Lewis (2001). As some reviewers pointed out (e.g. O'Brien, 2004 for the emotional and behaviour difficulties area), the diversity within these groups reduces any pedagogic significance of the category. This is a key point that relates to the origin of categories in the special education field in the administrative and resource allocation purposes (this relates to the discussion in Chapter 2).

The individual differences position assumes that general teaching strategies are adapted to individual needs. Here the concept of *continua of teaching strategies* was useful to capture the appropriateness of more intensive and explicit teaching for children with different patterns and degrees of difficulties in learning. This made it possible to distinguish between the typical adaptations in class teaching for most children and the greater degree of adaptations required for those with more significant difficulties in learning. These are adaptations to common or general teaching strategies, what have been called 'specialised' adaptations, or 'high-density' teaching. The Lewis and Norwich (2004) scheme identified various continua of teaching strategies from low to high intensity that covered strategies such as providing opportunities for transfer, shaping task structure, providing examples to learn concepts, provision of practice to achieve mastery, provision of task linked feedback and checking for preparedness for the next stage of learning. These varied, for example, from autonomous pupil-led (low intensity) to explicit and teacher-led (high intensity) or from larger steps, longer-term goals emphasis (low intensity) to small discrete, shorter-term objectives emphasis (high intensity).

This concept of continua of teaching strategies has some resemblance to a US version of a continuum of instruction (Mercer et al., 1996). Mercer identifies a single continuum from explicit (most teacher assistance) to implicit (least teacher assistance) instruction. The continuum is about the movement from teacher regulation through shared regulation to student regulation of learning. But, what Mercer introduces is the theoretical basis for different positions on the continuum, associated with different learning theories (behavioural, social constructivist and individual constructivist). Mercer's key point is about the importance of flexibility about teaching approach and not to adhere to one theoretical model, often underpinned by particular ideological commitments. This is an interesting model because it relates to the discussion of the tensions between different education models or visions in Chapter 4. Mercer argues for ideological flexibility as being more in keeping with actual teaching practices and more suited to the range of approaches required in teaching more diverse classes. As part of this analysis, he identifies student and curriculum factors that lend weight to opting for one or other approach on the continuum. For example, more explicit approaches (more teacher assistance) are relevant to early struggling with content or when content is sequential, while more implicit approaches (less teacher assistance) with early success with content or content is more conceptual. This flexible approach is also evident in another US analysis of different theoretical and ideologically based teaching approaches (Knight, 2002). In this analysis, Knight distinguishes between what he calls constructivist and Intensive-Explicit (IE) teachers. Though he does not talk about a continuum, which might be seen to imply easy movement between positions, he talks about 'crossing boundaries', which indicates what is involved in breaking away from model adherence. His argument is to identify points of convergence between these approaches to enable better integration and flexibility of teaching approach.

This interest in resolving tensions between different teaching approaches has wider relevance across teaching and education. But it does also have specific relevance to the education of children with disabilities and difficulties. The more explicit (Intensive-Explicit) approaches have been strongly associated with special education, while the more implicit (constructivist) approaches have been used in general teaching (Hardman and Dawson, 2008). The above arguments for flexibility and moving between connected positions sets the background to understanding how teaching comes to be split between ordinary and specialised kinds.

Teaching involves a cluster of strategies and if general strategies are applied at the high-intensity end of the continua, the methods might appear to be different from a cluster of methods at the low-intensity end. Though the specific methods might be different from one end of a strategy continuum to another, they are not qualitatively different in terms of strategy, and so the methods are not simply dichotomised. This tendency to split the continua into distinct types, especially for programmes of teaching of children at the ends of the continua of attainments, is reinforced by the historical separation of children with significant disabilities/difficulties in separate settings and schools. There can also be professional and parental interests in seeing the teaching in these separate settings as distinctive. But it is also important to recognise that adopting a continuum of teaching strategies approaches does not ignore that teaching suited to children with learning disabilities/difficulties might be inappropriate for average or high-attaining pupils. It is to reject representing teaching in dichotomies (e.g. teaching that involves extensive and varied practice to achieve mastery *versus* teaching that involves limited practice) and to accept a continuum concept (e.g. extensive and varied *to* limited practice). It is also to question the uncritical use of the term 'specialised teaching'.

Concluding comments and example

In discussing the specialisation of pedagogy, it is also relevant to consider the interdependence and relation between what counts as general and specialised teaching. It has been said that the more general teaching is adapted and flexible to address the needs of a greater range of needs, the less specialised teaching will be required (TDA, 2009). This inverse relationship between the general and specialised reflects this interdependence. Often this flexibility comes from approaches used for those with disabilities/difficulties being used more widely: the application of the 'many kids' argument discussed above. These approaches can then be adopted and adapted in general teaching approaches. The effect is that what is generally provided changes and, as seen in the Wave model (discussed in Chapter 3), additional provision is provided to a wider group than those with disabilities/difficulties, so blurring the distinction between traditional 'special' and 'general' teaching.

This relationship between specialised and general teaching can be seen in contemporary ideas about teaching children with dyslexic or significant literacy difficulties. Singleton (2009) and Rose (2009) talk about 'specialist dyslexia teaching' as 'structured', 'cumulative' and 'sequential'. Various principles and strategies are identified with this specialisation. For example:

- using multisensory methods for teaching and encouraging multisensory learning;
- planning and adapting the teaching programme to meet individual needs;
- teaching a structured programme of phonics;
- building in regular opportunities for consolidation and reinforcement of teaching points already covered.

Analysis of these kinds of strategies indicates that they may all be used in general teaching, implying that they are not specific to those identified as 'dyslexic'. However, the reference to structured consolidation and reinforcement indicates greater intensity of these strategies.

The key point about this way of thinking about specialisation of teaching is that it is about intensification and personalisation. This implies that there are no specialised teaching strategies specific to dyslexia or specific literacy difficulties, in the sense that they are qualitatively different from those used generally. In this sense the argument that there is no teaching basis to the identification of dyslexia has some validity (Gibbs and Elliott, 2010). However, a category may be useful to understand generalised learning strengths and difficulties associated with the category, which can be considered as hypotheses for the personalized intensifying of general teaching strategies for particular children (see Ravet, 2011). Linking this conclusion back to Chapter 3, the significance of a category, such as dyslexia/specific literacy difficulty, even if it does not have clear-cut distinguishing features, is not for identifying specific teaching strategies, but for knowledge that can be used tentatively to adapt the personalised intensification of the teaching of general strategies.

6
INCLUSIVE SCHOOLING

Introduction

Having examined the *what* and *how* of teaching and learning in the two previous chapters, this chapter focuses on *where* this takes place in schools. Talk about inclusion in education or inclusive education is often taken to be about where children and young people are schooled, whether in a special school or regular or ordinary school. For a child with a disability or difficulty to go to a special school or an ordinary school is a decision about the child's individual educational needs and kinds of opportunities offered by the educational setting. But, it is also about the purposes of schooling in society that are not only about individual learning and attainment but about social cohesion and development.

In the few decades since the adoption and international use of the inclusion term, it has accumulated a positive role in social policy, including educational policy. However, inclusion and inclusive education are also contested and problematic in relation to the design of schooling. It is sometimes said of inclusive education that it has become a global movement (UNESCO, 2005), but others have questioned this position. For example, Armstrong et al. (2010) talk about an inclusive education movement as having been in many respects an illusion. This has been because of the disparities in what is understood by inclusive education and how it has been practised internationally. In this chapter I will discuss the origins of the interest in inclusion/exclusion, how inclusion came to replace talk about integration and how inclusion in education became identified with all aspects of diversity in education. Definitional differences will be shown to reflect different value and social-political positions. Practical issues in implementing and designing inclusive schools and practices will be discussed and possible ways of addressing dilemmas about school differentiation will also be proposed.

Origins and significance of inclusion

As discussed above, inclusion in education came to international prominence with the UNESCO Salamanca Statement (UNESCO, 1994), which set out how special needs education for children with disabilities and difficulties was to be developed. The basic idea of the inclusive school is for all children to learn together regardless of any difficulties or differences. The inclusive school would recognise and respond to diverse needs (styles and rates of learning). However, this principle, even in 1994, was qualified by 'wherever possible', indicating that it might not always be possible and anticipating the continuing issues about the comprehensiveness of the inclusion principle. There are different views about the origins of this focus on inclusion, but two key developments can be identified. First, the growth and influence of the disability movement and disabilities studies refocused attention on discrimination and the barriers to participation experienced by disabled people, including children and young people. Special schools were seen as barriers to participation and opportunities and this led to calls for the closure of special schools (Thomas and Vaughn, 2004). As discussed earlier in this book, the promotion of the social model of disability played a large part in this critique of special education, special educational needs and special schooling. This refocused interest on how ordinary schools could be restructured or reformed to accommodate the diversity of learners. From this interest it is clear how the idea of an inclusive school would emerge.

But, an interest in the reorganisation of ordinary schools and the building of their capacity to accommodate more learner diversity did not have to be done in the name of inclusion. It could have been promoted as it had been prior to 1994 in terms of integration. In fact in the UK that was exactly how this interest was promoted in the 1970s and 1980s as illustrated in the Warnock Report (DES, 1978). So, why was there a change of terms? It is interesting that those who promoted a whole-school approach to planning for special educational needs in the 1980s (Thomas and Feiler, 1988) were the ones who in the 1990s were involved in the promotion of the inclusive school (Thomas et al., 1998). Integration was qualified as having different aspects, such as locational integration, social integration and functional or curricula integration (Warnock Report types; DES, 1978). It is revealing that inclusive education has been formulated as different from integration, which was portrayed as being about locational integration. The social and functional aspects of integration, which corresponded more closely to the concept of inclusion as social and academic participation in local ordinary schools, was overlooked. There may be two reasons for this terminological switch. One is that inclusion was framed as about organisational change, while integration (in its locational aspect) could be framed as about the placement of individuals in ordinary school without social and school organisational change. This can be linked to the opposition set up by social model advocates between the social model (focused on social change) and the individual or medical model (focused on individual change). But, though placement could be portrayed as individually focused, social and functional integration of an individual child with a disability or difficulty would necessarily involve some organisational change at class and even at school level, and therefore, involve some organisational change. So, the silence about social and functional integration could be attributed to the influence of the social model. It is notable that not all proponents of inclusive education interpreted integration as about individual placement; for example, Booth and Potts (1983) saw integration as having school reform implications.

The other factor related to this terminological switch was the development of policies about social inclusion and exclusion. Social exclusion was initially used in France in the 1970s as a term to mean 'the rupture of social bonds' (De Haan, 2000: 25) and to refer not only to the poor but also disabled people, abused children and other disadvantaged groups. The idea of the new term was to refer to new kinds of social problems, such as unemployment and fundamental changes in family life, for which previous welfare policies and provision were seen as inadequate. The use of social exclusion has also been attributed to the unpopularity in France of the British concept of 'poverty'. This has been attributed to the French interest in the values of solidarity as an alternative to utilitarian individualism and socialism (Silver, 1994). This focus on reducing social exclusion became more established in the European Union, written into treaties and underpinned by EU funding. Its wider international adoption was also evident; for example in New Zealand (Peace, 2001). In the UK, from 1997 the new Labour government focused its social policy or attacking social exclusion, though perhaps not using the term with the specific meaning attached to its original French use. The Labour government was looking for a progressive policy principle to set alongside and perhaps moderate its commitment to a quasi-market approach to social policy, which it inherited from the previous Conservative government. Social inclusion, as the opposite of social exclusion, introduced the idea of solidarity, which justified the welfare state in terms of social integration.

Though the policy terms 'inclusion' and 'inclusive' are therefore relatively new, the underlying values of equal opportunity, social respect and solidarity have a long history. Social inclusion derived its meaning partly from being the opposite of social exclusion, which has been taken to refer to processes in which individuals and entire communities are blocked from rights, opportunities and resources; for example, housing, employment, healthcare, civic engagement, democratic participation and due process (Power and Wilson, 2000). What defines social exclusion in this formulation is that these rights, opportunities and resources are seen as ones normally available to most members of society as they are central to social integration. It is interesting that social exclusion/inclusion is linked here to social integration (and the term 'integration'), in which all people are said to participate fully in the life of the community. Also, that social exclusion is the leading concept means that social inclusion has come to be defined as the opposite of social exclusion, that is, reducing social exclusion leads to social inclusion. This leaves social inclusion as a relatively unspecified positive term.

As Sennett (1999) has argued, social inclusion has its own logic, as part of his analysis of how social inclusion has been diminished by contemporary capitalism.

Though Sennett has analysed social inclusion practices in work settings, he argues that this analysis is relevant to understanding social inclusion in other organisation settings such as schools. He identifies three elements to social inclusion practices: 1) mutual exchange; 2) that the exchange has some elements of ritual; and 3) the ritual has witnesses who judge the behaviour of individuals. The importance of the witnessing of mutual exchange rituals is to underline mutual accountability between workers and managers. These mutual exchanges may be symbolic but they function to signal that members of the organisation are noticed and listened to by those in authority. Social inclusion in a work setting has been undermined, argues Sennett, through the growth of market flexibilities and the relative loss of mutual obligations and commitments between workers and their managers. This has had the effect of decreasing the significance of social inclusion and increasing the importance of autonomy as a source of honour. Sennett is not denying the value of autonomy as an important source of honour, but wants to show how the rise of autonomy brings with it the 'horrors of dependency' (p. 5), which can be seen as demeaning: a source of social dishonour. His key point is that in the current corporate world, with its centralisation of command in a technical-managerial elite, those who implement the commands are left without guidance and are not in relationships which support witnessed mutual exchanges. The importance of mutual exchange and mutual need that can bind people together is central to this analysis of social inclusion. It has relevance to the organisation of the school system in countries where academic standards are set centrally (by governments and by senior schools leaders), where schools become more autonomous and teachers are expected to deliver to the centrally set standards.

Another way in which the initial origin of social exclusion has influenced ideas about social inclusion has been though the framing of social exclusion in terms of being deprived of social recognition. Social recognition in this analysis depends on a full citizenship that enables full participation in the life of a community (Honneth, 1996). Honneth considers this citizenship to include economic, social and political participation. Social inclusion can therefore be seen as primarily about various kinds of participation in a community. This emphasis on social recognition is relevant to criticisms of ethnic and immigrant integration where the minority group is expected to assimilate to the majority or dominant group in a way that denies recognition of their distinctive ethnic and cultural ways. In this criticism, assimilation involves fitting in and suppressing or denying some distinctive characteristics. Social inclusion has therefore been defined from one perspective to imply that the 'struggle for recognition' requires that the 'mainstream' community accommodate to the minority.

However, this posing of assimilation (minority fitting in) as an opposite to accommodation (majority adapting) is not the only way of analysing how minority groups relate to majority ones. Berry (1997) proposed an alternative way as regards ethnic mixing and identity in terms of: 1) the retention–rejection of minority ways and 2) adoption–rejection of dominant group ways. Assimilation in this scheme is when individuals reject their minority ways but adopt the dominant ways.

Separation is a rejection of the dominant group's ways while retaining one's own ways and marginalisation is a rejection of one's own and the dominant group's. In this scheme, integration is the retention of one's own ways and the adoption of the dominant group's ways, sometimes associated with what has been called bi-culturalism. Though Berry's scheme applies to the ethnicity area, it is also relevant to the disability and difficulties one. The bi-cultural stance is evident in how deaf people can communicate within their signing communities but also operate in the mainstream communities (Gregory, 2004). The idea of bi-cultural identity formation has also been advocated as relevant to children with autism (Myers et al., 2012). Berry's scheme also shows that fitting in need not be inconsistent with retaining one's own ways. This possibility connects with a different model, supported here, where assimilation (the minority fitting in) and accommodation (the 'mainstream' adapting systemically to the minority) can be complementary social processes, with the one involving the other. There are therefore two distinct and inconsistent perspectives on accommodation. One sees it as complementary to assimilation, and rejects the 'purely accommodationist' social model because it is believed that many people with disabilities would select certain abilities if given the opportunity (Hughes, 2010). The other perspective sees accommodation as a binary opposite of assimilation (Thomas and Vaughn, 2004).

Inclusive education and schooling: issues and tensions

Applying ideas about social inclusion to education in keeping with a social model of disability was not going to be without its problems. These issues arise partly from the historical role of education and partly from issues associated with inclusion as a general value. As Sayed and Soudien (2003) point out, education has been not only about access and social mobility but also about social selection. In this way, education can be socially inclusive and exclusive. Also, talk about inclusive education has often failed to talk about different 'differences'; differences have been overlooked in terms of who is included/excluded. This is the criticism that inclusion assumes that 'one size fits all', when policies and practices might need to vary depending on the aspect of diversity. This relates to another criticism, summarised by Sayed and Soudien, that although inclusive education is meant to go beyond disability to cover other aspects of diversity, such as race, class and gender, there is little specification of how these different aspect interrelate. These authors also remind us that the dichotomous talk about inclusion–exclusion assumes that people always want to be included: that there is a movement from excluded to included. This may be so for many people, but some may wish to be in a bi-cultural position and others to be separated.

Another problematic aspect of the concept of inclusive schooling is that it assumes that inclusion can alter the status quo in society. An inclusive school cannot ensure that young people will participate in the wider community outside school. Schools may be able to influence society, but schools are nevertheless also subject to wider social structures and processes (Bernstein, 1970). Schools already serve various social and economic interests and inclusion is proposed for school systems in many countries that are often already selective and tracked into different kinds of schools. In the case of UK (England), for example, the principle of inclusion needs to be seen within the historical movement for comprehensive or common schools for all children and young people. In this way the principles of inclusion connect with a longer-term political vision about schools, especially about secondary schools for all. However, this varies by country. In countries with a tradition of common schools (e.g. Scandanavian countries), inclusion connects with this vision of schooling. But, in other countries, which have established differentiated secondary schooling (e.g. Germany and the Netherlands), inclusive education comes into tension with the basic organisation of the school system.

It is useful to consider a specific country to illustrate these points in more detail. I will examine briefly the issues in England. Central to the debates about the organisation of English secondary schools has been the selection of children at age eleven for either a more academic education in grammar schools or in secondary modern schools where a less academic/vocationally oriented education was provided. Special schools had their place in this differentiated school system where 'general ability' assessment played a large part in the selection process for these kinds of schools. The vision of schools for all, irrespective of gender, social class, religion, ethnicity or ability, meant that more provision was to be made for children with disabilities and difficulties in ordinary schools. From this perspective, special schools were seen as less favourable or totally unacceptable settings for children with special educational needs. Since the 1980s when legislation required the education of children with disabilities and difficulties in ordinary schools, subject to certain conditions, the proportion of children in special schools reduced from about 1.8 per cent (1983) to about 1.3 per cent (2000) of the school population (Norwich, 2002b). Since then the proportion in special schools has been largely unchanged at about 1.1 per cent (depending on the formula used: Ofsted, 2010). Parallel to special schools, there are still state-funded grammar schools (about 5 per cent of funded secondary schools; Politics.co.uk, 2012). Despite the historic move away from grammar to comprehensive schools from the 1960s, there was no national legislation to close state-funded grammar schools; it was left to local authorities to make this decision. This coexistence of grammar and comprehensive schools resembles the coexistence of special schools and ordinary or mainstream schools.

The conditions for inclusive education were probably optimal during the Labour period of government (1997–2010) when social inclusion became a central pillar of social, economic and educational policy. But, at no time has the inclusion agenda impacted on the continuation of schools based on religious affiliations or independent fee-paying schools. Despite the development of inclusive education policies and strategies during the Labour period and more inclusive talk and efforts to enhance inclusive practices, there was little political agreement about social inclusion as social cohesion. This has been shown in the recent Conservative and Liberal Democrat Coalition policy on special educational needs (DfE, 2011). This questioned and opposed the previous government's 'bias to inclusion'. What the government meant by 'bias to inclusion' seems to be more about the previous government's inclusive-oriented policy initiatives rather than extensive inclusive practices and developments. The coalition schools policy, in line with its wider social policies, has been towards greater school diversity and parental choice. This has involved some schools becoming independent of local authorities (academies programme) and the setting up of 'free schools' by parents, teachers and/or voluntary organisations. Inclusion in this policy context is confined to individual placement decisions (special or ordinary school) by parents: inclusion as a private not a public matter of social policy. The term 'inclusion' seems to carry too many social solidarity connotations for a right-wing-leaning government.

Debates about inclusion

The current English debates about inclusion in education reflect differing policy orientations that express distinct ideological and political commitments. Though there was a consensus during the Labour period of government about using the terms 'inclusion' and 'inclusive education', the different and conflicting perspectives and conceptions were often obscured. For example, the last Labour government defined inclusion, in its reply to the House of Commons Select Committee Enquiry into special educational needs, as about:

> the quality of a child's experience and providing access to the high quality education, which enables them to progress with their learning and participate fully in the activities of their school and community.
> *(DfES, 2006a: section 28)*

This focuses on quality experience and access, progression in learning and participation in school and community, but makes no reference to children being in their local community schools. Having special schools is compatible with this definition of inclusion. This shows how far government formulations about inclusion went beyond and in contradiction to the original intention associated with inclusion. An earlier definition of an inclusive school by the national inspection agency Ofsted had similar implications. In guidance to inspectors and schools (Ofsted, 2000), an inclusive school was presented as one where 'teaching and learning, achievement and attitudes and well-being of every person matters' (p. 4). Though this definition extended inclusion beyond special educational needs and disability to include gender, ethnicity, social background and so on, it did so as the above government definition did, in terms of learning and achievement. It also ignored the social participation aspect of inclusion that is clearly defined in the Inclusion Index's approach to inclusive education, in terms of:

> the participation in the cultures, curricula and communities of *local schools*.
> *(Booth et al., 2000: 3; italics added)*

In this definition of inclusive education, participation is multifaceted and is in local schools. Inclusion in this view is about restructuring schools so that they respond to the diversity of children in their locality (Ainscow et al., 2006). What is open to interpretation in this reference to 'local schools' is whether participation might be in a cluster or grouping of local schools in a neighbourhood, one of which might be more specialised for children with disabilities and difficulties. For example, in a locality there may be a cluster of four interconnected schools: a secondary with three primary schools and in one of the primary and the secondary schools there are resourced units/special classes. Would participation of some children with disabilities in a unit in one of these schools in this cluster of schools represent participation in local schools? This is the question about the level of organisation within and between schools which has the capacity to accommodate children with disabilities and difficulties. One option is that capacity is designed at the school level, where all accommodations are made within each school, that is, fully inclusive ordinary schools. The opposite option is that capacity is designed at the local authority level, where accommodations are designed not only within but also between schools. In this option, it is the local authority system that is inclusive by having ordinary and special schools. This was the option favoured by the Labour government (DfES, 2006b).

As Table 6.1 shows, these two options are not the only levels at which capacity can be built for the range of disabilities and difficulties. Table 6.1 uses a notional small English local authority with 45 schools to illustrate some of these options. The design of the school system involves three types of accommodations:

1. Adapted primary/secondary schools: where physical, social and learning adaptations are made for the majority of children with disabilities and difficulties.
2. Adapted primary/secondary with units: where schools are adapted as in 1 above but in addition there is additionally resourced provision for children requiring more specialised provision.
3. Special schools: for provision not available in 1 and 2 above.

Option 1: this represents a commonly found pattern of provision in English local authorities where all schools make some adaptations, but some primary and secondary schools in addition have additionally resourced units, perhaps for hearing impairment or designated for speech and language impairment. In addition there is a set of special schools.

Option 2: this is similar to option 1 in having capacity still built in at local authority level, but more is built into primary and secondary schools with more adaptations in all primary and secondary schools and more resourced units in some of these schools. In this option the number of special schools has reduced from seven to two. This second option is an important one as it represents what some would have considered as best practice in inclusive education, as of 2010 at the end of the Labour period of government. An authority such as Newham in east London will have reduced its special school population since the 1990s and built in capacity at primary and secondary school levels, but still have some special schools (CSIE, 2005).

TABLE 6.1 Levels at which capacity for disability/difficulties is organised: distribution of types of school within a notional local authority

Levels of organising capacity							
1 Local authority (LA)	Adapted primary	Adapted primary + unit	Adapted secondary	Adapted secondary + unit		Special School	total
	26	4	6	2		7	45
2 LA	Adapted primary	Adapted primary + unit	Adapted secondary	Adapted secondary + unit		Special School	Total
	22	8	4	4		2	40
3 Clusters + LA	Cluster type 1: Adapted primary (3–4) / Adapted secondary (1) / Adapted primary/secondary + unit (1–2) — 5–7			Cluster type 2: Adapted primary (3–4) / Adapted secondary (1) / Special school (1) — 5–6		Special School	2
4 Clusters	Adapted primary (3–4) / Adapted secondary (1) / Adapted primary/secondary + unit (1–2) — 5			Adapted primary (3–4) — 6 / Adapted secondary (1) / Special school (1)		Special school (1)	3
5 School	Adapted primary	Adapted primary + unit	Adapted secondary	Adapted secondary + unit			4
		24		4			
6 School	Adapted and resourced primary		Adapted and resourced secondary				8
	30						

Options 3 and 4: these represent capacity design where accommodations are made more at a locality level for groups of five to seven schools. Some clusters might involve special schools (type 2) and some not (type 1). The point of the clusters is to enable interchange between member schools through their proximity and organisational links. Option 3 represents a local authority where there are still a couple of special schools which do not fit into the cluster organisation. In option 4, there are no special schools outside cluster organisations and only special schools linked formally to primary and secondary schools.

Option 5: this represents capacity design where accommodations are made in all primary and secondary schools, so there are no special schools, only units, but not cluster-level units.

Option 6: this represents capacity design where accommodations are made at all primary and secondary schools, where there are neither special schools nor resourced units either. All schools have additional resources associated with units where required. This is the option implied in the position that opposes all separate provision as segregating and excluding and aims to provide learning support for all in ordinary schools (CSIE, 2002).

Some commentators are likely to see option 5 and 6 as 'something of an utopian ideal' (Low, 2007: 9). Low opposes what he calls full inclusion (that the general school system can be geared to provide for all kinds of disability as an integral part of provision) with what he calls 'moderate inclusion' based on a presumption towards inclusion ('so far as humanly possible', p. 6). In arguing against the position of the Centre for the Study of Inclusive Education (CSIE), he suggests that their argument for a single inclusive system of education that is adapted to the interests of every child is probably the national school system. This is clearly not an inclusive system at the level of local schools. He also responds critically to the common explanation given by full inclusion proponents of children who do not thrive in ordinary schools. This is the explanation that *all* failure to thrive is due to poor resourcing and inadequate implementation of proper inclusion. Low accepts that *some* failure to thrive may reflect inadequate resourcing and implementation and that such occurrences should not immediately lead to setting up separate provision. But, he questions whether this means that all examples of failure to thrive cannot be examples of inclusion. If this is how the term 'inclusion' is used, he argues, then inclusion cannot be associated with any problems or limitations. If someone suggests an association with negative experiences, then the experience is immediately redefined as not inclusion, but as something else; for example, as about integration (Disability Equality in Education, 2005; Roulstone and Prideaux, 2008). As Low notes, this move puts inclusion beyond empirical evaluation, a move that protects its purity but also makes it difficult to define and put into operation. This protective use of the term 'inclusion' could also explain the move, noted above, to define inclusion as having no relation to integration.

Along similar lines, Pirrie and Head (2007) note the continuing failure of inclusion proponents to give an adequate definition of the term. Part of putting inclusion beyond empirical evaluation is to make it a 'self-insulating concept' and consider it as a long and unending process – a road to travel rather than a destination. As Ainscow et al. (2006) put it: 'inclusion is seen as a never ending process' (p. 25). Pirrie and Head consider that much of what is said about inclusion is about the aura associated with the term (justice and compassion, equality, fraternity and human rights) rather than its definition. For them it is a 'passionate intuition' that has entered educational policy, practice and research. These authors see this commitment to a radical view about inclusion as a 'fiction' that has led to the disappearance of disability and a failure 'to recognize individual differences and the frequently painful lived experience brought about by impairment' (p. 28). They suggest that this has led to a crisis of belonging. By drawing on Bauman's analysis of the contemporary fragmentation of social dissent, they suggest that the emergence of 'disabilism' as a militant player in the 'recognition wars' is an example of this fragmentation (Bauman, 2004).

Stretch in the language of inclusive schooling

The terms 'inclusion' and 'inclusive' have come to be used in many different ways. For example, when the English inspection agency (Ofsted) refer to schools having an inclusive approach, they mean a caring and supportive school environment, not necessarily one that practises no behaviour exclusions. This was also shown in a recent study of secondary teachers' beliefs about inclusive schooling. These teachers' concept of inclusive schooling involved schools which admit a diversity of pupils including those with significant disabilities, schools that welcome everyone irrespective of background and where teachers feel responsible for the learning and achievement of all pupils. But, their concept of an inclusive school also involved some exclusion on account of behaviour and some recommending of pupils for special schools (Ylonen and Norwich, 2012).

That some aspects of inclusive schooling can be endorsed, but not others, has been attributed to the lack of clear definitions, which has left space for different politically oriented interpretations (Rix, 2011). Rix sees this as the reason for governments representing special schools internationally as having a role in an inclusive system. However, the growth of the choice and diversity model of schooling (sometimes called a neo-liberal model) in education policy in the UK (England) led the previous government to introduce some specialisation to secondary schools. Though this was mainly a 'subject' specialisation (e.g. modern languages or science), secondary schools could also adopt an area of special educational needs (e.g. cognition and learning as a second specialism), while special schools could also become specialist schools. Specialist schools were meant to be forward-looking providers with links to the wider community and other schools in their specialist areas. Rix studied the discourse used by a sample of these specialist special schools to see how they positioned themselves in the school 'market' (Rix, 2011). He found that many of these special schools presented themselves as 'inclusive', by either taking 'inclusive' to mean making all feel welcome, to refer to their outreach work in ordinary schools or to the way that Ofsted, the inspection agency, had judged their provision as 'inclusive'. He also found evidence that the language of the social model (e.g. barriers) was used in ways that proponents of the radical social model would criticise as more associated with a 'deficit model'. Barriers were not just external factors but internal impairments or disabilities.

Rix's response to this loose use of inclusive language was to call for a more prescriptive use of terms, so that inclusive education would be defined more in terms of the nature of school settings than individual rights. So, he called for a representative principle to be adopted in ascribing inclusiveness to schools. The principle is that:

> the community and organizational structures of the setting are representative and inclusive of a full cross-section and local community in all that it does.
>
> (p. 275)

The point of this principle is to shift the focus from the individual (whether as rights or needs) to the collective, so that all school settings met this principle. Rix considered that this would have the effect that 'segregated providers' such as special schools could not be representative without ceasing to be selective and separate.

Though Rix justifies this principle as reflecting a liberal democratic view of social justice, he does not explain how the principle's collective focus fits with the individual focus of liberal theories of justice (Artiles et al., 2006). Also, how would a representative principle be applied? Would it be applied in terms of all dimensions of diversity (e.g. ethnicity, religion, gender, disability, social background) or only some dimensions? But, also the authority to implement this principle would require a national democratic mandate and even if this were secured, there may still be regional or local areas that resisted central control on this matter. These issues are raised not because the representative principle has no value, but rather to indicate that there are other considerations that also have to be taken into account.

Specialisation of schools

I will now discuss the implications of a representative principle for the design of schools in terms of what we currently accept as a legitimate specialisation of schools. For this analysis I will use the term 'specialisation' to refer to schools that are specialist in terms of their intake of children and/or their curriculum focus. Specialist is usually seen to be the opposite of generalist. Another related way of talking about this distinction is in terms of the common school and a differentiated system of schooling. Table 6.2 shows some of the key dimensions of specialisation. These dimensions go well beyond disability specialisation, but they also show how some of the key dimensions of specialisation are widely accepted forms of differentiation (e.g. by age), while others have a long history and continue to be associated with some contention (e.g. religion and gender specialisation). The significance of these dimensions of specialisation differs between countries and changes over time within countries. In the UK (England) specialisation by funding

TABLE 6.2 Possible dimensions and options for generalist–specialist schools

Dimensions	Design options		
Funding:	Private (parents pay)	Maintained (tax payers)	Commissioned (taxpayers at private schools)
Commonality–differentiation			
Age:	Mixed (all) age	Primary–secondary	Elementary–middle–high
Gender:	Mixed gender	Single gender	
Religion:	Mixed secular	Single faith	Mainly single faith
Ethnicity:	Mixed ethnicity	Supplementary school	
Attainments–abilities:	Mixed attainments-abilities	Academic/Grammar	Technical/vocational
Subject area:	Mixed subjects	Mixed with subject specialisation	Mainly subject specialist; some mixed subjects
Learner exceptionality			
Disability:	Mixed abled–disabled	Single/mixed disability specific only	Disability specific mainly + some abled
Language medium:	Mixed majority + minority languages	1st language only	Mainly 1st language + some minority language
Gifted/talented:	Mixed	Mixed + some gifted/talented specific	Arts/music or maths specific

(private versus state funding) has special significance in the socio-economic structure of the country compared to other countries, particularly those with a republican constitution (e.g. France and the USA). Similarly, specialisation by attainment-abilities has a particular history in the organisation of secondary schooling in England. This concerns the place of grammar schools for higher-attaining young people in relation to the comprehensive school system.

As discussed above, the continued existence of special schools for some children with disabilities and difficulties alongside primary and secondary schools that accommodate children with disabilities and difficulties has some parallels with the retention of grammar schools. Both reflect continued parental interest in specialised schools for their children. This coexistence reflects the balance of power between central and local governments and parents, though there are also differences between grammar and special schools. Some parents may have little option but to accept special school, if no other schools are willing to accommodate their children. It is this element of compulsion that has led special schooling to be stigmatised, compared to grammar schools that have a more elitist and favoured aura. What is interesting is that differentiated secondary schooling is still well established in Europe and this tends to be associated with a special school system: a two-tracked school system (EADSEN, 2003). This is where provision for students with disabilities and difficulties is organised into a largely separate general and specialist system.

While age specialisation is probably the most accepted form of school specialisation internationally, ethnic specialisation has been the most controversial. Ethnic specialisation has been an expression of racism and oppression in countries such as the USA and South Africa in the twentieth century. Ethnic specialisation is rejected in many countries, though in the UK there is some ethnically based supplementary schooling, some of which is associated with religious faith.

Though there is more to say about the other dimensions of specialisation set out in Table 6.2, there are three key points that arise from this analysis. The first is that the inclusive school which welcomes and accommodates children with disabilities and difficulties has to be seen within the wider context of the other dimensions of schooling. These dimensions have historically represented more dominant interests than those of disability; for example, religion (faith), funding source and attainments/abilities. Second, the position that inclusion and the inclusive school go beyond disability involves a very complex political commitment to the design of schools that involves these other dimensions. Third, reference to inclusive schooling is likely to be relative to some but not all dimensions. A church school may be inclusive in welcoming and admitting children with severe disabilities, but this will mostly be if the children with disabilities are church-going, less likely for those who are non-believers.

Returning to Rix's representational principle, it is evident that schools may be more representative in relation to some dimensions than others. Whether schools can be fully representative on all dimensions raises questions that go well beyond the usual considerations of disability and inclusion – beyond rhetorical assertions about celebrating diversity, unifying the system and the radical transformation of the school system. It is also clear that the specialisation of schools will reflect the school's purposes and this connects to questions about the commonality–differentiation of the curriculum discussed in Chapter 4. As with curriculum design, school design may reflect some balance between being more and less representative of the local community. There is another critical point about this principle. The local community may not reflect the range of people and cultures in a wider area or the country. This depends on whether different groups and cultures live alongside each other or are separated by cultural, religious, ethnic and social class factors. Where there is demographic separation, this undermines a locality model of inclusion and raises larger policy questions about the location of housing and schooling (this is discussed further in Chapter 8).

Within school specialisation or differentiation

Not only are there issues about generic–specialist schooling, but even within a generic or inclusive school there are further questions about academic and social participation in local ordinary schools. There are questions about the organisation and grouping of children within a school. It is unclear whether 'participation in local schools' implies and requires that children with disabilities and difficulties will be in ordinary classrooms for most or all of their learning. This question will be discussed in terms of the generic–specialist grouping of learners in schools. Florian (2010) in her analysis of inclusive pedagogy, as discussed in Chapter 5, implies that children are not withdrawn from the class learning community that is established as part of inclusive pedagogy. However, the CSIE, a pressure group associated with the Inclusion Index, accepted in its charter that some children with special educational needs can spend *part of their time* outside the ordinary classroom (Thomas and Vaughn, 2004). This concession to part-time withdrawal raises a further question. Are part-time placements in off-site settings for appropriate and time-limited learning compatible with inclusive education, if the children are still members of ordinary schools and classes? This specific CSIE position could be seen as a step towards justifying some separate grouping and settings, and shows an interconnection between included and separate settings and provision.

Table 6.3 shows some of the key dimensions and the options for grouping children within schools. As expected the key dimensions are similar to school design dimensions, as are some of the frequently used options; for example, age grouping. As with schooling, there can be coexistence between mixed attainment grouping and some part-time and/or limited period withdrawal on the grounds of disability/difficulties. Though studies show that inclusive schools tend to use flexible grouping of children (Dyson et al., 2004), proponents of inclusive schools tend to be silent about the justification and acceptability of the balance between mixed and specialist grouping.

TABLE 6.3 Possible dimensions and options for generic–specialist grouping

Dimensions	Grouping options			
Age	Mixed age groups	Vertical age groups (in smaller schools)	Limited + specific purpose mixed age groups (e.g. literacy)	Age year groups
Gender	Mixed gender groups	Single gender (subject specific)	Single gender (all subjects)	
Attainments–abilities	Mixed attainment groups	Cross-curriculum/ general ability setting (tracking)	Subject specific + mixed attainment (setting/ tracking)	Subject specific only
Disability	Mixed abled+ disabled groups	Part-time + temporary disability specific; rest mostly mixed groups	Mostly part-time disability specific; rest mixed	Mostly disability specific
English 2nd language	Mixed 1st + 2nd language groups	Part-time withdrawal + ordinary class	Mainly withdrawal	
Social–emotional disadvantage	Mixed groups	Part-time withdrawal + ordinary class	Mainly withdrawal	

Multidimensionality and recent challenges to inclusive schooling

One of the central problems about the use of the inclusion term in education has been its multidimensional nature and the inability to find common ground between interest groups over these dimensions. The six ways of thinking about inclusive education, identified by Ainscow et al. (2006), illustrate this point:

1. Focus on SEN/disability.
2. Response to disciplinary exclusion.
3. All groups vulnerable to exclusion (beyond disability).
4. Developing school for all (common school).
5. Inclusion as 'education for all' (UNESCO initiative).
6. Principled approach to education and society.

These authors, as discussed above, opt for the sixth approach, the principled one that starts from values, but does not address the problem of the generality of the inclusion concept. They do, however, make reference to the dimensions of inclusion as involving presence, participation and achievement, which is a good starting point for analysing the multidimensionality of inclusion.

The multidimensional aspects make it hard to know how to use the term, unless people qualify its use (e.g. to say placement inclusion or participation inclusion), which has mostly not been the case. This affects the everyday use by parents and teachers, as well as policy makers in schools, local authorities and central government. This problem has been recognised in the UK. For example, the Education Select Committee of the House of Commons in their report on Special Educational Needs (House of Commons, 2006) urged the government to work harder to define exactly what it means by inclusion.

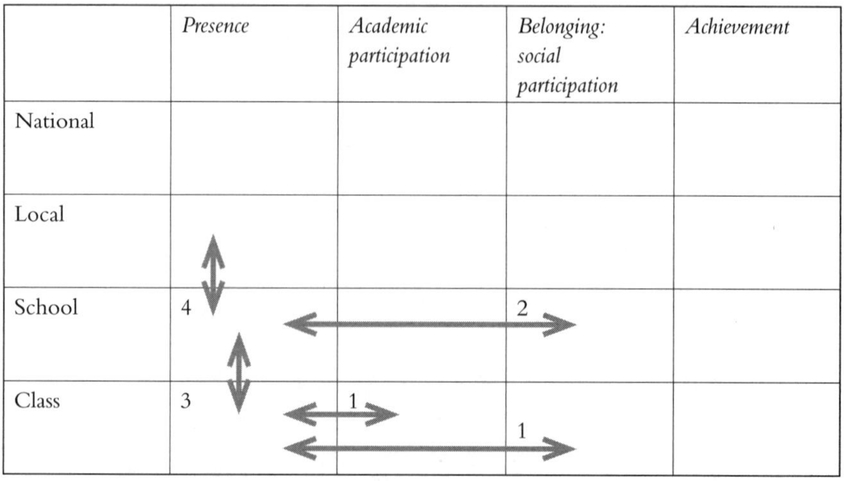

	Presence	*Academic participation*	*Belonging: social participation*	*Achievement*
National				
Local				
School	4		2	
Class	3	1	1	

FIGURE 6.1 Dimensions and levels relevant to inclusion

Figure 6.1 illustrates these four dimensions at four levels of use. The five arrows illustrate some of the tensions in the meaning of inclusion that are set up by the different dimensions and levels of inclusion. At a class level, children with disabilities and difficulties might be included in terms of presence, but might be neither academically nor socially participating (arrow 1). At a school level, children with disabilities and difficulties might be present in the school (placement inclusion), but not feel like they belong there (belonging exclusion) (arrow 2). In terms of presence, children with disabilities/difficulties might be a member of an inclusive school (placement inclusion), but outside ordinary class groupings; for example, in a special class (academic exclusion) (arrow 3). Similarly, a specialised school for children with disabilities might be separate from ordinary schools (placement exclusion), but be in an inclusive school system at local authority level (system inclusion) (arrow 4). From this analysis, we can expect that there is a possibility that when the term 'inclusion/exclusion' is used, with reference to some dimension and at some level, that what is called inclusive might be described as exclusive in terms of another dimension or level. For example, in Greece separate special classes in ordinary schools of children with disabilities and difficulties are called 'inclusion classes'. In the UK withdrawal units for pupils presenting behaviour difficulties have been called 'inclusion centres' (Preece and Timmins, 2004). They are called inclusive because they provide for children who might otherwise not be included in ordinary schools, but they could also be described as excluding with regard to academic participation.

The most significant recent challenge in the UK to contemporary ideas and practice associated with inclusive education came from Mary Warnock, chair of the 1978 Government Committee that endorsed integration. She rejected educational inclusion as being 'all children under the same roof', preferring a learning concept of inclusion, which is about 'including all children in the common educational enterprise of learning, wherever they learn best' (Warnock, 2005). Her perspective on inclusion can be seen to prioritise *engagement in learning* over placement, a view which has also been recently proposed for the area of education of children and young people with social, emotional and behaviour difficulties by Cooper and Jacobs (2011). Research also shows that some teachers working in separate settings see a degree of withdrawal to a separate setting as being inclusive in the sense of making it possible for certain children to engage in learning the same curriculum as other children (Norwich, 2008).

This tension between 'inclusion' as engagement in learning (wherever is best for learning) and as participation in local schools for all is the central point of current contention in the UK and other countries about the principle of inclusive schooling for children with disabilities and difficulties. Farrell (2006) is a rare example of someone who argues for the celebration of special schools in terms of 'providing the best education possible for children with special educational needs' (pp. 1–2). His argument for special schools, like Warnock's, is that inclusion has come to be seen as more important for schools than education. This argument is an interesting one as it sets up education as not being about inclusion. At the root of this disagreement are differences in basic assumptions about the purposes of schooling and society. There are two key underlying differences here: first, about the individual versus the social functions of schooling, and second, about the related knowledge-centred versus a society-centred position about the design of school programmes (as discussed in Chapter 4). Farrell and Warnock veer towards an individualist knowledge-centred position, while many proponents of inclusive education and schooling veer towards a social society-centred position. In a debate between Mary Warnock and myself over her 2005 position (Warnock and Norwich, 2010), I argued that schools can have both social and individual development functions and that maximising participation in schools for all is also a social educational aim, not something different from education. In rejecting the education versus inclusion dichotomy, I was adopting the stance that I have argued for in this book: that tensions need to be recognised and addressing them requires resolutions to be found, resolutions that may involve some balancing and trading off between principles.

Continued protection of the purity of inclusion

In questioning false dichotomies I am revisiting the argument from Chapter 1 that presented some of the difficulties with a social model of disability (one that is posed as antagonistic to an individual model). In doing so I am questioning, as does Low (2007), the logic of splitting which goes from 'X is not only individual ...' to 'X is only social', where X can be 'disability' or the 'purposes of schooling'. It is possible to critique the social model while still recognising important social dimensions in interaction with individual ones. However, some current proponents of inclusion have criticised key aspects of the national and international policy adoption of inclusion as well as the above critiques of inclusive practices as a 'retreat to traditional stances' (Ainscow, 2007: 128). Barton (2005) was another who was very critical of Warnock's SEN policy paper, depicting it as naive, arrogant and ignorant, with especial criticism of her ignoring the position of disabled people who had called for the end of segregated education (Alliance For Inclusive Education, 2004). The problem with this kind of critique is that it assumes that all disabled people follow the same line, or even the one espoused by the Alliance for Inclusive Education. The positions of Low (2007) and Shakespeare (2006), two disabled authors referred to in this book, are not supportive of the closure of all special schools (see Chapter 7 for more on parental and children/young people's positions to special schooling).

A common theme in this attempt to protect the purity of inclusion has been the critical portrayal of attempts to integrate elements of the social and individual models of disability as the 'resilience of the special educational episteme' (Slee, 2008: 103). Slee's analysis of inclusive schooling and education, as discussed above, is that it is 'troubled and troubling'. It is troubled because of policy respectability that has led to it becoming disconnected from its original political intent, to be troubling. According to Slee, inclusive education should be a 'radical provocation'

(p. 103), or as Allan (2005) suggests, an ethical project. Allan's critique of the Scottish replacement of 'special educational needs' by a wider concept of 'additional support needs' in 2005 is that this represents a 'repetition of exclusion' (Allan, 2008b). The new system and language are seen by her to create exclusion because it is a version of inclusion that sets limits on who goes to ordinary schools and is about the management of difference. In a similar way, Armstrong (2005) has represented the Labour government's stance as reconstructing inclusion within a traditional special educational framework.

Slee presents inclusive education as an attempt to disrupt the dichotomy between regular and special schooling. He introduces the idea of the 'irregular school' as a proxy for inclusive schooling to distance his concept of the inclusive from the reductive use of the term in current policy and practice. Irregular comes to mean the opposite of regular as a mark of how far regular schools have to go to become inclusive. So his call for irregular schools is part of the provocation, part of the position that inclusive education should be troubling. This idea of a radical change to ordinary schools has a certain history in UK approaches, as shown by Dessent's (1987) analysis using the phrase 'making the ordinary school special', which was an attempt to reconceptualise ordinary schools to have the capacity to welcome and provide for the diversity of pupils.

These critiques of the 'inclusive school' have been in terms of the wider critique of a neo-liberal approach to social exclusion/inclusion, which deregulated markets and introduced market-type principles into public services. Roulstone and Prideaux (2008), in relation to the English social policies of the new Labour government (1997–2010), have shown how inclusive education policy was related to the government's wider social inclusion agenda. They also present the Labour approach to inclusive education as opposed to one based on human rights, where the former is conditional and subject to types and provisos and the latter as unqualified and part of a wider struggle and radical transformation. Armstrong (2005) in a similar kind of critique of Labour inclusion policies portrayed the government's use of inclusion as taking transformatory values from the disability movement and turning them to the regulating and normalising functions of the 'neoconservative state' (p. 149). Armstrong argues that the political concept of inclusion was lost in legislation as inclusive schools were represented merely as impairment friendly schools. Equality, in his analysis, is reconceptualised as conformity to narrow performance criteria and that the focus on performance and standards promoted exclusion for those not meeting these standards.

Concluding comments

In this chapter I have discussed the complex issues and tensions involved in inclusive schooling. It is evident that the design of schools cannot be seen outside the wider political and social context of the purposes and functions of schools within society and the economy. This is even more so with the rise of the economic human resource purposes of schooling in governmental policies. Schooling needs to be seen also within the wider global economy and how this influences national educational policy and the place of inclusion within it. However, recognising these wider contexts and finding ways to counter their negative influences is not necessarily best done by adopting conceptual and value schemes based on dichotomies, such as transformational versus conservative. Conservative is seen as a damning attribution from a perspective that embraces unconditional rights to be educated alongside one's peers in terms of what is 'truly inclusive' (Roulstone and Prideaux, 2008: 26). Recognising any degrees or limits to or tensions over inclusion is dismissed as 'conservativism' (Slee, 2010: 109). But, what is 'truly inclusive' and what is involved specifically in new ways of seeing inclusion (Allan, 2008a) remain unspecified and unclear. Going beyond an indignant oppositional attitude to specifying a positive position tends to be described in generalities that raise as many questions as they provide ways forward. Armstrong et al. (2010) present inclusive education as a hope and belief in the possibility of 'fair and just relationships between people' (p. 138). In an earlier piece, Armstrong (2005) talked about promoting equity and recognising and supporting diversity. These philosophical and research issues will be examined further in Chapter 8.

7
PARENTS AND CHILDREN
Participation, partnerships and preferences

Introduction

In this chapter I examine issues that arise in the participation of children with difficulties and disabilities and the partnership of their parents in their education. These are central issues in any analysis of inclusive education. Inclusive values are defined in terms of participation which is represented as doing things in collaboration with others, but also about 'making choices about and having a say in what we do' (Booth and Ainscow, 2011: 11). Not only is inclusion and participation about children's collaboration and making choices but also the collaboration and choice making of families and school staff. This dual aspect to inclusion and participation is shown, for example, in sections of the Inclusion Index. Here inclusion is said to be about increasing the participation of all in the 'cultures, communities and curricula in local settings' (p. 20), but it is also about 'listening to the voices of children and acting on them' (p. 20). The same dual aspect is found in the way 'participation' is represented:

> participation is about active engagement in learning. It is about involvement in decisions about one's life. It also entails the important right not to participate, to assert one's autonomy against the group by saying 'no'.
> *(pp. 22–23)*

It is notable that despite a statement of 'a right to ... assert one's autonomy', there is no reference in the 15 inclusive values underpinning the Inclusion Index to autonomy, liberty or freedom as a key inclusive value. Nor is there discussion of whether the dual aspects of inclusion and participation (collaboration and choice making) are compatible or are in tension. The other option is that autonomy is a minor aspect in inclusive theory and practice. This is consistent with it not featuring in the set of key inclusive values and that it is hardly reflected in the actual content of the Index. There is only one reference to children being involved in their own learning under the 'Evolving Inclusive Practice' section C2.4. Only two of the 23 questions in this section (questions d and f: 162) are about whether school practices take account of children's own preferences about what they learn. Interestingly, these are not questions about the critical issues about where they learn and with whom, which might be seen as equally important areas where children might express their views.

The growth in importance of the child's voice over the last few decades has been stimulated by Article 12 of the United Conventions about the Rights of the Child:

> States Parties shall assure to the child who is capable of forming his or her own views the right to express those views freely in all matters affecting the child, the views of the child being given due weight in accordance with the age and maturity of the child.
>
> *(UNICEF, 1989: Article 12.1)*

Since the UK ratification of this Article, there have been key policies and legislation promoting child participation and voice in various areas of social policy. The Convention has also been ratified in other countries too, though not all countries. The USA had not ratified the Convention because of its perceived potential to undermine the authority of adults (Kilbourne, 1998).

The Ladder of Participation (Hart, 1992), an influential model of child participation, identifies eight rungs of a ladder with the three lowest ones framed as non-participation (manipulation, decoration and tokenism). The five next rungs represent increasingly progressive forms of participation (assigned but informed, consulted and informed, adult-initiated shared decisions with children, child initiated and directed, and child-initiated and shared decision with adults). The UK climate has become strongly 'pro-child participation', a movement that some have represented as a moral crusade (Lewis, 2010). Lundy (2007) has criticised how Article 12 has become commonly misunderstood and over-simplified under its various advocacy banners, such as 'pupil voice' or 'the right to participate', in a way that has undermined its significance and potential impact. Her argument is that child participation cannot be seen in isolation; it is interconnected with other human rights, so Article 12 has to be seen in relation to other Articles in the Convention. Article 3 is about the child's 'best interests' being a 'primary consideration'; this implies that children are dependent on others to represent their rights and best interests. So, there is potential for a tension between a child's 'best interest' and 'child participation'. But as Lundy (2007) argues, this does not mean that the right to have their views given due weight is to be abandoned. Rights theorists have considered that child autonomy is to be limited only if the child's preferred course of action interferes with their development or restricts their choices in an irreparable way (Freeman, 2000). In a similar way both Article 5 (about adults' right to provide appropriate direction and guidance) and Article 19 (about the right to be safe) can come into conflict with Article 12. As regards Article 5, for example, the tension has to be resolved in such a way that parental guidance reduces as the child matures and then eventually may come to an end. So, Lundy (2007) re-formulates Article 12, not only in its relationship with other Articles, but also in terms of four factors (voice, space, audience and influence) to support its more successful implementation.

This introduction has highlighted a key tension concerning participation, the tensions between participation and protection, which will be discussed in this chapter in relation to children with difficulties and disabilities. The other key tension to be examined in this chapter will be the one examined in previous chapters: the tensions arising from additional or different provision, the dilemmas of difference – wanting to have one's difference recognised without being stigmatised. These tensions arise for children in forming their own views about educational provision and for parents in exercising their guidance and direction for their children. Both tensions can be seen in the three-way relationship that arises in education between the child, her/his parents and the education providers (local authorities and teachers). The chapter will start with an examination of the views and participation of children with difficulties and disabilities followed by their parents' perspectives and partnership. In the final section there will a discussion of another tension between parental choice and equity of provision that has become central to special needs and inclusive education policy in the UK (England).

The views and experiences of children with difficulties and disabilities

Research about the views of children and young people about their educational provision is diverse in its focus on different areas of difficulties/disabilities and range of research methods. What follows is not meant to be a systematic review but illustrative of some studies that indicate the experienced tensions about 'difference' in relation to education. In a small-scale Finnish study, Jahnukainen (2001) conducted in-depth interviews with 23 ex-students who attended special classes in mainstream schools for emotional and behaviour difficulties about their experiences. The findings show that these students experienced tensions or dilemmas about their provision; while recognising the positive aspects about their relationships with their teachers and small teaching groups, they also experienced negative aspects about labelling associated with going to these classes. In another small-scale UK study, Polat and Farrell (2002) interviewed former pupils of a residential school for emotional and behaviour difficulties. A large majority was very satisfied with the quality of education, care and support they received; for example, smaller classes and one-to-one attention. The school was for most of them the only setting where they had been listened to and could express their feelings in a supported way. However, they had two areas of major concerns, forming relationships with the opposite sex and the negative impact of being labelled for attending the special school. However, this mixed picture was not found in Hornby and Witte's (2008) in which 21 graduates were overwhelmingly positive about their experiences of attending a residential special school for children with emotional and behaviour difficulties 10–14 years earlier. These graduates were also very negative about their ordinary school experience before going to special school. Caution is required in interpreting these studies as the research methods are not always clear. It is also difficult to generalise given the diversity of factors that can affect personal experiences; there is also testimony from 'special school survivors' of their alienation and sense of exclusion by attending special schools (Rae, 1996).

In a larger-scale study of primary and secondary-aged pupils identified as having moderate learning difficulties (MLD) in ordinary and special schools, Norwich and Kelly (2004) found that most pupils expressed positive evaluations of their schools and the teaching they received, while a significant minority expressed mixed views. While the majority in both settings preferred their current school, a significant minority (mostly secondary-aged boys) in special school preferred to be in a mainstream setting. A significant proportion of these pupils with MLD in the mainstream preferred learning support in withdrawal settings, not in their own classes. A notable finding of this study was the high incidence of reported 'bullying' in both settings. These findings are discussed in terms of experienced tensions or dilemmas about difference.

Parallels to the above findings were evident in a more recent Northern Ireland study of the perspectives of pupils in two secondary, two primary and a special school (Ryan, 2009). This study indicated how the 'reasonable adjustments' required by disability legislation could be better made by involving pupils with difficulties and disabilities in decision making about their support. The study also illustrated how common settings for all, such as dining halls, could be experienced by pupils with disabilities and difficulties and those without as excluding because they were felt to be intimidating. However, a separate learning support unit was a place where pupils felt secure and included. There were also several instances in the study of experienced tensions; for example, a pupil with visual impairment provided with a reading slope to enable enhanced reading, but not using it as it made him feel different from others, and a pupil with autistic spectrum disorder finding visually stimulating classrooms problematic.

Similar findings were identified in a larger-scale English study of parents and children with disabilities for the Disability Rights Commission (Lewis et al., 2006; Lewis et al., 2007). There were 75 children and young people with a wide range of disabilities and difficulties across the various strands of this study, many of whom valued their independence, autonomy and involvement in decisions about their schooling. Support for their learning from their perspectives was not just about applying additional provision, but being consulted regularly about their views and their preferences. Some children and young people were aware that their views might conflict with their parents, especially over risk taking. For some, mostly those with learning difficulties, questions about being different or disadvantaged, in comparison with their peers, was a sensitive issue. However, a large majority of children and young people were in favour of a range of mainstream and special settings that provide flexible ways of meeting diverse needs (Lewis et al. 2006). For example, young people in a specialist unit in an ordinary school saw the unit as providing a refuge from hectic school life and place to do their homework. Few young people in the sample were against special schools, with a majority seeing the need for choice between different provision settings.

This study also showed the highly individualised, varied and ambivalent nature of these children's and young people's views about their identity and language used. While some were empowered by accepting a disabled identity, others, including some at special schools, did not see themselves as disabled or that the term 'disability' applied to them. Some experienced tensions over using the term 'disabled' – resenting having to use it while accepting that it was 'really handy' (Lewis et al., 2006: 13). This kind of finding has parallels in an in-depth study of 20 D/deaf young people (Skelton and Valentine, 2003). Many of these young people did not consider being Deaf as a disability, but as a difference about language and culture. However, as these researchers show, many of these young people found themselves in an in-between position. On one hand, they did not consider themselves disabled, but on the other, they received disabled support grants, without seeing the contradiction. The study also illustrated how some of these young people switched between a deaf identify (where hearing impairment is seen as a disability) to a Deaf identity (where it is not) on a pragmatic basis.

Similar positions to the above ones were expressed in a European project involving 78 young delegates with a range of disabilities from 29 different European countries (EADSEN, 2007). Most of these young people, who were in secondary education in ordinary schools and vocational education, were overall satisfied with their education and felt that improvements had been made during their school careers. However, there were continuing challenges that included accessibility of education, teachers' attitudes and teacher training to understand and respond to their needs. Inclusion was valued as bringing diverse people together, improving social skills and positively challenging. These young people agreed on their rights to be respected and not discriminated against. They concluded that:

> We have the right to the same opportunities as everyone else, but with the necessary support to meet our needs; we have the right to make our own decisions and choices; our voice needs to be heard.
>
> *(p. 21)*

However, some experienced issues with inclusive education as one young person remarked:

> Inclusive education has been both the most horrible and the most beautiful challenge I had to face.
>
> *(p. 13)*

Though all delegates in ordinary educational settings very much favoured inclusion as the best option, as did some in separate settings, there was still a small number in separate settings who preferred what to them was a protected separate environment. The overall conclusion, as in the Lewis et al. (2006) study, was 'to give everyone the freedom to choose where they wanted to be educated' (EADSEN, 2007: 22).

Participation in practice

Concerns have been expressed about how child participation and voice have been implemented not only in research but also in practice (Lewis, 2010). The practical adoption of child participation in education, as in other service spheres, can be seen as a way of confining a very radical agenda that can threaten adult authority (Fielding, 2004). In relation to the 2001 English SEN Code of Practice, Armstrong (2005) has suggested that the Code frames pupil voice in a form that serves professional decisions. However, Lewis's (2010) argument is that 'listening better includes hearing silence and that silence is not neutral or empty' (p. 20): it communicates non-verbally a person's position and perspective. In this section I will discuss briefly some of the issues associated with the 2001 SEN Code of Practice, which has operated in England over the last ten years and called for pupils to have their views understood, to have choice and to be involved in decisions about their education (DfES, 2001a). The Code, as May (2004) notes, presents an unparalleled official commitment to the participation of pupils with difficulties and disabilities, but it is weak on clarifying what is involved in participation. Related terms are used interchangeably; for example, 'partnership', 'involvement', 'consultation' and 'participation'. Not only was the Code not legally binding, but it has also left pupils open to teachers' varied interpretations of participation. May (2004) also raises various limiting factors that affect the scope of pupil participation in practice; for example, that the Code is basically about managing the identification of pupils' special educational needs rather than their learning and that it has an excessive focus on verbal participation to the exclusion of non-verbal expressions.

However, some promising but varied participation practices were shown in a larger English study pupils with a range of SEN areas in 18 schools (4 secondary, 14 primary) that were selected for having promising participation practices (Norwich and Kelly, 2004). The study covered teachers, teaching assistants, SEN coordinators and LA officers as well as pupils with SEN (91 overall) and without SEN. But, the picture that emerged showed wide variations in participation practice: from consulting pupils through the entire individual educational planning and review process to guiding children to certain targets and providing some targets while others were negotiated. Though the most common methods of eliciting views was by talking, other methods, such as written, computer-based pictorial or visual, were also used. The focus covered reviewing progress, preferences and general well-being in a range of contexts, such as while away from lessons, and while doing some other activity. Pupils with SEN were also included in general participation practices: at school level (in social and environmental aspects of the school or school-wide behaviour policies) and at class level (class circle time activity and negotiating content of learning within curriculum constraints). Overall the findings indicate promising practice but inconsistencies between policy and practice. This was most evident in the analysis of barriers to participation identified by pupils with SEN compared to those identified by adults. Adults tended to identify child factors as barriers (e.g. cognitive competence), while children with SEN tended to identify teacher and school factors as barriers. All adult groups were in agreement over barriers to do with cognitive and communication difficulties and excessive demands or threat to a child. But, children agreed with adults on only two barriers, about children's unwillingness to participate and difficulties in building trust relationships. The other five factors identified only by children were about doubts about teachers keeping confidentiality, being unapproachable, token consultation, positive consequences slow in coming and pupils not being able to control what is done with their views.

Limits to participation and tensions between participation and protection

One of the continuing issues is whether there are limits to seeking and taking account of pupils' views. The Code of Practice was influenced by Article 12 of the UN Convention in advocating participation based on 'age, ability and past experience' (DfES, 2001a: 124). For some, any provisos to participation are to be avoided, because it can lead to the exclusion of a significant minority of those with disabilities and difficulties from participation (Rose, 1998). Subsequent national guidance and policy also emphasised the need for adult training to make participation work (DfES, 2004). The SEN Toolkit (2001) recognised that adaptations were required to enable some to participate, but that it may not be possible to identify the feelings of children with 'profound needs' (section 18 Toolkit: 3).

Whether it is meaningful to determine the views of pupils identified as having profound and multiple learning difficulties (PMLD) is a contentious issue (Harding, 2009). Harding suggests in line with the Mental Capacity Act (2005) that there be no assessments of incapacity in general, rather that functional capacity is decided in relation to specific issues. This legislation also requires that appropriate forms of communication are used for each person and that the person be able to produce a response including non-verbal ones. However, Ware (2004b) raises doubts about the extent to which people functioning at a pre-intentional level can form views about complex matters. She distinguishes between a negative reaction to an event and inferring from this a negative view about something. As Harding (2009) points out, some of the literature relates not to PMLD, but to pupils with 'little or no communication' or those with 'learning disabilities'. This underlies the importance of individual assessments of capacity in specific contexts, not in broad category terms and finding methods to foster pupil voice (Wright, 2008). However, even if an assessment concludes that a particular pupil cannot form a view about some important matter, some have distinguished between 'direct' and 'indirect' advocacy. In indirect advocacy others make assessments 'from a wishes and feelings perspective' about 'what the child would want to say if he or she was able to do so directly' (SEN Regional Partnership, 2004: 3). This is a similar view to that advocated from a philosophical perspective by Nussbaum (2009): that a guardian be empowered to exercise a person's functions in their interest of people with 'profound disabilities'. There are clearly risks of bias associated with this (see debates about facilitated communication: Jordan et al., 1998), but as Nussbaum argues, steps are required to identify appropriate guardians, as is done in other areas where guardians are appointed.

The Norwich and Kelly (2004) study concluded that pupils were clear about the difference between expressing their views and preferences about their education and their negotiation and decision sharing about these matters. This was in line with the UN Convention distinction between expressing a view and having that view given due weight (UNICEF, 1989). The study also identified various barriers to participation. As noted earlier in this book, a common response is to find ways of removing barriers. But some barriers are harder to overcome, as discussed above, when pupils with PMLD might be unable to form a view of a particular matter. In other cases the barrier might be another value, as found in the views of some adults in the Norwich and Kelly (2004) study: when participation was seen as too onerous, threatening self-esteem or drawing attention to weaknesses. This finding also reflects the general tensions identified in the UN Convention between participation and protection. Child social care literature has also recognised the tension between participation and protectiveness (Healy, 1998). However, when some authors recognise this tension, the protectiveness is sometimes dismissed as getting in the way of participation. For example, Percey-Smith and Thomas (2001) turn participation into a means of securing protection and then argue that their book provides examples of adults failing to protect children. This reflects a tradition of suspicion that adults cannot be authentically protective of children. And, while decisions about where children have their schooling are not as high stakes as some care decisions that involve brutal neglect and abuse, the issues are similar. Though ideas about good enough parenting and appropriate schooling vary and in some sense involve social constructions (see discussion in Chapter 8), this does not justify opting out of or retreating from decisions about these matters. Healy (1998) argues for a participatory approach to child protection that involves openness and clarity, where assessments are accessible and accountable. Similarly, were child participation in education to be limited by protective considerations, such decisions would need to be justified in an accessible and accountable way.

Concepts of parental partnership

Parental involvement and partnership in the education of children with disabilities and difficulties has been a long-standing educational issue. This has been particularly so in the UK where there have been changes in the pattern of relationships and balance of power between parents, schools and local authorities (Lamb, 2009). Underlying these relationships, as Vernon (1999) recognised, are some key questions:

1. To what extent is promoting partnership and development of provision for children with disabilities and difficulties about the relationship between parents as individuals and collectively?
2. How is partnership with these parents best promoted at school: by focusing on the parents of children with SEN or by focusing on the parents of all children?

One of the risks in putting these questions into this form is that they call for either/or answers, rather than seeing partnership as both an individual and a collective matter and partnership in relation to disability/difficulties as integral to general partnership approaches.

As in child participation, there is a similar Ladder of Participation relevant to parent engagement/participation in their children's education, though it was formulated about engagement in the area of Planning (Arnstein, 1969). Some time ago, Wolfendale (1983) contrasted parents as clients and as partners. As clients, parents were cast as dependent, peripheral to decisions and potentially inadequate; as partners, they were actively involved in decisions, having equivalent expertise and contributing to services. Wolfendale's concept of parents as partners is similar to the more complex definition of partnership by Pugh et al. (1987):

> a working relationship that is characterised by a shared sense of purpose, mutual respect and willingness to negotiate. This implies a sharing of information, responsibility, skills, decision-making and accountability.
>
> (p. 5)

This is an interesting definition as it places partnership in terms of a continuum of parent–teacher relationships that range from non-participation, through support, participation and partnership to control. This has some similarities to Arnstein's (1969) Ladder. In Pugh's notion, partnership is less than parent control and more than parent support, but though partnership involves more parental control than participation, these authors do not specify the difference between participation and partnership. In another version participation has also been defined as the same as partnership (Riddick, 1996). Wolfendale's idea of parents as clients and Pugh's concept of non-participation are also important as they clarify what is taken to be the opposite of partnership. This is where Bastiani's (1987) historical analysis of changing concepts of parent–teacher relationship is useful. Bastiani refers to the assumption, linked to the Plowden Report (1967), that parents who did not support their children's education require compensation. This compensatory assumption relates to parents as clients and as non-participators. The compensatory concept has been criticised as a deficit model of parenting that overlooked wider social and economic influences on parenting (Power and Clark, 2000) and ignored parents' interests in their children's education.

Parent partnership and perspectives in practice

The participation of the parents of children with disabilities and difficulties in decisions about their children's schooling has been promoted increasingly in principle and practice in the UK and internationally over recent decades (Kyriazopoulou and Weber, 2009). However, in England there have been continuing reports about parental dissatisfaction and their lack of confidence in the system of identifying educational needs, planning and provision for their children with difficulties/disabilities (House of Commons, 2006; Rogers, 2007; Lamb, 2009). Much has been written in the policy, practice and research literature about the background to these issues, including conflicts in the system of statutory assessment and statementing (Warnock, 2005), bureaucratic and procedural inefficiencies, inadequate central government standards of provision (House of Commons, 2006). 'Strategic ambiguities' in government principles have also been identified in analyses of parental experiences of 'parent partnership' practices (Pinkus, 2005) as well as partnership principles not put into practice (Norwich et al., 2005).

But, it has also been noted that the relatively high levels of reported parental satisfaction in the system have often not been acknowledged in policy debates (Lamb, 2012). In a review of relevant international research on parental satisfaction levels, Parsons et al., (2009) note that satisfaction levels revealed in UK-based studies, including their own, show generally high satisfaction levels as do comparable US studies. Whitaker (2007) has suggested that surveys conducted by voluntary disability specific organisations of their member parents tend to find higher levels of dissatisfaction because this may be the reason that these parents joined the organisation initially. These higher dissatisfaction levels are then communicated to government and come to influence government policy assumptions about parental perspectives to the SEN/disability education system. For example, Whitaker's (2007) survey in one local authority of parents of children with autistic spectrum disorders showed that 61 per cent (of 172 parents) were satisfied or very satisfied with mainstream education provision. However 39 per cent were dissatisfied, with these parents differing from the 'satisfied' ones in terms of the degree to which parents believed that staff understood their children's conditions and needs and staff willingness to listen and respond flexibly to these needs. Difference between parents and professionals over children's needs has also been shown in US research (e.g. Lake and Billingsley, 2000). As Parsons et al.'s (2009) review indicates, this is similar to other UK and Canadian studies, showing a substantial minority of dissatisfaction. In addition, the research picture is also one of satisfied parents having had to go through frustrations and battles to secure the current more satisfactory provision.

Overall the UK research literature on parent perspectives on partnership is sparse and piecemeal (Truss, 2008), covering different areas of disability and difficulties, identified before or during schooling. Many studies tend to be about communication problems, bureaucratic difficulties experienced with statutory assessment and the battling experienced by some parents (Lewis et al., 2006). Studies on parental attitudes using systematic measures and large samples have tended to be done in other countries, mainly in the USA, not the UK, as reviewed by de Boer et al. (2010). In five of the ten studies in this review, parents held mainly positive attitudes while in the other five they revealed mainly neutral attitudes. However, while parents of typically developing children showed more positive attitudes, those with children with disabilities/difficulties did not have clear attitudes to inclusive education and were not in favour of it as regards their own child. The study also showed that neither parent age nor gender were factors related to inclusion attitudes. But, parents with higher socio-economic status, higher education qualifications and more experience of inclusion tended to have more positive attitudes. Also, parents were more positive about inclusion for children with sensory and physical disabilities than behaviour problems and cognitive disabilities. These conclusions need to be interpreted with caution as inclusion was defined in variable ways across the studies. The review also did not bring out the finer points that individual studies found. For example, in one of the reviewed Australian studies (Elkins et al., 2003) many parents of children with disabilities/difficulties favoured inclusion (as ordinary school placement), some would if additional resources were provided, but a small group of parents still favoured special placement. However, de Boer and colleagues' interpretation of the difference in attitudes to inclusive education between parents with and without children with disabilities/difficulties is interesting. They suggest that parents of typically developing children were more positive about inclusion perhaps because they could see its benefits, but knew less about it through personal experience. By contrast, those with children with disabilities/difficulties seemed to be 'consuming' the achievements of the inclusion movement and were critical of how it functioned in practice.

Tensions and dilemmas in parental perspectives

However, not only do studies show varied parental perspectives, but there are also a few which show some tensions within parental perspectives. For example, Westling-Allodi's (2007) small-scale Swedish study of parents with children who have intellectual disabilities (eligible to go to separate units in ordinary schools), showed parents holding different attitudes about the suitability of these units for their children. Some were positive about units, having both defensive and assertive motives, while others were critical, seeing learning as better in regular class settings, their child as unique and not fitting general categories of need. But, there were also ambivalent parents, whose children attended units but who were critical of a 'culture' of low expectations and a lack of novelty. This study also revealed that 'critical' and 'ambivalent' parents were unsure about the benefits of battling for their preferences: they might get the resources and their preferred setting, but they felt that if staff were not supportive, then it might not work.

Runswick-Cole's (2008) study of parental perspectives also found a range of parental perspectives that were analysed in three groups. Parents in the first group (wanting nothing but ordinary school) focused on overcoming pedagogic barriers rather than within-child factors and were sceptical about professional judgement (tending to a social concept of disability). For the second group (committed to ordinary school, but changed to special school), this was in response to feelings of exclusion, inflexibility or lack of resources in ordinary school. They experienced dilemmas and were described as 'stuck between a rock and a hard place'. The third group (committed to special schools) saw the separate setting as the best opportunity for a 'normal' life and used more medicalised and within-child factor talk (tending to an individual/'medical' concept of disability). The evidence for this typology linking school preference to disability model is not transparent and so it is hard to see if parental perspectives might be mixed and reflect balancing, as shown in Landsman's (2005) US study of mothers of children with newly diagnosed disabilities from a range of social backgrounds. Landsman (2005) found that these mothers' concepts of disabilities did not comply simply with either medical or social assumptions. Their concepts tended to comply with a medical model in seeking to improve child opportunities for enhancing their child's functioning, but complied with a social model in rejecting aspects of a problem-based view of impairment. Landsman concluded that neither medical nor social models fully accounted for parents' perspectives.

There are also a few studies that illustrate some of the tensions and dilemmas experienced by parents over the identification of their children as having a disability/difficulty, which can be seen to reflect dilemmas of difference. Hansen and Hansen (2006) examined in a Canadian study the 'flux of dilemmas' parents experienced over treatment decisions for their sons with ADHD diagnoses. Their strongest dilemma was a 'balancing act' over weighing functional improvement (in home environment and academic performance) with negative side effects (now and in the future). Rogers (2007) in a UK study examined the significance of the diagnosis of their children as having a disability/difficulty for 24 parents with a range of diagnoses. Shock, disappointment, denial and emotional pain were used to make sense of these parents' experiences with parents represented as experiencing emotional dilemmas over diagnosis. For the parent their child's difference from others can become 'difficult' because of coming to terms with 'loss of an idealised child', the challenges of parenting and securing appropriate educational provision (McLaughlin et al., 2008).

In a more recent study, Russell and Norwich (2012) examined the function of an autistic spectrum disorder (ASD) diagnosis through in-depth interviews with 17 parents, some who had a diagnosis of ASD for their child and others who avoided this diagnosis. Analysis showed that these parents experienced dilemmas over whether to retain the 'normal' status of their child (to avoid stigma; to defend 'normal' status) or to 'normalise' the child through diagnosis and subsequent intervention (to access resources, professional support and be absolved from blame). Along with the second strategy, some parents tried to reframe and de-stigmatise ASD and some even tried to recruit other parents to seek ASD diagnosis. This parental reframing strategy corresponds to how teachers and other support professionals who recognise a dilemma over disability/difficulty identification resolve it by seeing the value of identification while seeking to promote positive images of disability (Norwich, 2009). Though there is a need for further study of these issues, the above summary indicates some evidence that parents experience tensions over identification and educational provision, where differences are experienced as dilemmas.

Choice–equity dilemma in education provision for children with disabilities and difficulties

It was clear in the above section that studies indicate that parents and their children with disabilities and difficulties value some choice about their educational provision, including some separate setting options. This is consistent with the observation made by Clarke (2010) that the value of choice is not confined to those with strong market-oriented policy commitments. Emancipatory movements, such as the feminist and disability ones, have advocated some degree of choice on certain matters. This is also reflected in the position that choice and control of opportunities for people (including children and young people) with disabilities and difficulties can be seen to have developmental benefits for them (Rose and Shevlin, 2004) and advance the autonomy of people with cognitive disabilities (Wolff, 2009a). These points show that adopting the language of choice and autonomy by an emancipatory movement is inconsistent with a strict dichotomy found in the inclusive literature between market-based choice policy approaches and state-based citizen rights approaches. Inclusive theorists and advocates tend to portray choice/market approaches (sometimes called neo-liberal) as opposed to and abhorring state intervention (Liasidou, 2012). As one US author concluded from a critique of the neo-liberal market approach: 'working for equity and inclusion is bound to be a struggle' (Brantlinger, 1997: 23). Central to the opposition between markets and equity is the historical relationship between choice and inequalities: in market relations, choice is connected to the reproduction of material inequality (Clarke, 2010). However, as will be argued below, the choice–inequality relationship does not imply that there is no positive role for choice where it is appropriately regulated.

For the purposes of considering the tensions between choice and equity in this section, the terms 'choice' and 'equity' will be used to characterise the oppositions between collective versus individualist policy and political positions. Equity will be taken to mean fair equal opportunity and is associated with the public realm, state involvement and citizen rights, while choice will be taken to stand for the private consumer approach based on markets (Clarke, 2010). Like some of the other tensions examined in this book, tension between choice and equity arouses deep political commitments that come to conceal important aspects of the relationship between opposed principles, in this case between markets and state intervention. As the economist Kay (2004) has argued, so-called 'free markets' only work if there is a state that enforces property rights and contracts and regulates the market in certain ways, that are not natural but socially constructed. All markets involve some degree of state regulation; all choice is therefore within some framework of regulations. As Clarke observes (2010), the very term 'school choice' is a misnomer;

in the English system, parents have a right to state a school preference that might not be met. All choice is circumscribed by bureaucratic and regulatory factors. So, what is needed here, as Brighouse (2002) has suggested, is the distinction between the irrational enthusiasm for or criticism of markets and what is consistent with reason and empirical evidence. At the root of this over-enthusiasm or over-criticality is an approach to oppositions (choice versus equity) that splits off the one from the other, to condemn the one (choice) and to idealise the other (equity). Another approach, which has been illustrated in this book, is not only to recognise the tension between the principles, but also to see the connection between them and see some value in both positions. This is to approach the positions as reflecting plural values that can lead to dilemmas. This is how the relationship between equity and choice comes to be framed as a dilemma.

Many radical critics of school choice overlook that some kind of school choice is already more pervasive in the UK and other Western-style countries than is often believed. In England, choice has been central to school systems since 1988 Educational Reform Act (Ball, 2008) introduced by a Conservative government. It has been noted that there has been little difference between successive government school policies since then: the Labour 1997–2010 government continued such policies, as has the current Conservative–Liberal Coalition Government (Brighouse and Swift, 2010). It has also been pointed out that all OECD countries allow parents to send their children to private schools, have housing markets that allow parents to purchase houses in desirable schools areas and implement a degree of choice between government schools (Brighouse, 2012). Brighouse's key argument is that though choice can undermine equality, this is no reason to reject choice. Based on the assumption that there is not likely to be school improvement policies in the UK and USA that do not depend on choice in some way, Brighouse suggests that:

> The issue is not, if you like, whether choice compromises equity, but rather *which feasible system of choice does best with respect to equity.*
>
> (p. 7; italics in original)

Brighouse's point is that even a no-reform approach gives choice a hidden role as in the neighbourhood schooling model used in much public schooling, where children go to their local neighbourhood schools which often reflect the range of socio-economic advantage. Children from economically poorer backgrounds in this model go to lower-achieving schools and children from more advantaged backgrounds to higher-achieving schools, as their parents can move house more easily, especially in urban areas.

However, there are several objections to choice-based schemes: 1) that 'hidden choice' preserves the sense that schools are in the public sphere and avoids treating education as a commodity; 2) that it might benefit the more advantaged of the less advantaged, not the very least advantaged; and 3) that for schools to be able to expand and contract according to demand, there needs to be some spare capacity.

There is not space to go into these arguments in depth, but Brighouse's responses are worth summarising briefly. He suggests that treating education as a commodity to some degree is unavoidable and unobjectionable. Whether it is wrong to exchange a good such as education and whether markets destroy the value of a good depends on the specific kind of good. In relation to education, Brighouse is sceptical whether it does so, but he recognises that this is a hard question to settle without empirical analysis. Here he suggests that several points need to be made. One is that it is not education or learning that is exchanged but schooling. School choice cannot assure learning as that depends on the learners' active engagement. Also, schooling depends on trained and educated teachers who are paid to promote learning; teaching is a vocation but is also a paid job. So, education might be driven out by school choice, but it is not inevitable that it will be. Brighouse also does not see the 'most advantaged among the less advantaged' as a serious objection; it is the purist argument that rejects some reduction in inequality because it does not go further. On the spare capacity argument, he contends that spare capacity is an extra cost to the choice model, but it has to be compared with the costs of other reform models that improve the relative achievement of lower achievers.

Brighouse's claim is that choice mechanisms can be a valuable part of a reform strategy aimed at social justice, and that in regard to the USA and UK it will be an essential part of effective reform with these aims (Brighouse, 2002). But, there are other key parts to this kind of 'universal regulated voucher' model, two that are very relevant to educating children with disabilities and difficulties. These are that the monetary value of vouchers needs to be progressive enough to ensure that schools will be willing to take and be able to teach those who are hardest to teach and that participating schools cannot charge any top-up fees (Brighouse and Swift, 2010). This is a very different model to a universal unregulated voucher model, which his analysis shows is unlikely to promote equity. Though Brighouse has little to say about choice schemes for children with disabilities and difficulties, his analysis of different choice options does lead to three key questions that are relevant to this field of provision:

1. To what extent do providers have the power to select their clients (formally and informally)?
2. To what extent does residence determine access to providers?
3. How well calibrated is per-unit funding to individual needs?

(Brighouse, 2012: 13)

Brighouse's analysis of specific versions of the regulated voucher model can be seen as an attempt to resolve the choice–equity dilemma. Interestingly, there has been little policy analysis of provision for children with disabilities and difficulties in terms of this dilemma. Gray (2010), in the context of English school SEN and inclusion policy, has identified two possible resolutions of the dilemma: 1) in terms of equity and individual choice and 2) in terms of collective consumerism. Option 1 would involve an independent assessment of children's special educational needs that would be translated into a monetary value for parents to use to secure services for their children. Gray raises some problems with this option:

- Who will do the assessment and how? If by assessors who are independent of local authorities, how would these be educationally relevant and dependable?
- How will additionality be defined? How to avoid the risks of definitions that are too narrow and so overlook important needs or too broad and incur the growth of financial costs?
- How to avoid perverse incentives? How to avoid parental strategies emphasising their child's difficulties to enhance the value of budget and providers raising their costs to create access barriers?

The second resolution option, with its origins in the tradition of the UK cooperative movement, focuses on collective consumerism. There is a long tradition of democratic collectivism in Britain that some see as an alternative to state interventionist policies (Muir, 2012). This can include forms of democratic local control, direct citizen participation and/or community-owned or public service mutuals. One version of this resolution would involve governments, local authorities and/or schools consulting with groups of users (Vernon, 1999) in policy review and making. Gray discusses some issues involved in this collective consumer model (e.g. who will represent the users), but does not address the wider issues raised by Brighouse and the role of a regulated voucher model. Nor does he consider whether both individual parent choice in a regulated model and collective consumerism could be integrated in some ways.

Concluding comments

This chapter is being written just as the government is about to legislate for a more choice-based approach to provision for children with disabilities and difficulties in English schools. This will involve new rights for parents to state a preference for any state-funded school including the new types of school operating outside the local authority system, Academies and Free Schools, and have these preferences met subject to specific conditions. Parental preferences for schools will not be met if: 1) the school is unsuitable for the child in terms of age, ability or SEN; 2) placement has a negative effect on the education of other children; and 3) that placement uses resources inefficiently (DfE, 2012). Though the government has initiated pilot developments across the country to test out its broad ideas, legislation is going ahead before lessons have been learned from these pilots. Nor is it clear whether individual budgets for parents will cover additional teaching services or just outside-school support for their children. But, central to any regulated choice scheme is whether schools have the power to select children with disabilities/difficulties (Brighouse, 2012). The current government has no plans to change the responsibilities placed on schools to admit, provide and engage with children with disabilities/difficulties. At present the overall responsibility for these children lies with local authorities, which belongs to a state provider model, not the developing market for schools model. The government's position is that the three conditions on meeting parental preferences is justified because it balances parental preferences, the needs of individual children, the needs of other children and the efficient use of resources. There is a silence about the situation of schools, in which they have to operate in a market that inclines them to avoid taking on the hardest-to-teach children, including those with disabilities/difficulties. This analysis shows that the school choice model that is being adopted for children with disabilities/difficulties in England is far from the conditions for a regulated choice model that aims for justice.

Three key dilemmas have been analysed in this chapter: participation–protection, difference as enabling–stigmatising and equity–choice dilemmas. Though examined separately, the first and third are about autonomy and control and though they operate in different spheres, there are connections between them as they relate to the triangular relationships between children–adults (including parents and teachers) and responsible organisations (local authorities and schools). Choice and participation reflect autonomy because expressing views that make a difference involves exercising some choice. Adults intervening on behalf of children and a state enacting equity policies can be seen as responsible agents protecting the rights of the less advantaged. How these dilemmas relate to other dilemmas that have been examined in this book will be the focus of the next final chapter.

8
PHILOSOPHICAL AND RESEARCH ISSUES

Introduction

Several of the conceptual and value issues that emerged in previous chapters will be addressed in greater depth in this chapter. One of the aims of this chapter is to highlight the problems with positions that are often represented as dichotomies. This has been evident in much of the thinking in this field; for example, in setting up an opposition between special needs and inclusive education, rights and needs discourse and positioning the social model as opposed to the medical (individual) model of disability. Another aim of the chapter is to focus on the uncertainties and ambivalence about the position of disability in relation to the concepts of 'difference' and 'diversity' as used in positions about inclusion and inclusive education. On one hand, inclusion is said to be about more than disability and is relevant to all learners (Slee, 2010), but on the other hand, there have been critiques of the international agenda and practices associated with Education for All (EFA) as having overlooked those with disabilities (Miles and Singal, 2010). Though 'inclusion' and 'education for all' policies can have common commitments in principle, the contexts in which these terms are used and how principles are applied in practice tend to reflect the positions of different interest groups.

The overlooking of disability in 'diversity' or 'difference' can also be seen to reflect the abstract language of inclusion as about 'responding to the diversity of needs of all' (UNESCO, 2009: 8). General concepts such as diversity and difference can therefore be interpreted as minimising differences: a homogenising tendency Cigman (2007b). Inclusion has also been criticised for not recognising or denying that some differences can be experienced as 'difficult' (Rogers, 2007). A third aim of this chapter is to examine the nature of difficulties and disabilities, what it means to say that they are 'real' or 'socially constructed'. This theme is about differing positions about the principle of inclusion and various philosophical assumptions about knowledge and the objects of knowledge. This leads into the final sections of the chapter that examine philosophical issues that underpin different research traditions or 'paradigms'.

Conceptions of Inclusion

Various distinctions and qualifications about inclusive education have been proposed since the mid-1990s. Slee (2010) says that inclusive education is not a technical problem to be solved through compensatory measures and that it ought to 'declare itself as a far more radical and creative enterprise. It is simultaneously a tactic and an inspiration. It is also a statement of value' (p. 108). Allan (2008a), along similar lines, has argued for inclusion as an ethical project and as involving an ongoing struggle. She has recognised that in translating inclusion into practice, teachers have experienced frustration, guilt, exhaustion and even a sense of futility, but she still sees this as a process to be committed to: 'we can be never done with the project of inclusion' (p. 164). These positions have been associated with 'radical inclusion' in the UK (Cigman, 2007a) or 'full inclusion' in the USA (TASH, 2012). Cigman (2007a) contrasts radical inclusion with moderate inclusion in terms of different interpretations of special schools. From her perspective, in radical inclusion special schools means segregation, exclusion, feeling excluded, humiliated by labels and a neglect of human rights. By contrast, in moderate inclusion special schools mean for some children integration, being included, a sense of belonging, being helped by a label and respect for human rights.

Differences over inclusion have also been presented in terms of 'responsible' versus 'irresponsible' inclusion. For example, Vaughn and Schumm (1995), in relation to learning disabilities in a US context, represented 'responsible inclusion' as about putting the student first, teachers choosing to participate in inclusive classrooms, having adequate resourcing, having a continuum of services and having the model developed and implemented by school. By contrast, what they called 'irresponsible inclusion' was about putting the place first, teachers mandated to participate in inclusive classrooms, resourcing not considered before establishing inclusive classrooms, having full inclusion as the only service model and having outside agencies directing guidelines for inclusion. This contrast also aligns 'responsible inclusion' with teachers' choice and local school decision making and 'irresponsible inclusion' with teacher obligation and outside policy directives. This raises an important issue in conceptions of inclusion about choice and control in policy decisions. Vaughn and Schumm's association of full inclusion with irresponsibility also touches on the issue discussed in the previous chapters about how we respond to practical problems in what are called inclusive practices. Some inclusion advocates have defended problematic practices as not really examples of inclusion, but due to either inadequate resourcing or poor implementation, presenting them as integration and not inclusion (Low, 2007). This protection of inclusion, its inviolability, reveals how it serves as the central social commitment and as an open-ended, long-term project.

In another related and more-in-depth analysis, Cigman (2007b) contrasts universalist with moderate versions of inclusion in terms of the extent to which regular schools should welcome and adapt to all children *without exception*, or adapt themselves *as far as possible*. Moderate is an unfortunate term to qualify a commitment to inclusion as it suggests half-heartedness. Low (2007) has gone for a different version of this principle, 'as far as humanly possible' (p. 6), to avoid a watering down of the commitment. I suggest that the term 'maximal' better captures this version of inclusion than the term 'moderate'. However, as Cigman argues, at the heart of this difference between universal and moderate (maximal) inclusion is disagreement about what is possible; for universalists this is a school where everyone can be included, while for moderates this might not be so. One of the issues here is what 'included' means in this disagreement. Both universal and moderate inclusionists might agree that inclusion is about engagement or participation in learning. But, engagement and participation have different connotations. Engagement has individual associations, implying that engagement is more important than where learning takes place. Participation has associations of being with others in a community, implying that this is in the regular school and class.

These disagreements are about marking out differences between learners in terms of what is appropriate for them and what they require – what is often called their personal needs. Where special schools are justified currently, this is usually in terms of broad curriculum requirements and pedagogic adaptations. No longer are they justified in terms of attributing disability or difficulty labels to individuals. However, special schools and disability/difficulty categories are emblematic of what is considered to be segregating or excluding and so stigmatising and devaluing, in the arguments for universalist inclusion. Another point that is relevant to the use of the language of segregation and exclusion is that these words are often used to imply power relations, in which the children and parents are powerless victims of governments, agencies and professionals. This can be seen as evaluative language that condemns different or separate provision without analysing what is negative about the situation. One aspect of this negativity might be the voluntary–involuntary nature of these practices: do parents and children have any say or power to influence decisions about education? Where they do, then different or separate provision might not be experienced as excluding or devaluing. This is where Cigman presents a revealing analysis of the universalist position in terms of Margalit's ideas about a decent society that does not humiliate its people (Margalit, 1996).

Margalit distinguishes between ascribing humiliation as a matter of fact to a person or group of people, whether self-ascribed or by others, and *having a good reason* to feel humiliated. This is an approach to humiliation and other emotional responses that asks for reasons for feelings. Though it is an approach that goes against the current practice of separating feelings from reasons as a way of respecting feelings, it is an approach that does ground feelings in social situations. As Cigman notes, feelings such as humiliation are responses to situations, and their reasonableness or not provides a basis for criticising the social conditions that generate the feelings, so justifying social change. The point behind the psychological and normative ascription of humiliation is also that feelings might become inappropriate, too little or too much. For example, feelings that might have been appropriate in some situations might not change as situations change. Cigman uses these kinds of arguments to counter those advocating universal inclusion who present special schools and disability categories as inherently devaluing. She has two key points. One is that empirically some disabled people and children do not feel humiliated by special school attendance or the use of categories, while some may. The other is that children might have had good reasons to feel humiliated in the UK under the pre-Warnock system where children were sent to special schools if deemed 'handicapped' and parents had few rights to appeal such decisions.

Though I recognise the value of Margalit's distinction, I am not sure Cigman's application of it to this field deals with some current negative concerns about the school system. Though parents in the UK now make a contribution to the assessment process for significant disabilities and difficulties, there may be some compulsion in what provision they come to accept for their children. Most international educational systems for identifying children with significant disabilities and difficulties now separate the eligibility question (disability/difficulty identification) from decisions about education programme needs (the where, what and how questions). But, SEN and disability categories can still have negative connotations and usages. The main issues are not just the empirical ones, but also the normative ones about what counts as a good reason for feeling humiliated or devalued. If good reasons for being humiliated are critical to the use of labels and separate provision, then parents and young people who use labels and special provision can also judge what is a good reason for being humiliated. Decisions about the use of categories and separate provision are not only for policy makers and professionals. This relates back to the discussion in Chapter 3 about the conditions for the positive use of labels. In that chapter it was suggested that labels be used within a holistic and common framework that recognises a person's strengths and difficulties in context and in a positive and respectful way. Without such a system a person may have grounds for feeling humiliated.

Cigman's focus on avoiding humiliation also underlies her analysis of the part played by the value of respect in debates about inclusion. She argues that respect is not only about avoiding humiliation, but also about the freedom to determine one's own vital interests as well as not be treated as a means to others' ends: it is about autonomy. Her point is that the universalist position focuses exclusively on the avoiding of the humiliation aspect of respect and is oblivious of the autonomy aspect. For the universalist, this leads to a position where schools 'ought' to accommodate all children and provide a satisfactory environment for every child. This obligation ('ought') is expressed in the universalist rejection of the validity of practical difficulties in inclusion. But, as Cigman argues, ought is usually seen to imply 'can'; so if schools ought to accommodate all, then from a universalist postion, schools can do so. This is how she identifies the importance of possibility in universal inclusionist positions, in their commitment to realising this possibility. If universal or full inclusion is possible, according to Cigman, then there would be some empirical evidence for this possibility. Yet, as she and others have pointed out (Pirrie and Head, 2007), the current weight of evidence against this possibility is ignored, so leaving the concept of possibility lacking empirical meaning.

Another strand of Cigman's analysis of universalist inclusion is its critique of assumptions that differences between learners are 'real'. This was introduced in Chapter 3 as part of my analysis about the reality of difficulties and disabilities. As explained there, Cigman suggests that this denial of the reality of difficulties involves the adoption of a metaphysical position (social constructionist) about what exists (ontology) in support of an ethical position about inclusion. Her argument is that this denial functions to protect some children from stigma (humiliation) by removing the 'reality' of their difference. As argued in Chapter 3, Hacking's analysis of social constructionist theories is along similar lines: that what passes as knowledge is about consciousness-raising and often aims to change the status quo. The effect, according to Cigman, of this use of metaphysics to support an ethical position is that the debate is set up as an intractable battle between paradigms: you either hold this position or not. She then suggests that in this metaphysical mode the debates become polarised; rather than in practical ethics mode, where there is more thinking through of options and avoiding of false opposites. Hers is a position that recognises tensions and the need for imaginatively resolving these, similar to the approach adopted in this book.

A right to inclusion: a human right?

The language of human rights has become a dominant doctrine for judging the international moral order through the auspices of the United Nations. Human rights have been defined as moral guarantees that can be invoked because they are human beings; rights being high priority, requiring compliance and considered universal (as in the Universal Declaration of Human Rights: UDHR). Rights are not considered to be dependent on recognition and so they precede national sovereignty. They provide criteria with which nation states should adhere and against which national legislation and practices are evaluated under UN conventions (Fagan, 2005). With respect to human rights about education, Article 26 section 1 of UDHR states that:

> Everyone has the right to education. Education shall be free, at least in the elementary and fundamental stages. Elementary education shall be compulsory.
> *(United Nations, 1948)*

It is also interesting and relevant to the argument which I will develop below that section 3 also states that 'Parents have a prior right to choose the kind of education that shall be given to their children'. However, neither in the UDHR nor the Salamanca Statement (UNESCO, 1994), which made strong statements in favour of inclusive schooling, was there any assertion of a human right to inclusive education.

However, those who have been critical of special education and special educational needs have invoked a human rights approach both nationally and internationally. For example, in the UN Policy guidelines on inclusive education, there is reference to a human rights framework as an underlying framework (UNESCO, 2009). Also, Reiser (2012) in the revised commonwealth guide to implementing Article 24 of the UN Convention on the rights of people with disabilities explicitly links the implementation of inclusive education to these rights. Runswick-Cole and Hodge (2009) have argued for abandoning the language of special education needs in the UK, based on the claim that it has led to exclusionary practices, and its replacement with the concept of 'educational rights'. They claim that changing from needs to rights would be wide-ranging for policy and practice, without spelling out exactly what improvements this would have, other than avoiding using a term they consider to be associated with exclusion. The basic assumption of these authors is that language is powerful and important, so changing discourse is what matters. This is seen in the way they base their argument on an Italian rights-based approach developed in Reggio Emilia that uses the United Nations Convention of the Rights of the Child (UNICEF, 1989). This approach refers to children's 'special rights' not 'special needs'. But, Runswick-Cole and Hodge consider that because the term 'special' has some negative associations, it is best to simply drop it, whether this has implications or not for justifying additional provision or not. Though language is important, so are the principles and practices denoted by terms such as 'special' or 'additional'.

These authors' criticisms of both the concept of 'need' and 'special' will be discussed in the next section, but their reasons for replacing needs by rights reveals their own awareness of the limitations of this switch. They recognise the philosophical difficulties with rights-based discourse (Runswick-Cole and Hodge, 2009: 201) – that the universality of rights can be challenged (Fagan, 2005) and that political groups can manipulate the assumed universality, yet they still conclude:

> Nevertheless, the use of rights-based language has been used successfully to challenge exclusionary practices.
>
> *(Runswick-Cole and Hodge, 2009: 201)*

Their justification is not principled but pragmatic and political, in terms of how rights discourse has helped the disabled people's movement.

This political use of rights language has led to an inflation of rights claims; for example, the 2002 claim by the Centre for the Studies of Inclusive Education that there is a right to a mainstream school education (CSIE, 2002). It has been suggested that rights language tends to inflationary claims and that sometimes rights claims sound like they are duties (Cigman, 2007a). Such claims can imply that parents have a duty to send their children to mainstream schools and that such schools have a duty to accept all children. This inflationary use could come from the implication that for rights to be guarantees, some other agent or agency, usually an authority, has a duty or responsibility to make certain provisions. But, this responsibility applies only if the individual with the right decides to use their right; a right involves an entitlement or a guaranteed opportunity, not a responsibility. Human rights are usually about securing a basic minimum of the conditions for what is judged to be a good life; for example, Article 1 of UDHR is about free and compulsory elementary education. These are access rights to schooling that have driven the Education for All initiatives that apply to all children whether they have disabilities or not (UNESCO, 2005). These access issues are central to a broader concept of inclusive education and schooling, but there is a considerable gap between these basic access rights and the more complex rights claims for all children with disabilities to go to a mainstream or regular school and be in regular classes all or most of the time.

Claims for a right to inclusive education or schooling for every child preceded the more recent United Nations Convention on the Rights of Persons with Disabilities (UNCRPD: United Nations, 2006). Various national and international non-government organisations (NGOs) and networks contributed and advocated for inclusive education in the formulation of UNCRPD (see for example, Alliance for Inclusive Education, 2004). Article 24 of the UNCRDP refers to states ensuring 'an inclusive education system at all levels' and persons with disabilities not being 'excluded from the general education system on the basis of disability'. This Article continues:

d. Persons with disabilities receive the support required, within the general education system, to facilitate their effective education;
e. Effective individualised support measures are provided in environments that maximize academic and social development, consistent with the goal of full inclusion.

(United Nations, 2006: Article 24 (d) and (e))

Some organisations see the UNCRPD as a clear international statement endorsing inclusive education for disabled children, but the Convention's language is still about included/excluded from the 'general education system' and the provision of individualised support consistent with 'full inclusion'. Separate settings, such as separate classrooms and separate schools might be seen as part of the general education system, compared to some of the historic provision outside education. There is also some vagueness in Article 24e's reference to individualised support consistent with full inclusion: is this limiting the provision of individual support by the goals of full inclusion or is this recognising some tensions between individual support and full inclusion?

It is notable that while many countries have signed the UNCRDP, some have signed UNCRDP with reservations; for example, the UK (English) government because policy has been to have some specialised provision outside mainstream schools and because of the assumed need for parental choice. Those who oppose such reservations consider that too much emphasis is placed on parental choice rather than on the right of the child to be treated without discrimination. Whether going to a specialised separate setting is discriminatory is itself a continuing question that has been discussed above. Also, this playing down of parental choice goes against a key aspect of the original UDHR that parents have a prior right to choose the kind of education that shall be given to their children. That many people take human rights as self-evidently true (Fagan, 2005) and many countries signed the Convention without reservations, does not mean inclusive education can be simply justified as a human right. The self-evidence and moral force of human rights to many people means that rights are less contentious when it is about access to quality schooling. But, rights claims are more open to doubt and different rights can come to conflict when it comes to specialised settings for some children with disabilities. Nor does the pervasiveness of rights language conceal the long-standing nature of the dilemmas associated with human rights (Brown, 1997), which will be examined further in the next sections.

Special educational needs: what went wrong?

The criticisms of the concept of 'special educational needs' were set out in Chapter 2. In this section I will illustrate how the language and concept of needs are never far away from the language of rights and inclusion. The Salamanca Statement (UNESCO, 1994), which first introduced some of the key principles of inclusive education, relied on the concept of need, as shown in this excerpt:

> Education systems should be designed and educational programmes implemented to take into account the wide diversity of these characteristics and needs (statement 8).

Inclusion is defined in this international statement in terms of 'needs' which can be interpreted to mean *what is called for* or *required*. In the more recent UNCRDP, the language of needs has been replaced by the language of *requirement*, for example:

> Persons with disabilities receive the support required.
> *(UNESCO, 2006: Article 24e)*

Though the word 'needs' may have been dropped, the underlying concept of requirement associated with 'needs' has been retained.

Much of the criticism of the language of special educational needs or special needs derives from a critical version of a social perspective that associates 'needs' with an individual deficit model (Tomlinson, 1985). The term 'special', despite its positive lay usage, has also been suspect because of its associations with 'need'; which is seen as separatist and discriminatory. Usually examples are given of the negative use of these terms in everyday situations (Corbett, 1996: Runswick-Cole and Hodge, 2009). Though these examples are neither benign nor neutral, they reflect the underlying stereotypical and prejudiced attitudes to people with disabilities and difficulties in particular contexts as much as the negativity of the terms themselves. In this respect, addressing only the language and not the language in interaction with the underlying attitudes and contexts can lead to a superficial position.

In some English local authorities the term 'SEN' has been replaced by 'additional educational needs', to emphasise that provision was additional to what is generally provided. This contrasted with talk about different provision, which could be seen as divisive and separatist. The term 'additional support needs' came to replace SEN in Scotland as part of a policy development to make the field more inclusive of other children who had additional needs but not disabilities/impairments; for example, for children for whom English was an additional language (SEED, 2003). Similarly, the concept of 'additional needs' was introduced in England under the Every Child Matters initiative to include SEN and disability in addition to other areas of additional needs (DfES, 2006a). This also expressed a more inclusive approach to needed or required additional provision. However, as with the initial Warnock SEN concept, the wider more 'inclusive' additional needs concept has been seen by some commentators as more of the same negativity: the 'repetition of exclusion' (Allan, 2008a). Again, the objection seems to be that 'additional needs' marks out deficits, what Allan has called 'finding the pathological' (p. 35).

In the same way that the SEN term was seen as an expansion of negative labelling, so the additional needs concept is seen as widening the focus on vulnerability and the professional dominance that can go with formal conceptual systems. There is a point in this criticism of the use of the term 'need' with its associations of being needy, vulnerable and dependent. Initially SEN was defined in English legislation (1981 Education Act) to not include those for whom English was an additional language (EAL), keeping the needs of second language learners as separate from learners with disabilities/difficulties. More recently EAL has been included under the Scottish 'additional support needs' concept, but there are still some who oppose this move from an EAL perspective because the needs are seen to arise from different situations. This is a distancing from the vulnerable, which is even more evident in the way that additional provision for those seen as very able, or 'gifted and talented', are not usually seen as having 'special' or 'additional needs'.

My argument is not to deny problems with how the term 'needs' has been used, as argued in Chapter 2 (see the three-dimensions model of need in Chapter 2). Nor is it to deny the ambiguities and uncertainties of its policy use. It is to suggest that more analysis of the term and its place and use within a value framework is necessary to understand and address issues in this field. It is also to suggest that attributing specific needs to some cannot be considered outside the context of human needs for all. This implies that needs are not relevant only to the 'needy' or 'vulnerable' but to all, which can reduce the distancing or 'othering' associated with the use of SEN categories. Dependency is common to all humans, not just those identified as having disabilities/difficulties. This is where the significance of the concept of a continuum of need is evident (in contrast to clear-cut difficulty boundaries) in highlighting the links between different degrees of difficulty and human commonality. It is also important to appreciate that the justification for human rights links needs and rights. Human rights are difficult to justify without some reference to common human interests or needs, with rights seen as protecting basic human interests or needs (Fagan, 2005).

Doyal and Gough (1991) have argued that doubts and abuses of the idea of objective and general (or universal) human needs underlie recent social disillusion and scepticism. They questioned those who argue that it is morally safer and more justifiable to consider needs to be subjective preferences and that individual people and groups decide their own priority goals which they then call needs. These authors recognise that critiques of objective common human needs come from the political right and left wing. For the neo-liberal right, needs are seen as dangerous, with the risk of leading to authoritarian legislation, and even sometimes dismissed as metaphysical fantasy (Gray, 1983). For some on the left, needs are socially and historically relative and open to cultural domination or imperialism. Those in powerful positions can claim to know the interests and needs of those with less power, while ignoring their preferences. So, when 'needs' are used in this way they can be oppressive. However, human rights have also been used oppressively when only more privileged male whites were attributed rights historically. This shows that it is how these concepts are defined and used within a context and framework of values that matters.

Doyal and Gough's analysis rejects the idea of needs as biological or psychological drives in favour of another view of needs as goals that can be generalised to all people. However, in rejecting needs as biological drives, they are not detaching needs from physiological and psychological aspects of humanity. They do this by adopting the idea that these aspects *constrain* but do not *determine* choice and action. The concept they develop builds on the distinction between needs and desires/preferences; a distinction that is based on the idea that needs refer to 'goals which are believed to be universalisable' (p. 39). The key point in this analysis is that the way need is used, as shown in the term special educational needs, can hide why the goals are universalisable. For Wiggins (1985) the key aspect about a need comes from the serious harm resulting from not satisfying the need. So, not satisfying or meeting a need will be against someone's interest, whereas wants are not seen as linked to interests. From this comes the identified structure of needs statements: 'A person needs B in order to C', where it is not the universal aspect that matters, but the efficacy in leading to C and where without C there will be some harm. So, needs statements reveal instrumentality to goals that can become obscured, as often happens when it said of a child that s/he has a special need, without clarifying the goal without which there will be some harm.

From this analysis it is clear that needs depend on clarifying what counts as serious harm and by implication what flourishing and well-being involve. But, if there is disagreement about what is serious harm to well-being, then there can be no consensus about basic needs; which is why, as Doyal and Gough suggest, there are such debates about social policy and morality. So, if there is no escape from one's own culture to find some neutral ground on which to approach need satisfaction, then no clear distinction can be made between needs and wants/preferences. This is the relativist position that Doyal and Gough resist. Their case is based partly on the analysis of the grammar of needs language and partly by appealing to basic and deep human intuition. Wants imply knowing the object of what is desired, while needs do not imply knowing what is needed; for example, vitamins for good health. You can also be said to need something that you do not want; this implies that its use involves something beyond subjectivity, something that exists independently of preferences, depending on what Wiggins calls 'the way the world is' rather than 'the workings of my mind' (Wiggins, 1985:152). But, as Doyal and Gough argue, this is not to accept a simple biological determinism (Midgley, 2005). Their other argument is an appeal to a 'deep moral conviction throughout the world' (Doyal and Gough 1991: 44) that there are basic needs that are generalisable. Their position is not a metaphysical one about an absolute and final set of needs, but that there is a normative force that cannot be easily ignored. In many respects this kind of argument resembles the one for the justification of basic human rights, where the case for them is felt to be morally powerful and one without which a decent life would be hard to imagine (Fagan, 2005). In relation to one of the central tensions discussed in this book, the tensions between realism–relativism have arisen again; last time it was in relation to that nature of knowledge in the design of the curriculum and teaching in Chapter 4. This crucial issue will be addressed again later in this chapter in connection with ontological and epistemological assumptions in research about disabilities and inclusive education.

Based on this position, Doyal and Gough (1991) suggest that basic needs involve physical health and autonomy which are seen as universal in the sense of applying to all human beings, while basic need 'satisfiers' reflect cultural and historical diversity. The link between the 'universal' needs and these relative and local satisfiers are what they call *intermediate needs,* the set of characteristics that generally and positively contribute to basic needs (physical health and autonomy). These involve: nutrition and clean water, protective housing, non-hazardous work setting and environment, health care, security in childhood, significant primary relationships, physical security, economic security, basic education, safe birth control and child-bearing. There are several reasons for starting to introduce this outline theory of human needs. First, it shows that talking about educational needs cannot stand alone: it depends on the interconnection between intermediate needs and the social pre-conditions for need satisfaction. Educational needs are, for example, closely linked to primary relationships, security in childhood and physical health. Second, justification for talking about special or additional educational needs would have to set out what is said to be required within a broader framework of basic and intermediate needs. Third, in this theory basic and intermediate needs provide the basis for what all humans are entitled to, what they might be said to have a basic right to. In this way there are connections between this kind of formulation of needs and human rights. And fourth, a theory such as this connects ideas about basic and intermediate needs with capabilities, the concept introduced by Amartya Sen (Sen, 1985). Doyal and Gough theory draws on Sen's idea of well-being; in particular his distinction between functionings and capabilities, which will be discussed in the next section.

The promise of a capability approach

What Doyal and Gough's theory of need has in common with the capability approach, particularly the one developed by Nussbaum (Nussbaum and Glover, 1995), is the aim of developing a fully universal conception of human capabilities/needs which is dynamic and open-ended, one that is built on a critique of relativism (Gough, 2003). Nussbaum questions three well-known arguments against universalism: 1) from cultural variability and relativity; 2) from the good of diversity; and 3) from paternalism. The argument about capabilities/needs as culturally relative ignores that real cultures are evolving and open, drawing on other outside ideas and practices. As for the good of diversity argument, Nussbaum agrees that this is acceptable until practices cause people some harm. As discussed above, 'causing harm' can be seen as itself relative, but this kind of persistent relativism flounders because of its negative implications (it undermines any expectation that others will stand by or have any concern about one's own personal rights/needs) and ignores commonly held moral convictions. The paternalism argument against universalist approaches can also be seen as double-edged. It is often traditional systems that oppose human rights that are paternalist and controlling. When outsiders attribute human rights to members of a culture, they are endorsing opportunities for members to think and choose for themselves. Though some people interpret universal human rights/capabilities as an outside imposition, it is for those who are affected by the opportunities related to these rights to judge whether rights are alien and unacceptable. It is not for those defending a certain status quo to speak for or against rights. Doyal and Gough's criticism of relativism goes further than Nussbaum's in pointing out how various versions of it denounce universal standards only to support their use when it suits their positions (Doyal and Gough, 1991).

One of the reasons for current interest in capability approaches in the field of disabilities and difficulties (Nussbaum, 2009) is its growing prominence in normative and development economics as well as philosophy. This has led people to see its relevance to the disability field (Mitra, 2006) and special educational needs and inclusive education (Terzi, 2005). The capability approach has addressed various kinds of diversity in a global and development context and been seen as the basis for an approach to social justice allied to a human rights framework. Terzi (2010), who has introduced this approach in the educational field as regards disability, has presented the capability approach as relevant to formulating a principled approach to what is a just educational provision for students with disabilities/difficulties. I consider that another reason for interest in this approach is the limitations and disappointment with current ideas in sorting out issues in the field, both with special educational needs and more recently with inclusive education.

What the capability approach has to offer that breaks new ground is its focus on positive flourishing and opportunities. Hughes (2010) summarises this by saying that the capability approach is about everyone becoming more able to do and become. For Sen a *functioning* is 'an achievement of a person: what she or he manages to do or to be' (1985: 12). As functionings are valuable, they are related to well-being.

Capabilities are those functionings that someone can choose and therefore are positive opportunities to flourish; they are not just freedoms from harm. The capability–functioning distinction reflects Sen's focus on interests and not just actions, which enable people to have capabilities that they can choose not to use.

The capability approach originates from a response to limitations in assessments that measure only desire satisfaction, resources or outcomes (Unterhalter et al., 2007). It focuses on real choices available to people, not just evaluating satisfaction with outcomes or resource input. One of the advantages of the capability approach is that unlike other theories of justice (e.g. Rawls, 2001), human diversity is assumed to be central to this normative framework.

Capability theorists propose that the approach can help define disability in a way that goes beyond the traditional opposition of medical and social models (Terzi, 2010). According to Mitra (2006) disability is a deprivation or limitation in capability or functioning:

> an individual is disabled if he or she cannot do or be the things he or she values doing or being.
>
> (p. 241)

However, other factors (e.g. poverty) can lead to capability deprivation, thus linking impairment/disability into wider social and economic factors relevant to disadvantage. Capabilities range from basic (nutrition, health) to complex (self-respect, happiness), so introducing a wider range of issues than the traditional health focus on disability. Another key aspect of the capability approach is that commodities (or goods) are useful only insofar as they enable functionings. Two people may have the same resources (e.g. money or food), but one may be less able to use these funds because of some personal or social factor, thus converting commodities into capabilities is a key issue from a capability perspective. This is the key way in which the capability approach differs from an approach that evaluates people's positions as regards resources rather than capabilities (Rawls, 2001: Pogge, 2004).

Terzi (2010) uses the capability approach to show how disability is relational in the sense that it depends on the interlocking of personal and social factors. In a similar way, Mitra (2006), based on a previous model by Altman (2001), proposed a three-factor model of disability in which the following broad factors interact to affect someone's capability to function:

1. Personal characteristics, for instance, age, and including impairment; for example, constant pain, sensory impairment.
2. Commodities and resources available; for example, higher costs to achieve a capability.
3. Environment; for example, physical and social barriers.

This model has a basic difference from the social model, as discussed in Chapter 2, in its recognition that impairment can deprive a person of a capability given a particular social context and resource availability. In this sense the capability approach to impairment/disability has links to the bio–psycho–social model adopted in the International Classification of Functioning (ICF: WHO, 1980; see Chapter 3 this volume). The ICF model of disability also makes a distinction between capacity and performance which corresponds to the capability/function distinction. As Mitra (2006) argues, for these reasons the ICF can be seen as a specific exemplification of aspects of a capability approach. However, as I argued in Chapter 3, the ICF still has strong links to the health sphere and needs further development to be applicable to education (c.f. Hollenweger's education development of ICF; Hollenweger, 2011).

Terzi (2005) has advocated the capability approach as relevant to questions about disability in education, suggesting that it goes beyond and helps resolve the dilemmas of differences (Minow, 1990; Norwich, 2008). There are two parts to her argument. The first is that the tension between a social and individual (medical) approach to disability is resolved because the capability approach represents disability in relational terms, as the interaction of social and individual factors. The second part is based on the capability approach's recognition of difference in a normative framework that aims for justice and equality. This, she argues, helps to avoid negative labelling associated with disability and special educational needs. As I have argued before (Norwich, 2008), it is unclear how this resolves specific dilemmas of difference experienced in education, which have been discussed earlier in this book. The capability approach does offer a justification for differential resource allocation in terms of a principled framework. In this sense it addresses the dilemma of difference, but not necessarily resolving it in practice, in terms of the experience and practice of differential resourcing and provision, and the significance attached to these arrangements.

The question of whether a capability approach resolves dilemmas of difference in theory is raised by Pogge (2004), but not in terms of this dilemma as such. Pogge has questioned the way that the capability approach evaluates individual differences to justify additional resources for people with disabilities. He refers to the way in which the capability approach treats differences as a moral concern of 'vertical inequality'. By contrast, differences (e.g. hair colour), that are irrelevant to moral concerns and so irrelevant to additional resourcing, are called 'horizontal inequalities'. Pogge's argument is that the capability approach by evaluating differences as resource worthy can lead to stigmatising people who are less well endowed than others. Pogge's position is to favour a 'resourcist' approach which does not consider personal characteristics as relevant to moral concerns. This resourcist approach focuses instead on equal resourcing as a way of avoiding the risk of stigmatising disabled people.

Pogge's position is therefore to avoid vertical inequalities to prevent stigma, but as Terzi argues, this means that there is no sensitivity to individual requirements. She suggests that the way that Pogge's resourcist position avoids vertical inequalities is to see disadvantage as socially determined or irrelevant. Terzi's argument is that the resourcist position cannot work out whether social arrangements are disadvantageous to a disabled person without reference to her or his functioning. And, such functioning cannot be considered to be fully social determined. So, Terzi draws attention to those differences in functioning that cannot be addressed by environmental changes; for example, when a visually impaired person cannot read social and non-verbal cues in social interaction (note that some differences in functioning can be addressed by environmental changes). She also points out that Pogge's analysis resembles the social model, which refuses to recognise any connection between impairment, disability and disadvantage. In opting for evaluating disabilities in terms of capability limitations, Terzi falls back on denying that recognising such a limitation is *necessarily* stigmatising, any more than it stigmatises other kinds of diversity (e.g. pregnant women). However, though there may be no good reason for stigmatising in terms of capability thinking, there may still be some stigmatising in practice. This brings the argument back to the point that the practical experiences of recognising impairment differences may be stigmatising, so bringing out a difference between resolving dilemmas of difference in theory and practice.

Nussbaum (2009), who has applied the capability approach to people with cognitive or intellectual disabilities, presents the approach as one that goes further than any other theory of justice in addressing questions of respect and equality. In this she is comparing the capability approach with Rawls's theory of justice as fairness based on social contract principles. However, she also recognises that the capability approach only presents a partial theory of social justice and one that sets only a social minimum. In this respect, Nussbaum is clear that the capability approach is not about full equality of capabilities but about reducing capabilities. She interprets Sen's position as being about the currency of justice, the question about the 'equality of what'. For Sen the currency of equality is capabilities and functioning, rather than resources or welfare. But, Nussbaum's approach to defining equality and adequacy is different from Sen's in important ways. She defines a list of ten 'central human capabilities' as a basic minimum as an entitlement that is relevant to a life with human dignity. Sen (1999), who avoids setting capabilities on a universal basis (with a view to designing a just constitution), refuses to endorse specific lists. He opts instead for taking local considerations into account using democratic social choice to decide on capabilities. For Sen, inequalities in capabilities do not have to make claims on governments, so that identifying such inequalities might say little about how they are rectified. Robeyns (2003) notes that Nussbaum with her focus on basic capabilities does not make the distinction between well-being/agency that Sen does. For Sen agency is the key aspect of a capability: as the functionings that someone chooses. Sen's position by contrast to Nussbaums's can also be seen to reflect a more communitarian perspective on entitlement and rights (Brown, 1997).

Deciding on basic capabilities does raise questions about the adequacy versus the equality of capabilities. Nussbaum argues that some capabilities require equality (e.g. capabilities associated with human dignity), but for other capabilities associated with instrumental goods, adequacy may be enough. But how does this distinction relate to educational capabilities and functioning? Are there educational capabilities that require equality and others adequacy and how is this to be decided?

The capability approach has been criticised for being too individualistic, especially by those adopting a communitarian philosophical perspective (Gore, 1997). However, Robeyns (2003) suggests that such criticisms fail to distinguish between ethical and methodological individualism. The capability approach involves ethical individualism in that it takes individuals as the unit of evaluation when considering different social arrangements. But, the capability approach does not depend on ontological individualism: it does not assume that only individuals and their properties exist or that explanations are only in terms of individuals. A related but different criticism of the capability approach is that it does not take enough account of social power and social constraints on choice (Hill, 2003). As Robeyns argues, the capability approach does not analyse the social institutions that underlie power and that have an influence on opportunities. She suggests that this opens the capability approach to different positions depending on the theory of choice adopted. If choice is seen as unconstrained as in economics compared to other fields, such as sociology and gender studies, where it is seen as more constrained, this leads to different normative positions. Robeyns's conclusion is that the capability approach is mainly about the evaluative space, and so can be used with widely different positions on social reality and relationships.

This analysis, while appreciative of the capability approach, points to the key limitations of the approach. It is this dependence on different theories of choice that denies to the capability approach any contribution to the current debates about placement of children with disabilities and difficulties in separate special schools. Is placement in a special or ordinary school a matter of private–personal choice or a matter for public–democratic social choice. The current UK (England) government sees inclusion in school placement as a private matter, not a public policy matter, so its criticism is of the 'bias to inclusion' (DfE, 2011). This tension between choice and equity is central to public policy issues in the UK (Clarke, 2010), as was discussed in the last chapter. Though there has been growing interest in a capability approach to the field of disability in education (Terzi, 2005; Florian et al., 2008; Reindal, 2009), it is important to avoid excessive expectations of what it can offer. This requires critical awareness of its incompleteness and that it needs to be integrated with other approaches. However, the capability approach does provide a renewed ethical approach by highlighting inequalities and providing conceptual resources to address issues in the disability and education field.

Researching inclusive education

In the final sections of this chapter I will examine in more detail some of the epistemological and ontological issues that arise in research about inclusive education. Clough (2000) presented a framework of different approaches relevant to inclusive education, which included: 1) psycho-medical approach; 2) sociological response; 3) curricular approaches; 4) school improvement approach; and 5) disability studies critique. This diversity of research assumptions has been characterised as fragmented, conflicting and not leading to productive dialogues (Dyson and Howes, 2009). This conflict can be illustrated by the stance taken from a disability studies perspective by Oliver (1999) from an emancipatory research perspective that characterises other approaches, called 'research as investigation', as 'parasitic' (p. 183). For Oliver, the solution to parasitic research is not just one of commitment: giving up 'the pursuit of objectivity in researching oppression and decide on which side we are on' (p. 184). His critique extends to disability or inclusion researchers who make a living out of investigating disabled people and who despite their avowed commitment to improving the lives of disabled people, give priority to investigation and their careers over emancipation.

Oliver's trenchant position is in the tradition of research that is called critical or emancipatory, one that rejects approaches that are scientific (positivist) or interpretivist, because they do not prioritise social improvement over investigation. This tension between these traditions, or what some people call paradigms (Denzin and Lincoln, 2005), represents one of the three major dilemmas identified by Hammersley (2003) in social research. Hammersley represents these three tensions as intrinsic to education research and by implication are relevant to inclusive education:

1. What research requires *versus* what policymakers and other 'users' of research want: this tension is over the complexity and unpredictability of research and different agendas for research.
2. Basic *versus* applied inquiry: this is about the balance between 'pure' and practical research.
3. Commitment to the pursuit of knowledge *versus* commitment to social improvement.

The third dilemma represents researchers as having a dual agenda that is not always possible to meet. Commitment to the pursuit of knowledge may not always lead to social improvement; for example, someone may use the research conclusions to negative ends, and a commitment to social improvement may introduce bias into research or reject research knowledge that is seemingly a barrier to social improvement.

At the root of this tension between social improvement and research are different conceptions about the purposes of research. The critical tradition has historical links to Karl Marx's famous statement that 'philosophers have only interpreted the world in various ways, the point is to change it' (Marx, 1845). This tension between a critical and scientific concept of research is evident in different approaches to research on inclusion: is it a matter of evidence about what works or about values and rights? In empirical research about the workings and consequences of various kinds of provisions and settings – 'what works' – reviews of the evidence from international studies have identified a lack of appropriate studies and where there is evidence there is no 'clear endorsement of positive effects of inclusion' (Lindsay, 2007: 1). Some have commented that a general view about inclusion is not open to an empirical research approach, because of the diversity and multifaceted nature of inclusion and questions about it (Hegarty, 1993; Lindsay, 1997). But, there are basically different stances to the purposes and role of research. Lindsay (2007) advocates more focused studies into the mediators and moderators that support optimal education for children with disabilities and difficulties in order to develop evidence-based approaches. Booth (1996), by contrast, adopts a critical position to such empirical research by contending that as inclusion represents a value commitment, it is not subject to empirical validation. From this perspective, if children with a disability in an ordinary class are performing less well academically or socially than similar children in a separate setting, then this implies the need to examine how the ordinary class can be adapted. It does not constitute evidence about the consequences of inclusion. At the root of these positions are differences about values in research and the function and focus of research: is there a single overriding value (e.g. emancipation) versus the interplay between plural values (e.g. 'truth', 'authenticity', usefulness, social improvement) in education and research about education?

Much of the current criticism of evidenced-based approaches to education and inclusive education comes from those who adopt the contemporary form of scepticism, sometimes called postmodern or post-structuralist. These debates have been more vocal and intense in the US field of special education than in the UK, though evident here too (Allan, 2012). For example, Brantlinger (1997) analysed various publications by prominent US special education scholars, who have been wary of the principle of inclusion, the direction of the inclusion movement and criticised inclusion supporters for being subjective, ideological and political (e.g. Fuchs and Fuchs, 1994; MacMillan et al., 1994; Kaufman and Hallahan, 1995). Brantlinger's argument was that these authors were themselves very political and their assumed neutrality and objectivity are problematic. She branded them as traditionalists who see ideology in others but not themselves. This was based on their recurrent use of themes in their criticisms of inclusion supporters; for example, 'the enemy in battle', 'dreamer out of touch with reality' and 'demagogic methods'.

As Brantlinger says herself, it is probably best not to use the term 'ideological' as a term of criticism in these kinds of debates, given its emotionally loaded and ambiguous usage. But, it is interesting that she suggests that the inclusionist ideology is somehow more acceptable than the traditionalist special educationalists' version, because it is explicit and organic to an emancipatory approach to oppressive social structures. This position reveals again a response to the pursuit of knowledge versus social improvement dilemma that opts exclusively for social improvement and in so doing sets up a false dichotomy that favours the assumed advances of oppressed groups over rigour and clarity of ideas. This can be seen in Brantlinger setting up a doubtful dichotomy between the beliefs of traditional special education and inclusive schooling. Many with experience in this field would find it hard to subscribe to such a dichotomy. For instance, she attributes over-generalised beliefs to special education that are not warranted by the specific references she uses. For example, 'Special education teachers are more successful than general education teachers in instructing students identified as disabled' (p. 434) is based on one editorial that reports that there is little evidence that teachers can deliver particular kinds of instruction to students with high and low incidence disabilities in inclusion schools (Fuchs and Fuchs, 1997).

This kind of debate, sometimes called the 'science wars', has persisted as shown by the debate between Kauffman and Sasso (2006) and Gallagher (2006). Kauffman and Sasso start their attack by asserting that postmodernist ideas are 'intellectually bankrupt' (2006: 65). They argue that postmodernists refuse to answer direct and specific points and instead question the motives and politics of the arguer. These authors' major concerns are about what they see as the postmodern pessimism about 'finding truth or effective methods of intervention' (p. 67), based on the position that 'truth floats or is always constructed to suit the interests of those in power' (p. 67). Finding common ground with postmodern ideas is also rejected, because they see postmodern positions as intolerant of science as a tool for advancing education for those with disabilities and difficulties. In defending their position they align themselves with a correspondence approach to truth: that a statement's truth does not depend on who asserts it, but on its correspondence with evidence. They also deploy the usual criticism of relativism associated with postmodern thought: that by deconstructing knowledge and power the postmodern position undermines its own claims to knowledge and makes it impossible to challenge power.

Gallagher (2006), as someone more sympathetic to postmodern positions, is clear and open about the ethical drive behind postmodern and social constructionist ideas. Her approach resembles aspects of Hacking's (1999) analysis, discussed in Chapter 3: that the unmasking or deconstructionist aims of social constructionist thought reveals an ethical commitment. However, Gallagher's main point, one often found in postmodern argument, is that a science of education is not absolutely objective and so this partial objectivity opens scientific methods to subjectivity. This is the central sceptical core of postmodern thinking that has been considered to debase the currency of scientific-based knowledge in the social sciences. Research methods are not seen as neutral nor are observations theory free. Reality cannot be detached from how things appear to humans, there is no 'view from nowhere' and things do not exist apart from the meaning humans bring to them.

The basic problem with these positions is that the debates are not informed by the nuances, humility and wisdom that come from recognising the historic philosophical tensions that have perplexed humankind since Plato and Protagoras. Questions about inclusion in education, as argued previously in this book, do need to address these tensions rather than act them out in a futile 'phoney science wars' (Rorty, 1999). Gallagher (2006) seemingly tries to find common ground with Kaufman and Sasso (2006) by saying that they are in the same position – 'our inability to self-transcend' (Gallagher, 2006: 104) – leaving them with partial objectivity and partial subjectivity. But, this does not incline her to see any legitimate place for fallible science-based knowledge, only for an ethically driven constructivist position.

The problem with the kind of argument deployed by Gallagher is that it sets up a standard of 'absolute knowledge' and if any claims to knowledge fall short of this, then any kind of claim to objectivity in knowledge or 'realism' about what exists is rejected. Advocates of scientific knowledge rarely make such absolutist philosophical claims; they tend to adopt a position that recognises the fallible nature of any claims (Popper, 1972). Even Rorty (1989), who has been identified as postmodern in his philosophical thinking, distinguishes between a reality out there and descriptions of the world that are not. His pragmatic philosophical position is one that criticises a metaphysical realism, not a scientific realism based on the predictive power of empirically based science. Rorty (1999) also appreciates the tensions between fundamental intuitions about knowledge. So, he aligns himself with Hacking's (1999) analysis that resists the oversimplified dichotomy – knowledge as discovered or constructed – and expects more critical analysis of what 'social construction' and 'objectivity' mean. Docx (2011), in addressing whether the appeal of postmodernism has passed, suggests that postmodern thought represented a rejection of the totalitarian impulse (e.g. in Marxist thought) in its questioning that there is no single privileged standpoint. In so doing, he appreciates that postmodern stances challenged dominant discourses and so gave voice to marginalised groups and enabled injustice to be addressed. But, as Docx argues, by deconstructing everything, after the initial challenge presented by postmodern thought, confusion and uncertainty follow. When de-privileging all positions becomes established, what are we left with? As Rorty (1999) notes, critics of the postmodern position wonder why those who argue about social construction do not spend their time proposing some other social construction. Docx's analysis is that when confronted with what we are left with and 'what next?' questions, aggressive postmodernism has the negative unintended consequence of leading to an 'inert conservatism' where market principles dominate (p. 8). Despite its unmaking and deconstructing potential, postmodern scepticism also does not fit with a belief in the emancipatory nature of knowledge. Hammersley (2002) notes the contradiction between the idea of knowledge as emancipatory and a consistent application of scepticism. From this it follows that emancipatory research requires some positive conception of knowledge.

Inclusive education research methodologies

As in other areas of educational research, there are methodological conflicts in inclusive and special needs education research. Central to these have been stances taken to causal explanation and generalisations (sometimes called positivist) by those who support this mode of knowledge and those opposed to it who favour qualitative research approaches (interpretivist). These stances have often been called 'paradigms', drawing on Kuhn's analysis of scientific revolutions in physics. Sometimes, three paradigms have been identified following Habermas (1978): empirical–analytic (positivist), interpretivist and critical. The key aspect of the concept of distinct paradigms has been the assumption that there is a tight link between ontology (what exists), epistemology (what is it to know) and methodology (principles of research methods) (Crotty, 1998). A paradigm therefore cannot be criticised from the assumptions of another paradigm; the only criteria to evaluate some research must be internal to the assumed paradigm – the incommensurability of paradigms. However, there are serious questions about the concept of 'paradigms'. Not only is the very term questionable, given its origin in Kuhn's social analysis of a scientific revolution, but there are also negative consequences to this depiction of research stances. Paradigms in Kuhn's sense were different versions of physics theory as an empirical generalising science, not broad social research approaches based on different philosophical assumptions. Students learning about educational research are often presented with oversimplified and unsophisticated assumptions about paradigms; for example, that positivism has realist ontology, an objectivist epistemology and adopts experimental methodologies. There are also problems with the incommensurability assumption associated with paradigms, as it makes it hard to assess quality and merit in educational research across different methodologies. In addition, the strict distinction between paradigms implies a rejection of the mixing of methodologies and methods, despite the recent moves in this direction and away from methodological purism.

There are different views about mixed methodologies that bear on the usefulness of the 'paradigm' term and the philosophical assumptions underpinning educational research. Some authors see mixed methods as a third paradigm (Johnson and Onwuegbuzie, 2004), while others see this as a confusing position that reinforces the original false distinction between two paradigms (Gorard, 2010). From this perspective, research methodologies and methods can be detached from the epistemology from which they emerge. For Gorard, the key forgotten aspect of research is its design, which involves a choice based on the claims and conclusions to be drawn. Gorard (2010) also reminds us that the logic of analysis cannot be based on simple distinctions between quantitative–qualitative research. Commonalities are evident, for example, inductive and deductive analysis are used in both traditions, qualitative methods use concepts of the typical and degrees of frequency and qualitative researchers often adopt quality checks on research that resemble those used in quantitative research methods. From a different perspective, Luttrell (2005), whose background is ethnography, has argued for the value of sustaining epistemological tensions in educational research rather than dissolving them. However, she advocates a research community of practice where there is a continuum of quantitative and qualitative methodologies along with a range of hybrid strategies.

The justification for mixing methodologies and methods has been what some authors have called pragmatic (Johnson and Onwuegbuzie, 2004), in the sense that the selection of research strategy depends on its practical usefulness. Often the term 'pragmatic' is used in research in its everyday sense of doing what is convenient and practical rather than by some principle. This makes passing reference to pragmatist philosophy without becoming involved in the theoretical issues about the purposes of research. So, there are problems with this cursory use of pragmatist philosophy. As Scott (2007) has argued, if practical considerations determine whether a specific type of social research is appropriate, this concedes that current understanding takes precedence over alternative conceptions, and this leads to a relativism in what counts as knowledge. Pragmatism has been presented as offering an account of research that is pluralistic and goes beyond simple dichotomies, such as theory and practice. It focuses on research (inquiry) as resolving problems that present themselves in experience (Dewey, 1938) and considers that practice is the driving force for inquiry rather than theory. However, to avoid pragmatist ideas leading to a self-defeating relativism Alexander (2006) suggests that a limited conception of transcendence is required. This involves a transcendental pragmatism that is based on ideals that are not dependent on current human activities.

The point of the transcendental aspect in this version of pragmatist thought is to counter a sceptical relativist position, to make it unintelligible. In Alexander's version of transcendental pragmatism, knowledge of causation follows understanding of the meanings, purposes and concepts embedded in historical traditions. Educational knowledge is therefore first qualitative and when quantitative it is to make qualities that we seek to understand more precise. Three implications are drawn from this position. First, educational research requires explicit and well-defended visions of the good, giving prominence to philosophy and ethics. Second, though randomised controlled trials (RCTs) have some place in educational research, their relevance to educational practice depends on particular contextual factors and knowledge. Third, there is a need to take account of the purposive nature of educational practice in making use of empirical generalisations. For example, Fenstermacher (1988) uses the idea of the *practical argument* to relate generalised knowledge (technical rationality) with reflection-in-action. The practical argument links the expression of a desired goal through various premises (situational and empirical) to a particular practice intention. The situational premises relate to specific settings while the empirical premises are testable empirical generalisations. This concept of a practical argument reflects Dewey's interlinking of theory and practice.

Scott (2007) identifies three different approaches that have been used to reconcile quantitative and qualitative stances: alignment involves sequencing different designs in a research programme; compensation involves the use of different designs for different purposes (e.g. generalisation and illumination); and in translation the epistemic form from one stance is translated into another. Scott's point is that all these approaches operate at the level of methods and ignore epistemological and ontological considerations. He is also critical of the pragmatic or what he calls the a-epistemic resolution. His argument is that resolution should be at the ontological level, which is best done by critical realism, the philosophical position developed by Bhaskar (1989). This position was discussed in Chapter 2 in relation to models of disability. The key part of critical realism as regards educational research is that it is realist in recognising that material and social mechanisms exist whether observers know them or not. In this sense it is anti-radical constructionist, though it does not assume absolute knowledge at the ontological level. The realist level is inferred through a transcendental argument: generative mechanisms are inferred as real as these mechanisms are the condition required for causal explanations. It is notable that critical realism used to be called in an earlier version transcendental realism. This analysis shows that despite differences, there is a key similarity between transcendental pragmatism and critical realism. Both depend in different ways on a transcendental argument to avoid self-defeating scepticism and to establish the possibility of a 'view from somewhere'.

Concluding comments

The aim of the chapter has been to pursue some of the prior themes and arguments in the book into philosophical analysis. What has emerged in this chapter are not final solutions or resolutions, but more awareness of basic tensions between a sceptical relativism and some versions of realism. This has been applied to both the social ethical and the knowledge considerations that arise in inclusive education. In relation to educational research and knowledge, a transcendental pragmatist and critical realist resolutions have been discussed, though they are not without their own weaknesses (Hammersley, 2003: Pihlström, 1997). Critical realism has had little impact on thinking about special needs or inclusive education (Burnett, 2007), though as discussed in Chapter 2 it has been used to explore an interactionist concept of disability (Williams, 1999).

In concluding this chapter I want to draw attention to several central points that are relevant to moving forward. I will start with the importance of fostering productive relationships between different theoretical and research perspectives. Dyson and Howes (2009) have identified three ways that are relevant to inclusive education in which this can be done: first, critique needs to be more systematic, robust and even-handed; second, productive relationships can be built into the design of programmes of research; and third, there needs to be more bridge-building between disciplines and greater interdisciplinary collaboration. The next two points exemplify this call for greater robustness in analysis and interdisciplinarity. The first point is about how people talk about 'social construction'. Much has been said about social constructionist perspectives which are unmasking in their ethical aims. This usage and its alignment with emancipatory ethics seems to overlook that there is another version of 'social construction', one in which material things are used by humans for certain social and institutional purposes. When used for social purposes this produces social objects and social facts that have a certain reality. According to Searle (1995), this reality does not depend on individual preference or views but social and institutional functions and their common acceptance. So, the concept of 'disability' could be ontologically intersubjective in the sense that it serves commonly accepted social functions (e.g. entitlement to additional resources). This social existence can produce social facts about disability that can be investigated with an objective epistemology. In other words, disability can be examined for causal relationships with other factors.

The final point is to exemplify how greater depth of critique can take us beyond a simple three 'paradigm' classification of educational research paradigms into positivist, interpretivist and critical, often attributed to Habermas (1978). Habermas's intention in identifying these approaches to knowledge was not to construct a typology of self-contained research methodologies, but to develop a critical philosophy or theory about knowledge and its links to human interests. This involved recognising the distinction between the historic Greek idea of pure theory, disconnected from human practices, and the idea of theory as critique. The central idea in Habermas's conception is of knowledge constituting interests, those interests that drive the purposes and methodology of knowledge construction. In the empirical–analytic approach that involves the testing of law-like generalisations (sometimes called positivist), the interest is technical control over objectified processes. In the historical–hermeneutical sciences, the focus is the understanding of meaning and interpretation of texts. Such inquiry is seen to be directed to achieving consensus in a framework of understanding derived from a cultural–historical tradition: a practical cognitive interest. In critically oriented sciences the goal is to go beyond generalised causal knowledge and practical interpretive understanding to identify regularities that express relations of dependence and power that can be transformed. The key to determining the validity of critical propositions is the self-reflection of those to whom the regularities apply. Habermas's analysis exposes the technical interests concealed in the dominance of the empirical–analytic sciences, while recognising that the power of these sciences derives from their unswerving application of their methods without reflecting on these interests. By focusing on the driving role of human interests, Habermas also shows the links between knowledge and values, expressing similar perspectives to some of the pragmatic philosophical positions discussed above.

9
CONCLUSIONS

Introduction

In this book I have examined tensions and dilemmas that arise from the principles and practices of inclusive education in relation to the education of children and young people with disabilities and difficulties. Though the focus has not been on inclusion in its most general sense, this analysis reflects back on the coherence and usefulness of more generalised ideas and values in inclusive education. Also, while drawing on sources and experiences outside the UK, the detail has been grounded in the systems operating in England.

The terms 'inclusion' and 'inclusive' have become pervasive in society and education, not just in the education of children with disabilities and difficulties. They are used for talking generally about being welcoming, accepted and belonging in groups, organisations and society (e.g. Wrigley, 2003). I have examined how the term came into use in recent decades to represent a contemporary mix of the values of equal opportunity, social respect and solidarity. I have also suggested that it is this mix of values that has contributed to the significant ambiguities in its meaning and use and to the tensions examined here. In this chapter I set out the conclusions by revisiting the initial distinction between hedgehog and fox stances and then summarise the kinds of dichotomies, tensions and dilemmas that arise in educating children with disabilities and difficulties. I also show how these tensions and dilemmas involve not only dilemmas of difference but also tensions between participation–protection, choice–equity and underlying philosophical dilemmas about what exists as real or relative and about knowledge as serving investigatory or emancipatory purposes. There is also a summary of how these tensions have and can be resolved, but this is done more in terms of principles than practical examples. My assumption is that these theoretical positions frame how practical issues are approached and therefore influence how policy and practice decisions are made.

Central position

I have used and applied Isaiah Berlin's distinction between the hedgehog and fox ways of thinking and valuing to understand issues in inclusive education. In so doing I have aligned the hedgehog stance with what I have called ideological purity and the fox stance with ideological impurity: the hedgehog has a single vision and knows one big thing, while the fox knows many things, pursues plural values and recognises some tensions between them. Berlin (1990) suggested that the fox stance does not try to fit varied experiences and values into an unchanging all-encompassing unitary vision, as does the hedgehog stance. When the fox stance goes beyond critique and seeks resolutions to tensions, a pure coherent position is not expected. It is also suspicious of a style of thinking that sets up over-simplified dichotomies and favours one element to the exclusion of others to fit this single principle or position. I have also suggested an extension to the hedgehog–fox distinction by identifying two typical approaches to value and philosophical tensions. In the hedgehog stance, the elements or principles in tension are split from each other with one or more invested with negativity and rejected, while one is invested with positivity and strongly endorsed. There is also in a hedgehog stance an account of a progressive switch or turn from one perspective to the opposite with no connections recognised between these principles. In the fox stance, by contrast, there is openness to connections between the elements or principles in tension. Positive and negative judgements are not confined to one or other element; it is not about either/or but both/and. Resolutions are sought which combine plural values as far as possible with these resolutions open to change over time. But, because values sometimes conflict, there will be hard choices (or dilemmas) that entail some trade-off, some less than perfect solution, involving an 'irreparable loss' (Berlin, 1990: 13). Finally, the hedgehog–fox distinction is better seen as being along a dimension or continuum of difference. This is in keeping with the fox approach adopted in this book and with Berlin's own use of the distinction.

The other central argument in this book is that the tensions and dilemmas in inclusive education involve not only dilemmas of difference (difference as enabling–stigmatising), but also tensions about autonomy–control (between participation–protection, choice–equity) as well as underlying philosophical dilemmas about what exists (as real or relative) and about knowledge (as serving investigation or emancipation). The dilemmas of difference and of autonomy–control can be seen to reflect, following Dahl (1982), dilemmas of plural democracy. In his analysis, individuals and organisations ought to have some autonomy but also be controlled as they have the potential for injustice. Dahl identifies six forms of this dilemma: 1) rights versus utility; 2) a more exclusive versus more inclusive demos; 3) equality amongst individual or amongst organisations; 4) uniformity versus diversity; 5) centralisation versus decentralisation; and 6) concentration versus dispersal of power. The dilemmas of difference align with the more exclusive versus more inclusive demos and the uniformity versus diversity tensions, while the autonomy dilemma aligns with the centralisation versus decentralisation and concentration versus dispersal of power tensions. Seen in this way the central dilemmas related to the education of children with disabilities and difficulties can be linked to wider political and policy issues in a plural democracy.

Addressing tensions and dilemmas in inclusive education

In this section I will summarise why it is important to address these tensions and dilemmas and discuss the approach adopted in addressing them. The main reason why addressing them is important is to maintain integrity in one's stance to problems and issues. This is about the intellectual honesty of avoiding denial and facing difficult experiences, on one hand, and being authentic about values that do and should guide personal and social affairs, on the other. A related reason for addressing tensions and dilemmas is to reduce unnecessary conflicts between opposing positions. This is made possible by seeing the connections between opposing positions, seeing them as different while not conflating them. The kind of unity that results from addressing tensions and resolving dilemmas is not a final definitive and unchanging conclusion: there are no final solutions. In the fox-oriented stance taken in this book, there are different resolutions according to context and perspective. However, some resolutions may endure as settlements over a period of time, but are still open to review with changing circumstances. The kind of unity that can be achieved through this basic stance derives from the shared human experience of engaging in the process of addressing tensions and resolving dilemmas whether as persons, organisations or States. It is a shared endeavour that can bind across difference.

As discussed above, when there are plural values, the aim is to 'have it both or all ways' as far as possible, while recognising that there may be continuing tensions and residual losses. Past resolutions of the autonomy–control and the difference (or differentiation) dilemmas have determined the shape of the current education system. The position of inclusive education in international conventions, national legislation and school systems in practice shows the extent to which inclusive/commonality resolutions to dilemmas of difference make up the current settlement. This settlement has also been built on equity/protection-oriented resolutions to the autonomy–control dilemmas. This settlement has been questioned in some developed countries (e.g. UK, USA) with the rise of interest in and implementation of more choice and participation-oriented resolutions. The implications have been a challenge to various ideas about inclusive education particularly universal or radical versions. This way of thinking about addressing tensions and resolving dilemmas sets the ideas and prospects of inclusive education in a different light. It is also distinct from two other approaches. One is to be indifferent to the tensions and dilemmas, and just combine elements and principles in a relatively uncritical way. The other approach, with which I have been more engaged in this book, approaches the tensions by splitting and polarising the elements, rejecting the negative while working and promoting the positive. The latter reflects the radical or universal inclusion position, which I have examined critically in the book.

I now summarise the key points from the preceding chapters in terms of the approach I have just outlined. Starting with the concept of inclusive in inclusive education, it was clear that the term covers several dimensions and operates at different levels – being multidimensional and multilevel. This relates to the ambiguity in its meaning and the tensions that arise such as 'all under the same roof' versus 'engagement in learning wherever best'. It also underlines how being included with respect to a group or setting may involve being excluded with respect to another: inclusion can go with exclusion. This suggests that using the terms 'inclusion/inclusive' with the dimension and level specified would obviate some of the confusion.

Models of disability

It was argued in Chapter 2 that the opposition between special educational needs and disability in terms of individual deficit ('medical' model) versus social imposition/oppression ('social' model) is untenable. Underlying these tensions are different conceptions of knowledge about disability, knowledge serving emancipatory purposes (as a model for social and political action) and knowledge serving causal explanatory purposes. Tensions within social perspectives on disability also show the impact of different assumptions about the purposes of knowledge production. Oppositions between disability as oppression or disadvantage and special needs as the needs of the individual or the needs for school change (the inclusion turn) are false. The distinction between disablism and disability was also seen to clarify the confusion between disability as a 'restriction on activity' (social) and as 'restricted activity' (individual). So, I argued for a theoretical resolution that integrated concepts of disability as socially and materially produced in an interactive model of disability. This was based on realist assumptions about disability as emergent from bio-social interactions. An integrative model also related to the false splitting between individual and social theories of learning and the development of abilities and disabilities. The policy and practice implications are that both status enhancement reflecting social changes and personal enhancement reflecting individual changes are appropriate, though there are continuing issues about the priority of emphasis of these strategies (Woolf, 2009b).

Identification and categories

Chapter 3 illustrated how terms and category use vary internationally and nationally reflecting a conflation of meanings; for example, the language of needs and of difficulties, and the tension between continua and categories. The use of 'special educational needs' revealed ambiguity between need as the resources and teaching required and as a softer way of referring to difficulties/disabilities. Similarly, 'learning difficulties' has ambiguous meaning as intellectual/cognitive difficulties and as generic difficulties in English legislation for all areas of SEN. The scope of related terms is not always clear and reflects differing positions about who is covered and who not. Categories or labels can have costs and benefits depending on the purpose, perspective, context and kind of label. So, a distinction can be made between 'being a problem' (becoming blamed/humiliated) and 'having a problem' (which can be addressed positively). When learner categories are not taken to represent how things are (realism), but as socially constructed (relativism), this can reflect how ontological positions can be used to support ethical positions (Hacking, 2006; Cigman, 2007a). For example, saying that dyslexia is a social construction can mean that the term need not exist, is bad and should be abandoned. One resolution to this dichotomy is to regard categories as referring to both natural (or indifferent) kinds of things (biological bases) and socially constructed (interactive) kinds of things. Another approach is to regard categories as terms of practical usefulness for intervention and resource claim purposes.

Debates about the value of categories express a dilemma of difference about whether identifying a disability/difficulty is enabling or stigmatising. A theoretical resolution of the dilemma can adopt a three-dimensions model of needs or requirements within a framework that respects all requirements that are: 1) common to all; 2) specific to some; and 3) unique to the individual. A practical resolution of this dilemma can involve combining commonality and differentiation strategies. For example, improving the general school system to better provide for diverse needs alongside individual identification. Remaining issues are addressed by minimising labelling, focusing on strengths, not just difficulties, while being sensitive about labels. Resolutions start with commonality approaches as far as they go, then differentiated approaches come to be used, but where they start depends on how geared the common system is to the diversity of individual needs. This is the basis for the three tiers, or Wave, model (Response to Instruction/teaching strategy) that connects general to specialised teaching. These are used in assessment for teaching or intervention rather than just for labelling. Though non-responding in the RTI strategy can be seen as opposed to individual child assessment, the latter can be used following and with the response to teaching strategy. This model of assessment and identification is based on an interactive model of disability, and can be linked to a bio–psycho–social model associated with an educational version of the ICF (Hollenweger, 2012).

Curriculum

Ideas about inclusive curricula can overlook basic tensions between knowledge-centred, person-centred, society-centred and effectiveness-centred models of what is worth learning. For example, competency/performance models have been seen to threaten core curriculum subjects. Teaching subject knowledge, when seen as facts and information, has been opposed to teaching generic skills, which are thought to be necessary to generate future knowledge. This can be resolved by seeing skills as necessary to advance knowledge, while recognising that using skills depends on knowledge and understanding (Alexander, 2009). The difference between a knowledge-oriented and a skills-oriented curriculum approach expresses opposing epistemological positions about the nature of subject knowledge: whether it is related to social position and interests (a relativist position) versus unrelated and unaffected by the particular knower (a realist position). Young (2007) resolves this tension through a social realist integration that rejects knowledge as either connected to specific situations (relativist) or as context free (Platonic realism). In his position, knowledge is a collective product of the mind (the social aspect) but becomes independent of it (the realist aspect).

A curriculum dilemma of difference (or differentiation) is experienced in curriculum design for all aspects of diversity (e.g. the tensions between vocational and academic programmes (Judge, 1981)), not just over disability and difficulties. Resolutions involve recognising that there are not final solutions to dilemmas, dispensing with historical resolutions and seeking a contemporary balance between values and constraints. Resolving the curriculum differentiation dilemma for disabilities and difficulties was illustrated by identifying four elements: 1) general aims/principles; 2) broad areas of learning; 3) specific content programmes; and 4) class teaching schemes. When combined in terms of when these elements are common to all or differentiated for some, there are five broad options: two where all elements are common to all or differentiated for some, and three veering more to commonality or more to differentiation. The first two 'pure' options are neither politically desirable nor socially viable. In two of the three other options, there can be some areas of learning and specific programmes that are different for some, while the general aims and principles are common to all. When curriculum areas or specific programmes are differentiated or specialised for disability/difficulties, this could be when programmes aim to accept/circumvent an impairment or to remediate functional difficulties. This resolution contrasts with teaching to common specific programme goals in ordinary schools when adaptations are to the level of learning, mode of presentations/response or learning climate and relationships. But, it is possible to adopt both a differentiated circumvent/remedial programme strategy and a common programme adaptation one. Universal design has also sometimes been presented as an alternative to specialised programmes, because of its aim to build in adaptations in advance. This may be one way of avoiding differentiated elements to common programmes, but such advance design may not be universal, implying that specialised programmes may still be required (Shakespeare, 2006).

Pedagogy

Teaching strategies that are useful for specific groups, it was argued, can also be useful for other children too (the 'many kids' argument). However, useful for some others may not necessarily be useful for all children. Inclusive pedagogy also depends on whether inclusive is taken in a universal or moderate sense of the term (Cigman, 2007a). In its universal sense inclusive pedagogy is taken as all learning together, being responsive to individual differences, avoiding ability labelling, grouping or withdrawal (Florian, 2009). But, as a concept and practice, it is based on false dichotomies. Extending what is available in the general class can be seen as extending/adding to generic teaching for some children. Assuming that all children can learn and their learning abilities can change is compatible with recognising learning dispositions. Recognising limits to learning also does not mean that limits are necessarily fixed. Similarly, responding to difficulties in learning as a teaching challenge and opportunity might require identifying a disability or difficulty, if this provides guidance about how to adapt teaching. Inclusive pedagogy, when inclusive is meant in its moderate sense, is therefore consistent with some specialised teaching. It is not a matter of either/or but both/and. However, there are risks of stigma whether selecting learning activities is teacher or child-led.

Inclusive pedagogy with its focus on communities of learners adopts a socio-cultural or social model of learning as participation, which was linked to the social model of disability in Chapter 2. Following a social v. medical model dichotomy, this sets up a split between social and individual models of learning, with the social embraced and the individual rejected. I have argued that though the social and individual levels of analysis are different, they are interconnected: learning as individual acquisition and as participation cannot be separated. Ravet (2011) integrates a rights- and needs-based pedagogic approach in a model which recognises rights to similar and different pedagogy, but talks about distinct rather than specialised pedagogy because the latter has connotations of separate teaching. The tiered Wave model is also relevant to the connection between generic and specialised pedagogy, where what counts as generic depends on how adapted and flexible generic teaching is to individual differences. The idea of a continuum of teaching strategies (Lewis and Norwich, 2004) in which generic strategies are intensified and personalised is also a way of connecting generic to specialised pedagogy. This is where difference is by degree rather than kind and is consistent with the individual differences model of pedagogy (where pedagogy is informed by 'common to all' and unique to individual requirements (see three-dimensions models of educational needs/requirements above). However, in the general differences model, where pedagogy is also informed by 'specific to some' requirements, knowledge about learners' functional difficulties can be relevant to adapting generic teaching strategies. Using specialist knowledge about, for example, autism, can be seen therefore to be part of an inclusive pedagogy.

Schooling

Inclusion in its universal form was defined originally to be opposed to integration, which was taken to be about placement and assimilation. However, this switch from integration to inclusion ignores the links between the two concepts and sets up inclusion as a self-insulating concept; where any failure to thrive by definition cannot be inclusion but is interpreted as integration. Assimilation is also to be replaced by inclusive accommodation, rather than seeing the interlinking between these processes. This is a bi-cultural resolution with the minority retaining some of their own ways while adopting some ways of the dominant group. Inclusion has also been defined as reducing exclusion, so implying that they are opposites. Yet, it is possible for an additional unit in an ordinary school to be inclusive, in providing access to mainstream school, but exclusive as children might sometimes be outside regular class lessons.

A continuum of provision has been seen as providing a resolution between the twin-track alternatives of special versus ordinary school placements for children with disabilities and difficulties. There are other modern forms of mixing elements of separate and general provision, such as, special schools dispersed into special units in ordinary schools, special schools located and connected to ordinary schools (co-located) and reverse integration (settings mainly for children with disabilities/ difficulties take in a diversity of children). Such resolutions have been criticised as flawed in terms of infringing rights (Taylor, 2001) and falsely assuming that provision in special settings cannot be moved to ordinary ones (Booth, 1994). But, these critiques equate provision with physical resources and ignore the curriculum and pedagogic aspects. Teaching might be extended in ordinary classrooms to take account of these adaptations, but there are dilemmas of difference to be confronted there too.

Participation, partnership and preference

When participation gives way to protection rights under some conditions, this does not mean that giving due weight to children's views in other conditions is abandoned. Accepting limits to children's capacity to form a view also requires an assessment of this capacity in relevant contexts, not in general terms, and using methods to foster the child's voice as much as possible. In cases of profound disability, guardians can represent views, though awareness is required of the risks involved in this resolution, which can be addressed to some extent through openness and accountability.

The dilemmas of difference that parents and their children with disabilities and difficulties can experience over labels and various forms of differentiated provision can be resolved through stigma-reducing strategies. This involves finding ways to reduce as far as possible the initial need to have visible differences in provision. If different provision is required, then the visibility of different labels, settings and teaching can be reduced or reframed in more positive terms. This will also include parental and child participation in designing adaptations. For some there is no tension between equity and choice (or parental preference) as parents and young people are seen to prefer that responsible agencies (government, local authorities or schools) provide appropriate adapted ordinary provision (inclusive). However, some may prefer mixed ordinary–separate provision and others to be separate. Where the equity–choice dilemma is recognised, resolutions can be about parents individually or collectively. In an individual regulated choice model, three conditions need to be considered: providers cannot select children, unless very exceptional and strict conditions are met (regulated admissions); residence does not determine access to preferred provision; and funding is calibrated to individual needs. Collective resolutions could also involve parents in collective consumer and citizen approaches, through direct parental consultation and participation and/or community-owned or public service cooperatively owned services (mutual organisations).

Philosophical aspects

The distinction between universal and moderate inclusion is based on different perspectives on the significance of separation and differentiation. Universal inclusion tolerates no separation as this is stigmatising and humiliating; moderate inclusion, which would be better called maximal inclusion, tolerates some separate differentiation. It was argued that universal inclusion is flawed in two ways: 1) it does not recognise that respect is engendered not only through avoiding humiliation, but also through enabling autonomy; 2) there is a difference between feeling humiliated and having a good reason to feel humiliated.

A human rights basis for inclusive education has been defined as opposed to a needs basis, which some see as exclusionary. Policies that link needs with inclusion are regarded as perpetuating exclusion. Sometimes it is implied that a right to access implies a duty to use these rights – which it does not. There is also an inconsistency between invoking universal human rights from an emancipatory social constructionist perspective, and then justifying their use for political/pragmatic reasons. Critiques of needs-based approaches also ignore that the language of rights is strongly connected to language of basic needs. It is not possible to consider special or additional needs outside the human needs of all; needs language is not just about those who are 'vulnerable' or 'needy'.

The debates about the relativist or realist nature of human rights and basic needs underlie significant political disagreements. For those on the political right, human rights can be a dangerous authoritarian threat, while for those on the left, rights can be used for cultural domination. The resolution adopted in this book rejects that there is a final formulation of basic rights and needs and that they are merely relative to culturally dominant groups. It assumes that there is an ethically intuitive normative force for something generalisable that goes beyond subjectivity and particular cultures. In one version, basic needs which can underpin human rights can be seen as 'universal' in being generalisable, with 'needs satisfiers' as historically relative and variable (Doyal and Gough, 1991).

Inclusive education research reflects diverse research methodologies and philosophical stances. There are differing positions about the purposes of knowledge about inclusive education: whether the purpose of knowledge is for social improvement or understanding, and whether knowledge is about 'what works' in inclusive education or about how to promote values and rights. This is the tension between emancipatory and investigatory conceptions of knowledge. Critical perspectives about a science of education (and of inclusive education) set up a scientific approach as aiming for absolute objective knowledge and then find it falling short. This is turned into its opposite, that scientifically based 'knowledge' is subjective, that there is 'no view from nowhere' and reality cannot be detached from how it appears. This critique exaggerates scientific aims, which are not about absolute but fallible knowledge. These points are related to the over-simplified position that knowledge is either discovered or socially constructed. The resolution adopted here is that in the same way that fully context-free knowledge is untenable, so strong relativism becomes self-undermining in making knowledge claims. Post-structural and postmodern positions can also lead to an undermining of emancipatory positions (Hammersley, 2003). The philosophical resolutions adopted in this book assume an interplay between sceptical relativism (how things appear) and a decentring realism (how things are). In the field of values, I have argued more for value pluralism than value relativism (Berlin, 1990). As regards knowledge I have veered in the direction of a critical or social realism, on one hand, and a transcendental pragmatism on the other, sometimes associated with a pragmatic realism (Putnam, 1993).

Concluding commentary

This book has engaged less with the education–inclusion debate – what is more important, education or inclusion? – which can be seen as a political left-wing/right-wing educational debate. To over-simplify, education on the right is about the individual's learning in a strongly knowledge-centred curriculum; on the left, education is about participating in a society-centred curriculum which aims to develop a more socially inclusive society. This is a debate about what is worth learning, the priority to individual or social interests and how schooling connects to wider societal aims. In educating children with disabilities and difficulties, ordinary school inclusion has been criticised for harming the individual educational interests of some children with disabilities/difficulties (Warnock, 2005: Farrell, 2006). In this perspective, the wider social value of children learning together is seen as secondary or overlooked. To many who in their professional practice adopt some kind of inclusive education, this is a strange position because they are strongly committed to the social purposes of education. This is also connected with negative professional and parental responses to the recent English government's criticisms of previous policy as biased to inclusion. For many, inclusion is seen as not only a private parental (or young person's) preference, but also a public policy issue about solidarity and social cohesion.

This book has engaged in debates positioned to the ideological left of centre, specifically on the tension between more radical or universalist and more moderate or balanced positions about inclusion in education. In examining various interrelated tensions and dilemmas, I have tried to keep my own detailed personal views and positions to the side. However, they will have inevitably been expressed in how the argument has been framed and balanced. Another way of framing these differences that leaves me feeling a little uncomfortable is in terms of transformational versus more conservative approaches to inclusion. If these distinctions were placed on a continuum, I would place myself towards the conservative inclusion pole. This is not because I see myself as a political conservative or opposed to social transformation, but because of personal queries about idealism, I veer more towards a 'realist' than a 'utopian' version of idealism. I cannot see the usefulness of rampant scepticism and criticism that cannot be turned eventually into creative and feasible policy and practical improvements. This underlies my arguments for a fox rather than a hedgehog style of thinking about inclusive education. In my view, one of the reasons for adopting this style of thinking is that it bridges divisions, crosses boundaries and so makes for better integrations. But, it also makes space for different perspectives within the limits set by embracing plural values. So, in stating some of my personal views, I recognise that others may adopt others. I see these continuing differences and tensions between progressive and conservative orientations as making for a flourishing intellectual and political life (Russell, 2004).

In conclusion, recognising and embracing plural values means that we cannot always have it all ways – sometimes we can and sometimes not. When not, balancing and hard choices are required and there will be some eventual loss that is hard to accept. So, the fox stance involves living with conflict and ambivalence both personally and socially. This can be seen as just a condition of our humanity. But, I would argue that there are also benefits in recognising this condition positively. On one hand, it gives a sense of personal and socio-political integrity, while on the other hand, it can promote a social cohesion by the mutual recognition of the shared experiences of addressing and resolving tensions and dilemmas. I conclude with a quote: it has been said that 'inclusion is good; full inclusion may be too much of a good thing' (Zigmond and Baker, 1996: 33). This is a colloquial way of bringing out a key point that there are other goods, the plural value position. And finally, I question whether the terms 'inclusion' and 'inclusive' deserve the prominence they have had, while still very committed to the underlying and historic plural values that have driven the endeavour.

REFERENCES

Abberley, P. 1987. The concept of oppression and the development of a social theory of disability. *Disability, Handicap & Society*, 2, 1, pp. 5–19.

Adelman, H.S. 1971. Learning problems: Part I. An interactional view of causality. *Academic Therapy*, VI, pp. 117–123.

Adelman, H.S. and Taylor, L. 2003. Rethinking school psychology (commentary on public health framework series). *Journal of School Psychology*, 41, pp. 83–90.

Ainscow, M. 1998. Would it work in theory? Arguments for practitioner research and theorising in the special needs field. In C. Clarke, A. Dyson and A. Millward, eds., *Theorising special education*. London and New York: Routledge, Ch. 2.

Ainscow, M. 2007. Towards a more inclusive education system. Where next for special schools. In R. Cigman, ed., *Included or excluded? The challenge of the mainstream for some children with SEN*, London: Routledge, Ch. 13.

Ainscow, M. and Muncey, J. 1989. *Meeting individual needs*. London: David Fulton.

Ainscow, M., Booth, T., Dyson, A., with Farrell, P., Frankham, J., Gallannaugh, F., Howes, A. and Smith, R. 2006. *Improving schools, developing inclusion*. London: Routledge.

Alexander, H.A. 2006. A view from somewhere: explaining the paradigms of educational research. *Journal of Philosophy of Education*, 40, 2, pp. 2056–221.

Alexander, R.J. 1992. *Policy and practice in primary education*. London: Routledge.

Alexander, R.J. 2000. *Culture and pedagogy: international comparisons in primary education*. Oxford: Blackwell.

Alexander, R.J. 2009. *Towards a new primary curriculum: a report from the Cambridge Primary Review. Part 2: the future*. Cambridge: University of Cambridge Faculty of Education.

Allan, J. 2005. Inclusion as an ethical project. In S. Tremain, ed., *Foucault and the government of disability*. Ann Arbor: University of Michigan Press, Ch. 14.

Allan, J. 2008a. *Rethinking inclusive education: the philosophers of difference in practice*. London: Springer.

Allan, J. 2008b. The repetition of exclusion. *International Journal of Inclusive Education*, 10, 2–3, pp. 121–133.

Allan, J. 2012. From inclusion to engagement: helping students engage with schooling through policy and practice. *European Journal of Special Needs Education*, 27, 1, pp. 129–131.

Allan, J. and Slee, R. 2008. *Doing inclusive education research*. Rotterdam: Sense.

Alliance For Inclusive Education 2004. *2020 The campaign to end segregated education*. London: Alliance For Inclusive Education.

References

Altman, B.M. 2001. Disability definitions, models, classification schemes, and applications. In G. L. Albrecht, K. D. Seelman and M. Bury, eds., *Handbook of disability studies*. Thousands Oaks, CA: Sage, pp. 97–122.
Ameson, A., Allen, J. and Simonson, E., eds. 2010. Policies and practices for teaching socio-cultural diversity; concepts, principles and challenges in teacher education. Strasbourg: Council of Europe.
APA 2000. *DSM IV-TR: Diagnostic and statistical manual of mental disorders –Text revision*. Fourth edition. Washington, DC: American Psychiatric Association.
Archer, M. 1995. *Realist social theory: the morphogenetic approach*. Cambridge: Cambridge University Press.
Armstrong, D. 2005. Reinventing 'inclusion': New Labour and the cultural politics of special education. *Oxford Review of Education*, 31, 1, pp. 135–151.
Armstrong, A., Armstrong, D. and Spandagou, I. 2010. *Inclusive education: international policy and practice*. London: Sage.
Armstrong, A., Armstrong, D. and Spandagou, I. 2011. Inclusion: by choice or by chance? *International Journal of Inclusive Education*, 15,1, pp. 29–39.
Arnstein, S.R. 1969. A ladder of citizen participation. *Journal of the American Planning Association*, 35, 4, pp. 216–224.
Artiles, A. J. 1998. The dilemma of difference: enriching the disproportionality discourse with theory and context. *The Journal of Special Education*, 32, 1, pp. 322–336.
Artiles, A.J., Bal, A. and King Thorius, K.A. 2010. Back to the future: a critique of response to intervention's social justice views. *Theory Into Practice*, 49, pp. 250–257.
Artiles, A.J., Harris-Murri, N. and Rostenberg, D. 2006. Inclusion as social justice: critical notes on discourses, assumptions, and the road ahead. *Theory Into Practice*, 45, 3, pp. 260–268.
Avramidis, E., Lawson, H. and Norwich, B. 2010. Difficulties in learning literacy. In D. Wyse, R. Andrews and J. Hoffman, eds. *The international handbook of English, language and literacy teaching*. London: Routledge, pp. 389–400.
Badley, E.M. 2008. Enhancing the conceptual clarity of the activity and participation components of the international classification of functioning, disability and health. *Social Science and Medicine*, 66, pp. 2335–2345.
Ball, S.J. 2008. *The education debate*. Bristol: Policy Press.
Barnes, C. and Sheldon, A. 2007. 'Emancipatory' disability research and special educational needs. In L. Florian, ed., *The Sage handbook of special education*. London: Sage, pp. 233–246.
Baron-Cohen, S., Scott, F.J., Allison, C., Williams, J., Bolton, P., Matthews, F.E. and Brayne, C. 2009. Prevalence of autism-spectrum conditions: UK school-based population study. *The British Journal of Psychiatry*, 194, pp. 500–509.
Barton, L. (2003) *Inclusive education and teacher education: a basis for hope or a discourse of delusion*. Professorial Lecture. London University: Institute of Education.
Barton, L. 2005. *Special educational needs: an alternative look*. Online: www.leeds.ac.uk/disability-studies/archiveuk/index.html (accessed 9.11.12).
Barton, L. (ed.) (1997) *The politics of special educational needs*. Lewes: Falmer.
Barton, L. and Tomlinson, S., eds. 1984. *Special education and social interests*. Beckenham: Croom Helm.
Bastiani, J. 1987. *Perspectives on home school relations: parents and teachers, vol. 1*. Windsor: NFER-Nelson.
Bauman, Z. 2004. *Identity*. Cambridge: Polity Press.
Benjamin, S. 2002. *The micro politics of inclusive education*. Buckingham: Open University Press.
Berlak, A. and Berlak, H. 1981. *Dilemmas of schooling: teaching and social change*. London and New York: Methuen.
Berlin, I. 1978. *The hedgehog and the fox*. Chicago: Ivan R. Dee Inc. Publishers.
Berlin, I. 1990. *The crooked timber of humanity*. London: Fontana Press.
Bernstein, B. 1970. Education cannot compensate for society. *New Society*, 15, 387, pp. 344–347.
Berry, J. 1997. Immigration, acculturation and adaptation. *Applied Psychology: An International Review*, 46, pp. 5–68.

Bhaskar, R. 1989. *Reclaiming reality: a critical introduction to contemporary philosophy.* London: Routledge.
Billig, M., Condor, S., Edwards, D., Gane, M., Middleton, D. and Radley, A. 1988. *Ideological dilemmas: a social psychology of everyday thinking.* London: Sage.
Blamires, M. 1999. Universal design for learning: re-establishing differentiation as part of the inclusive agenda. *Support for learning,* 14, pp. 158–163.
Booth, T. 1994. Continua or chimera? *British Journal of Special Education,* 21, 1, pp. 21–24.
Booth, T. 1996. Changing views about research on integration: the inclusion of students with special needs or participation for all? In A. Stigson, R. Curran, A. Labran and S. Wolfendale, eds., *Psychology in practice with young people, families and schools.* London: David Fulton Publishers, Ch. 8.
Booth, T. 2011. The name of the rose: inclusive values into action in teacher education, *Prospects,* 41, pp. 303–318.
Booth, T. and Ainscow, M. 2011. *Index for inclusion: developing learning and participation in schools.* Third edition. Bristol: CSIE.
Booth, T. and Potts, P. 1983. Integration and participation in comprehensive schools. *Forum,* 25, 2, pp. 40–42.
Booth, T., Ainscow, M., Black-Hawkins, K., Vaughn, M. and Shaw, L. 2000. *Index for inclusion: developing learning and participation in schools.* Bristol: CSIE.
Bourdieu, P. 1992. The left hand and the right hand of the state. Interview by Droit, R.P. and Ferenczi, T. Online: www.variant.org.uk/32texts/bourdieu32.html (accessed 3.8.13).
Brantlinger, E. 1997. Using ideology: cases of non-recognition of the politics of research and practice in special education. *Review of Educational Research,* 67, 4, pp. 425–459.
Brighouse, H. 2002. *School choice and social justice.* Oxford: Oxford University Press.
Brighouse, H. 2012. *School choice and educational equality.* Online: http://philosophy.wisc.edu/brighouse/ (accessed 8.11.12).
Brighouse, H. and Swift, A. 2010. School choice for those who have no choice. *Questa,* 1, pp. 6–10.
Brogan, C.A. and Knussen, C. 2003. The disclosure of a diagnosis of an autistic spectrum disorder: determinants of satisfaction in a sample of Scottish parents. *Autism,* 7, 1, pp. 31–46.
Brown, C. 1997. Universal human rights: a critique. *The International Journal of Human Rights,* 1, 2, pp. 41–65.
Burnett, N.B. 2007. Critical realism: the required philosophical compass for inclusion? In *Proceedings Australian Association of Research in Education: Research impacts: proving or improving?* Online: http://eprints.qut.edu.au (accessed 10.11.12).
Burt, C. 1937. *The backward child.* London: University of London Press.
Bury, M. 2000. On chronic illness and disability. In C.E. Bird, P. Conrad and A.M. Fremont, eds., *Handbook of medical sociology.* Fifth edition. New Jersey, PA: Prentice Hall, pp.173–183.
Carroll, J.B. 1989. The Carroll model: a twenty-five year retrospective and prospective view. *Educational Researcher,* 18, 1, pp. 26–31.
CAST 2006. Teaching every student. Online: http://www.cast.org/research/index.html (accessed 20.11.12).
Cigman, R., ed. 2007a. *Included or excluded: the challenge of the mainstream for some SEN children.* London: Routledge.
Cigman, R. 2007b. A question of universality: inclusive education and the principle of respect. *Journal of Philosophy of Education,* 41, 4, pp. 775–793.
Clarke, C., Dyson, A. and Millward, A., eds. 1995. *Towards inclusive schooling.* London: David Fulton.
Clarke, C., Dyson, A., and Millward, A., eds. 1998. *Theorising special education.* London: Routledge.
Clarke, J. 2010. Choice versus equity: antagonism in politics, policy and practice, in SEN Policy Options Group, ed., Choice–equity dilemma in special educational provision. *Journal of Research in Special Educational Needs,* 10, 3, pp. 237–247.

CLDD Research Project 2012. Briefing paper on Autism. Specialist Schools and Academic Trust Research project. Online: http://complexld.ssatrust.org.uk/uploads/9b%20 autism-briefing.pdf (accessed 31.12).
Cline, T. 2011. Diverging approaches to special educational needs in England and Scotland and their implications for children learning English as an additional language. *NALDIC Quarterly*, 8, 4, pp. 5–8.
Clough, P. 2000. Routes to inclusion. In P. Clough and J. Corbett, eds., *Theories of inclusive education*. London: Sage, pp. 1–34.
Conservative Party (2007) *Commission on Special Needs in Education*. Online: www.conservatives.com/tile.do?def=news.story.page&obj_id=137766 (accessed 21.11.12).
Cooper, P. 2004. ADHD. In A. Lewis and B. Norwich, eds., *Special teaching for special children: pedagogies for inclusion*. Maidenhead: Open University Press, Ch. 10.
Cooper, P. and Jacobs, B. 2011. *From inclusion to engagement: helping students engage with schooling through policy and practice*. London: Wiley.
Cook, B.G. and Schirmer, B.R. 2003. What is special about special education? *The Journal of Special Education*, 37, 3, pp. 200–205.
Corbett, J. 1996. *Badmouthing: the language of special needs*. London: Cassell.
Corker, M. 1999. Differences, conflations and foundations: the limits to 'accurate' theoretical representation of disabled people's experience? *Disability and Society*, 14, 5, 627–642.
Corker, M. and French, S. 1999. Reclaiming discourse in disability studies. In M. Corker and S. French, eds, *Disability discourse*. Buckingham: Open University Press, Ch.3.
Critchley, S. 1999. *The ethics of deconstruction*. Edinburgh: Edinburgh University Press.
Crotty, M. 1998. *The foundations of social research: meaning and perspective in the research process*. London: Sage.
Crow, L. 1996. Including all our lives: renewing the social model of disability. In C. Barnes and G. Mercer, eds., *Exploring the divide*. Leeds: Disability Press.
CSIE 2002. *The Inclusion Charter*. Bristol: CSIE.
CSIE 2005. *Segregation trends – LEAs in England 2002–2004*. Bristol: CSIE.
Developmental Adult Neuro-diversity Association 2012. *Neuro-diversity*. Online: www.danda.org.uk/p. (accessed 3.9.12).
Daniels, H. and Hedegaard, M. 2011. *Vygotsky and special educational needs: rethinking support for children and schools*. London: Continuum Publishers.
Dahl, R.A. 1982. *Dilemmas of pluralist democracy: autonomy and control*. New Haven, CT: Yale University Press.
Dart, G. 2007. Provision for learners with special educational needs in Botswana: a situational analysis. *International Journal of Special Education*, 22, 2, pp. 56–66.
Davis, A. 2008. Ian Hacking, learner categories and human taxonomies. *Journal of Philosophy of Education*, 42, 3–4, pp. 441–455.
Davis, P. and Florian, L. 2004. *Teaching strategies and approaches for pupils with special educational needs: a scooping study*. Research Report 516. London: DfES.
de Boer, A., Pijl, S.J. and Minnaert, A. 2010. Attitudes of parents towards inclusive education: a review of the literature. *European Journal of Special Needs Education* 25, 2, pp. 165–181.
De Haan, A.D. 2000. *Social exclusion: enriching understanding of social deprivation*. University of Sussex: Studies in Social and Political Thought.
Denzin, N.K. and Lincoln, Y.S. 2005. *The Sage handbook of qualitative research*. London: Sage.
Derrida, J. 1992. *The other heading: reflections on today's Europe*. P. Braut and M. Naas, trans. Bloomington, IN: Indiana University Press.
DES 1978. *Warnock Committee Report*. London: HMSO.
Dessent, T. 1987. *Making the ordinary school special*. London: Falmer Press.
Dewey, J. 1916. *Democracy and education: an introduction to the philosophy of education*. New York: MacMillan.
Dewey, J. 1938. *Logic: a theory of inquiry*. New York: Henry Holt.
DfE 1994. *Code of Practice: on the identification and assessment of special educational needs*. London: DfE.

DfE 2011. *Support and aspiration; a new approach to special educational needs.* London: DfE.

DfE 2012. *Support and aspiration: a new approach to special educational needs and disability – progress and next steps.* Ref. 000446. London: DfE.

DfES 2001a. *Code of Practice: on the identification and assessment of pupils with special educational needs.* London: DfES.

DfES 2001b. *SEN toolkit.* London: DfES.

DfES 2004. *Removing barriers to achievement: the government's strategy for SEN.* Annesley: DfES Publications

DfES 2005. *Data collection by type of special educational needs.* London: DfES.

DfES 2006a. *The common assessment framework for children and young people: practitioners' guide.* Annesley: DfES.

DfES 2006b. *Government response to Education and Skills Committee report on special educational needs.* London: DfES.

DfES/DRC (Department for Education and Skills/Disability Rights Commission) 2006. *Implementing the Disability Discrimination Act in schools and early years settings.* Nottingham: DfES.

Disability Equality in Education 2005. In defence of inclusion: Warnock challenges the right of disabled children to inclusion. *Times Educational Supplement,* 8 July.

Docx, E. 2011. Postmodernism is dead. *Prospect,* 185. Online: www.prospectmagazine.co.uk/magazine/postmodernism-is-dead-va-exhibition-age-of-authenticism/ (accessed 24.5.12).

Douglas, G. and McLinden, M. 2004. Visual impairment. In A. Lewis and B. Norwich, eds., *Special teaching for special children? Pedagogies for inclusion.* Maidenhead: Open University Press, Ch. 2.

Doyal, L. and Gough, I. 1991. *A theory of human needs.* Basingstoke: MacMillan.

Dumit, J. 2006. Illnesses you have to fight to get: facts as forces in uncertain, emergent illnesses. *Social Science & Medicine,* 62, 3, pp. 577–590.

Dupre, J. 1981. Natural kinds and biological taxa. *The Philosophical Review,* 90, 1, pp. 66–99.

Dyson, A. 1990. Special educational needs and the concept of change. *Oxford Review of Education,* 16,1, pp. 55–66.

Dyson, A. 1999. Inclusion and inclusions: theories and discourses in inclusive education. In H. Daniels and P. Garner, eds., *Inclusive education.* London: Kogan Page, Ch. 3.

Dyson, A., Farrell, P., Polat, F., Hutcheson, G. and Gallannaugh, F. 2004. *Inclusion and Pupil Achievement Research Report 578.* London: DfES.

Dyson, A. and Howes, A. 2009. Towards an interdisciplinary research agenda for inclusive education. In P. Hicks, R. Kershner and P. Farrell, eds., *Psychology for inclusive education.* London: Routledge, Ch. 13.

Ecclestone, K. 2004. Learning or therapy? The demoralisation of education. *British Journal of Educational Studies* 52, 2, pp. 112–137.

Edwards, D. and Mercer, N.M. 1987. *Common knowledge: the development of understanding in the classroom.* London: Methuen.

Edyburn, D.L. 2010. Would you recognise universal design for learning if you saw it? Ten propositions for new directions for the second decade of UDL. *Learning Disability Quarterly,* 33,1, pp. 33–41.

Egan, K. 1998. *The educated mind: how cognitive tools shape our understanding.* Chicago: University of Chicago Press.

Elkins, J., Kraayenoord, C.E. and Jobling, A. 2003. Parents' attitudes to inclusion of their children with special needs. *Journal of Research in Special Educational Needs,* 3, 2, pp. 22–129.

Eraut, M. 2007. Early career learning at work and its implications for universities. In N. Entwistle and P. Tomlinson, eds., *Student learning and university teaching. British Journal of Psychology* Monograph Series II, 4, pp. 113–133.

European Agency for Development in Special Educational Needs (EADSEN) 2003. *Special education across Europe.* Brussels: EADSEN.

European Agency for Development in Special Educational Needs (EADSEN) 2007. *Young voices: meeting diversity in education.* Brussels: EADSEN.

European Agency for Development in Special Educational Needs (EADSEN) 2011. *Teacher education for inclusion across Europe: challenges and opportunities*. Brussels: EADSNE.

Evans, J. and Lunt, L. 2002. Inclusive education: are there limits? *European Journal of Special Needs Education*, 17, 1, pp. 1–14.

Fagan, A. 2005. Human rights. *Internet Encyclopaedia of Philosophy*. Online: www.iep.utm.edu/hum-rts/ (accessed 2.11.12).

Farrell, M. 2006. *Celebrating the special school*. London: Routledge.

Farrell, P. 2000. The impact of research on developments in inclusive education. *International Journal of Inclusive Education*, 4, pp. 153–162.

Farrugia, D. 2009. Exploring stigma: medical knowledge and the stigmatisation of parents of children diagnosed with autism spectrum disorder. *Sociology of Health & Illness*, 31, 7, pp. 1011–1027.

Fenstermacher, G.D. 1988. The place of science and epistemology in Schon's conception of reflective practice. In P.P. Grimmett and E.L. Erikson, eds., *Reflections in teacher education*. New York: Teachers' College Press, pp. 39–46.

Fielding, M. 2004. Transformative approaches to student voice: theoretical underpinnings, recalcitrant realities. *British Educational Research Journal*, 30, pp. 295–311.

Fletcher, J.M. and Vaughn M. 2009. Response to intervention models as alternatives to traditional views of learning disabilities: response to the commentaries. *Child Development Perspectives*, 3, 1, pp. 48–50.

Florian, L. 2007. Reimagining special education. In L. Florian, ed., *The Sage handbook of special education*. London: Sage.

Florian, L. 2008. Special or inclusive education: future trends. *British Journal of Special Education*, 35, 4, pp. 203–207.

Florian, L. 2009. Towards inclusive pedagogy. In P. Hicks, R. Kershner and P. Farrell, eds., *Psychology for inclusive education: new directions in theory and practice*. London: Routledge, Ch. 4.

Florian, L. 2010. The concept of inclusive pedagogy. In G. Hallett and F. Hallett, eds., *Transforming the role of the SENCO*. Buckingham: Open University Press, pp.61–72.

Florian, L. and Black-Hawkins, K. 2011. Exploring inclusive pedagogy. *British Educational Research Journal*, 37, 5, pp. 813–828.

Florian, L. and Kershner, R. 2009. Inclusive pedagogy. In Daniels, H., Lauder, H. and Porter, J., eds., *Knowledge, values and educational policy: a critical perspective*. London: Routledge, pp. 173–184.

Florian, L. and McClaughlin, M., eds. 2008. *Disability classification in education: issues and perspectives*. Thousand Oaks, CA: Corwin Press.

Florian, L., Dee, L. and Devecchi, C. 2008. How can the capability approach contribute to understanding provision for people with learning difficulties? *Prospero*, 14, 1, pp. 24–33.

Frederickson, N. and Cline, T., eds. 1995. *Assessing the learning environments of children with special educational needs*. London: Educational Psychology Publishing.

Frederickson, N. and Cline, T. 2009. *Special educational needs, inclusion and diversity*. Second edition. Maidenhead: McGraw Hill.

Freeman, M. 2000. The future of children's rights. *Children and Society*, 14, pp. 277–293.

Frith, U. 1999. Paradoxes in the definition of dyslexia. *Dyslexia*, 5, pp. 192–204.

Fuchs, D. and Fuchs, L.S. 1994. Inclusive school movement and the radicalisation of special education reform. *Exceptional Children*, 60, 4, pp. 294–309.

Fuchs, D. and Fuchs, L.S. 1997. Editorial: lessons from welfare 'reform'. *Journal of Special Education*, 30, 3, pp. 229–231.

Fuchs, D., Fuchs, L.S. and Stecker, P.M. 2010. The 'blurring' of special education in a new continuum of general education placements and services. *Exceptional Children*, 76, 3, pp. 301–323.

Furedi, F. 2009. *Wasted: why education isn't educating*. London: Continuum International Publishing Group.

Gallagher, D.J. 2006. If not absolute objectivity, then what? A reply to Kaufmann and Sasso. *Exceptionality*, 1492, pp. 91–107.

Gardner, H. 2006. *Multiple intelligences: new horizons*. New York: Basic Books.
Gibbs, S.J. and Elliott, J.G. 2010. Dyslexia: a categorical falsehood without validity or utility. In T.E. Scruggs and M.A. Mastropieri, eds., *Advances in learning and behavioral disabilities: Vol. 2 Literacy and Learning*. Bingley: Emerald, pp. 134–149.
Goacher, B., Evans, J., Welton, J. and Wedell, K. 1988. *Policy and provision for special educational needs*. London: Cassell.
Goodley, D. 2007. Towards socially just pedagogies: deleuzoguattarian critical disability studies. *International Journal of Inclusive Education*, 11, 3, pp. 317–334.
Gorard, S. 2010. Research design: as independent of methods. In A. Tashsakkori and C. Teddlie, eds. *Sage Handbook of mixed methods in social and behavioural research*. London: Sage, pp.237–252.
Gore, C. 1997. Irreducibly social goods and the informational basis of Amartya Sen's capability approach. *Journal of International Development*, 9, 2, pp. 235–250.
Gough, I. 2003. *Lists and thresholds: comparing our theory of human need with Nussbaum's capabilities approach*. WeD Working Paper 01, The Wellbeing in Developing Countries Research Group, University of Bath, Bath, UK. Online: http://eprints.lse.ac.uk/36659/ (accessed 16.9.12).
Gray, J. 1983. *Mill on Liberty: a defence*. London: Routledge.
Gray, P. 2010. Choice and equity: a conflict of principle in services and provision for SEN? In SEN Policy Options Group, ed., *Choice–equity dilemma in special educational provision*. *Journal of Research in Special Educational Needs*, 10, 3, pp. 243–247.
Gregory, S. 2004. Deafness. In A. Lewis and B. Norwich, eds., *Special teaching for special children: pedagogies for inclusion*. Maidenhead: Open University Press, Ch. 2.
Grove N. 1998. English at the edge: a perspective from special needs. *Changing English*, 5, 2, pp. 161–173.
Habermas, J. 1978. *Knowledge and human interests*. London: Polity Press.
Hacking, I. 1999. *The social construction of what?* Cambridge, MA: Harvard University Press.
Hacking, I. 2006. Kinds of people: moving targets. British Academy lecture. Online: www.britac.ac.uk/pubs/src/_pdf/hacking.pdf (accessed 12.11.12).
Hammersley, M. 2002. Research as emancipatory; the case of Roy Bhaskar's critical realism. *Journal of Critical Realism*, 1, 1, pp. 33–48.
Hammersley, M. 2003. Social research today: some dilemmas and distinctions. *Qualitative Social Work*, 2, pp. 25–44.
Hansen, D.L and Hansen, E.B. 2006. Caught in a balancing act: parents; dilemmas regarding their ADHD child's treatment with stimulant medication. *Qualitative Health Research*, 16, 9, pp.1267–1285.
Harding, E. 2009. Obtaining the views of children with profound and multiple learning difficulties. *Educational and Child Psychology*, 26, 4, pp. 117–128.
Hardman, M.L. and Dawson, S. 2008. The impact of federal public policy on curriculum and instruction for students with disabilities in the general classroom. *Preventing School Failure*, 52, 2, pp. 5–11.
Hargreaves, D.1996. *Teaching as research based profession: possibilities and prospects*. London: TTA Annual Lecture.
Harris, R. and Burns, K. 2011. Curriculum theory, curriculum policy and the problem of ill-disciplined thinking. *Journal of Educational Policy*, 26, 2, pp.245–261.
Hart, R.A. 1992. *Children's participation: from tokenism to citizenship*. Florence, Italy: UNICEF.
Hart, S. 1998. A sorry tail; ability pedagogy and educational reform. *British Journal of Educational Studies*, 46, 2, pp. 153–168.
Hart, S., Dixon, A., Drummond, M.J. and McIntyre, D. 2004. *Learning without limits*. Maidenhead: Open University Press.
Haslam, N. 2003. Kinds of kinds: a conceptual taxonomy of psychiatric categories. *Philosophy, Psychiatry and Psychology*, 9, 3, pp. 213–217.
Hastings, R. and Remington, B. 1993. Connotations of labels for mental handicap and challenging behaviour: a review and research evaluation. *Mental Handicap Research*, 6, 3, pp. 237–298.

Hastings, R., Sonuga-Brake, E.J.S. and Remington, B. 1993. An analysis of labels of people with learning disabilities. *British Journal of Clinical Psychology*, 32, pp. 463–465.

Hatcher, P.J., Hulme, C. and Snowling, M.J. 2004. Explicit phoneme training combined with phonic reading instruction helps young people at risk of reading failure. *Journal of Child Psychology and Psychiatry*, 45, 2, pp. 338–358.

Hatzichristou, C. 2002. A conceptual framework of the evolution of school psychology: transnational considerations of common phases and future perspectives. *School Psychology International*, 23, pp. 266–282.

Healy, K. 1998. Participation and child protection: the importance of context. *British Journal of Social Work*, 28, 6, pp. 897–914.

Hegarty, S. 1993. *Meeting special needs in ordinary schools*. London: Cassell.

Hill, M. 2003. Development as empowerment. *Feminist Economics*, 9, 2/3, pp. 117–135.

Hodgson, A. and Spours, K. 2011. Rethinking general education in the English upper secondary system. *London Review of Education*, 9, 2, pp. 205–216.

Hodkinson, A. 2010. Inclusive and special education in the English education system: historical perspectives, recent development and future challenges. *British Journal of Special Education*, 37, 2, pp. 61–67.

Hollenweger, J. 2011. Development of an ICF-based eligibility procedure for education in Switzerland. *BMC Public Health*, 11, Supplement 5, pp.1–8.

Hollenweger, J. 2012. Using the International Classification of Functioning, Disability and Health Children and Youth version in education systems: a new approach to eligibility. *American Journal of Physical Medicine and Rehabilitation*, 91, 13, pp. 97–102.

Honneth, A. 1996. *The struggle for recognition: moral grammar of social conflicts*. London: Policy Press.

Hornby, G. and Witte, C. 2008. Looking back on school – the views of adult graduates of a residential special school for children with emotional and behavioural difficulties. *British Journal of Special Education*, 35, 2, pp. 102–107.

House of Commons Education and Skills Committee 2006. *Special educational needs. Third report of session 2005–06*. London: Stationery Office.

Howe, K.P. and Welner, K.G. 2002. School choice and the pressure to perform: déjà vu for children with disabilities. *Remedial and Special Education*, 22, 4, pp. 212–221.

Hughes, J. 2010. Defining disability in an age of enhancement. Online: http://ieet.org/index.php/IEET/IEETblog (accessed 28.2.12).

Imrie, R. 2004. Demystifying disability: a review of the International Classification of Functioning, Disability and Health. *Sociology of Health and Illness*, 26, 3, pp. 287–305.

Individuals with Disabilities Education Improvement Act (IDEA) 2004. Public Law No. 108–446 (2004). Online: http://frwebgate.access.gpo.gov/cgi-bin/getdoc.cgi?dbname=108_cong_public_laws&docid=f:publ446.108 (accessed 21.11.2012).

Jahnukainen, M. 2001. Experiencing special education. *Emotional and Behavioural Difficulties*, 6, 3, pp. 150–166.

Jeffrey, B. 2006. Creative teaching and learning: towards a common discourse and practice. *Cambridge Journal of Education*, 36, 3, pp. 399–414.

Johnson, R. and Onwuegbuzie, A. 2004. Mixed methods research: a research paradigm whose time has come. *Educational Researcher*, 33, 7, pp. 14–26.

Jordan, R. 2004. ASD. In A. Lewis and B. Norwich, eds., *Special teaching for special children: pedagogies for inclusion*. Maidenhead: Open University Press, Ch. 9.

Jordan, R., Jones, G. and Murray, D. 1998. *Educational interventions with autism: a literature review of recent and current research*. London: DfEE.

Judge, H. 1981. Dilemmas in education. *Journal of Child Psychology and Psychiatry*, 22, pp. 11–116

Jutel, A. 2009. Sociology of diagnosis: a preliminary review. *Sociology of Health & Illness*, 31, 2, pp. 278–299.

Kaufman, J.M. and Hallahan, D.P., eds. 1995. *The illusion of full inclusion; a comprehensive critique of a current special education bandwagon*. Austin TX: Pro-Ed.

Kauffmann, J.M. and Sasso, G.M. 2006. Towards ending cultural and cognitive relativism in special education. *Exceptionality*, 14, 2, pp. 65–90.

Kavale, K.A. and Mostert, M.P. 2004. *The positive side of special education: minimising fads, fancies and follies*. Lanham, MD: Scarecrow Education.
Kay. J. 2004. *The truth about markets: why some countries are rich and others remain poor*. London: Penguin.
Kelly, N. and Norwich, B. 2004. Pupils' perceptions of self and of labels: moderate learning difficulties in mainstream and special schools. *British Journal of Educational Psychology*, 74, 3, pp. 411–435.
Kilbourne, S. 1998. The wayward Americans – why the USA has not ratified the United Nations Convention on the Rights of the Child. *Child and Family Law Quarterly*, 10, pp. 243–256.
King-Sears, M. 2009. Universal design for learning: technology and pedagogy. *Learning Disability Quarterly*, 32, 4, pp. 199–201.
Kripke, S. 1980. *Naming and necessity*. Cambridge, MA: Harvard University Press.
Knight, J. 2002. Crossing boundaries: what constructivists can teach Intensive-Explicit instructors and vice versa. *Focus on Exceptional Children*, 35, 4, pp. 1–15.
Koch, T. 2011. Is Tom Shakespeare disabled? *Journal of Medical Ethics*, 34, pp. 18–20.
Kortering, L.J., McClannon, T.W. and Braziel, P.M. 2008. Universal design for learning; a look at what algebra and biology students with and without high incidence conditions are saying. *Remedial and Special Education*, 29, 6, pp. 352–363.
Kritzer J.B. 2011. Special education in China. *Eastern Education Journal*, 40, 1, pp. 57–63.
Kyriazopoulou, M. and Weber, H., eds. 2009. *Development of a set of indicators for inclusive education in Europe*. Odense, Denmark: European Agency for Development in Special Needs Education.
Lake, J. and Billingsley, B. 2000. An analysis of factors that contribute to parent-school conflict in special education. *Remedial and Special Education*, 21, 4, pp. 240–251.
Lamb, B. (2009) *Lamb Inquiry into parental confidence in special education needs*. London: DCSF.
Lamb, B. 2012. Support and aspiration: cultural revolution or pragmatic evolution? (SEN Green Paper policy paper). *Journal of Research in Special Educational Needs*, 12, 2, pp.107–121.
Landsman, G. 2005. Mothers and models of disability. *Journal of Medical Humanities*, 26, 2/3, pp. 121–139.
Laughlin, F. and Boyle, C. 2007. Is the use of labels in special educational useful? *Support for Learning*, 22, 1, pp. 36–42.
Lave, J. and Wenger, E. 1991. *Situated Learning. Legitimate peripheral participation*. Cambridge: University of Cambridge Press.
Lawson, H., Walte, S. and Robertson, C. 2005. Distinctiveness of curriculum provision at 14 to 16 for students with learning difficulties; opportunities and challenges. *British Journal of Special Education*, 32, 1, pp. 12–20.
Lawton, D. 1989. *Education, culture and the National Curriculum*. London: Hodder and Stoughton.
Lewis, A. 2010. Silence in the context of 'choice' voice. *Children and Society*, 24, pp. 14–23.
Lewis, A and Norwich, B., eds. (2004) *Special teaching for special children? Pedagogies for inclusion*. Maidenhead, Open University Press.
Lewis, A., Parsons, S. and Robertson, C. 2006. My school, my family, my life: telling it like it is. Executive summary. University of Birmingham. London: Disability Rights Commission.
Lewis, A., Davison, I., Ellins, J., Niblett, L., Parsons, S., Robertson, C. and Sharper, J. 2007. The experiences of disabled pupils and their families. *British Journal of Special Education*, 34, 4, pp. 189–195.
Liaisidou, A. 2012 *Inclusive education, politics and policymaking*. London: Continuum.
Lieberman, L.J., Lytle, R.K. and Clarcq, J.A. 2008. Getting it right from the start: employing the universal design for learning approach to your curriculum. *Journal of Physical Education, Recreation and Dance*, 79, 2, pp. 32–39.
Lindsay, G. 1997. Are we ready for inclusion? In Lindsay, G. and Thompson, D., eds., *Values and practices in special education*. London: David Fulton Publishers, pp. 89–103.
Lindsay, G. 2007. Educational psychology and the effectiveness of inclusion/mainstreaming. *British Journal of Educational Psychology*, 77, pp. 1–29.

Low, C. 2007. A defence of moderate inclusion and the end of ideology. In R. Cigman, ed., *Included or excluded: the challenge of the mainstream for some SEN children*. London: Routledge, Ch. 1.

Lundy, L. 2007. Voice is not enough. *British Educational Research Journal*, 33, 6, pp. 927–942.

Luttrell, W. (2005) Crossing anxious borders: teaching across the quantitative–qualitative 'divide'. *International Journal of Research & Method in Education*, 28, 2,183–195.

MacBeath, J., Galton, M., Steward, S., MacBeath, A. and Page, P. 2007. *The costs of inclusion*. Cambridge: National Union of Teachers/University of Cambridge, Faculty of Education.

MacMillan, D.L., Semmel, M.I. and Gerber, M.M. 1994. The social context of Dunn: then and now. *The Journal of Special Education*, 27, pp. 466–480.

Margalit, A. 1996. *The decent society*. Cambridge, MA: Harvard University Press.

Marks, J. 2000. *What are special educational needs? An analysis of a new growth industry*. London: Centre for Policy Studies.

Marx, K. 1845. Theses on Feuerbach. Online: www.marxists.org/archive/marx/works/1845/theses/index.htm (accessed 22.5.2012).

Masschelein, J. and Simons, M. 2005. The strategy of inclusive education apparatus. *Studies in Philosophy and Education*, 24, 2, pp. 117–138.

May, H. 2004. Interpreting pupil participation into practice: contributions of the SEN Code of Practice (2001). *Journal of Research in Special Educational Needs*, 4, 2, pp. 67–73.

McClaughlin, M. and Florian, L., eds. 2008. *Disability classification in education: issues and perspectives*. Thousand Oaks, CA: Corwin Press.

McClaughlin, M., Dyson, A., Nagle, K., Thurlow, M., Rouse, M., Hardman, M. et al. 2006. Cross-cultural perspectives on the classification of children with disabilities. Part II. Implementing classification systems in schools. *The Journal of Special Education*, 40, 1, pp. 46–58.

McDonnell, L.M., McLaughlin, M.J. and Morison, P. 1997. *Educating one and all: students with disabilities and standards based reform*. Washington, DC: National Academy Press.

McGuire, J.M., Scott, S.S. and Shaw, S.F. 2006. Universal design and its applications in educational environments. *Remedial and Special Education*, 27, 3, pp. 166–175.

McLaughlin, J. Goodley, D. Clavering, E. and Fisher, P. 2008. *Families raising disabled children: enabling care and social justice*. Basingstoke: Palgrave Macmillan.

Mead, G.H. 1934. *The works of George Herbert Mead vol. 1 Mind, self and society*. Chicago: University of Chicago Press.

Mental Capacity Act 2005. National Archives. Online: www.legislation.gov.uk/ukpga/2005/9/contents (accessed 6.8.12).

Mercer, C.D., Lane, H.B., Jordan, L, Allsopp, D.H. and Eisele, M.R. 1996. Empowering teachers and students with instructional choices in inclusive settings. *Remedial and Special Education*, 17, 4, pp. 226–236.

Messinger-Willman, J. and Marion, M.T. 2010. Universal design for learning and assistive technology: leadership considerations for promoting inclusive education in today's secondary schools. *NASSP Bulletin*, 94, 1, pp.5–16.

Midgley, M. 2005. *The essential Mary Midgley*. London: Routledge.

Miles, S. and Singal, N. 2010. The Education for All and inclusive education debate: conflict, contradiction or opportunity? *International Journal of Inclusive Education*, 14, 1, pp. 1–15.

Minow, M. 1990. *Making all the difference: inclusion, exclusion and American law*. Ithaca: Cornell University Press.

Mitra, S. 2006. The capability approach and disability. *Journal of Disability Policy Studies*, 16, 4, pp. 236–247.

Mittler, P. 2000. *Working towards inclusive education: social contexts*. London: David Fulton.

Molloy, H. and Vasil, L. 2002. The social construction of Asperger Syndrome: the pathologising of difference? *Disability and Society*, 17, 6, pp. 659–699.

Moore, D., Brown, D., Glynn, T., Hornby, G., Anderson, A. and Jones, L. 2004. *Specialist and resource teachers' role and training requirements*. Volume 1. Wellington: University of Auckland.

Morris, J. 1991. *Pride against prejudice: transforming attitudes to disabilities*. London: Women's Press.

Morton, J. and Frith, U. 1995. Causal modelling: a structural approach to developmental psychopathology. In D. Cichetti and D.J. Cohen, eds., *Manual of developmental psychopathology*. New York: Wiley, pp.357–390.
Muir, R. 2012. Social democratic public services. In J. Denham, ed., *The shape of things to come. Labour's new thinking*. London: Fabian Society.
Myers, J.A., Ladner, J. and Koger, S.M. 2012. More than a passing grade: fostering positive psychological outcomes for mainstreamed students with autism. *Journal of Developmental and Physical Disability*, 23, pp. 515–526.
NLS 2003. *Targeting support: choosing and implementing interventions for children with significant literacy difficulties*. National Literacy Strategy DfES 0201/2003.
Nordenfelt, L. 2003. Action theory, disability and ICF. *Disability Rehabilitation*, 25, 18, pp. 1075–1079.
Norwich, B. 1990. *Reappraising special needs education*. London: Cassell.
Norwich, B. 1993. Ideological dilemmas in special needs education: practitioners' views. *Oxford Review of Education*, 19, 4, pp. 527–545.
Norwich, B. 1996. Special needs education or education for all: connective specialisation and ideological impurity. *British Journal of Special Education*, 23, 3, pp. 100–104.
Norwich, B. 1999. The connotation of special education labels for professionals in the field. *British Journal of Special Education*, 26, 4, pp.179–183.
Norwich, B. 2002a. Education, inclusion and individual differences: recognising and resolving dilemmas. *British Journal of Educational Studies,* 50, 4 , pp. 482–502.
Norwich, B. 2002b. *LEA inclusion trends in England 1997–2001: statistics on special school placements and pupils with statements in special schools*. Bristol: CSIE.
Norwich, B. 2008. *Dilemmas of difference, inclusion and disability: international perspectives and future directions*. London: Routledge.
Norwich, B. 2009. Dilemmas of difference and the identification of special educational needs/disability: international perspectives, *British Educational Research Journal*, 35, 3, pp. 447–467.
Norwich, B 2010. Dilemmas of difference, curriculum and disability: international perspectives. *Comparative Education* 46, 2, pp.113–135.
Norwich, B. and Kelly, N. 2004. Pupils' views on inclusion: moderate learning difficulties and bullying in mainstream and special schools. *British Educational Research Journal*, 30, 1, pp. 43–65.
Norwich, B. and Lewis, A. 2001. Mapping a pedagogy for special educational needs. *British Educational Research Journal*, 27, 3, 313–331.
Norwich, B. and Lewis, A. (2007) How specialised in teaching children with disabilities and difficulties? *Journal for Curriculum Studies*, 39, 2, 127–150.
Norwich, B., Griffiths C. and Burden, B. 2005. Dyslexia-friendly schools and parent partnership: inclusion and home–school relationships, *European Journal of Special Needs Education,* 20, 2, pp. 147–165.
Nussbaum, M. 2009. The capabilities of people with cognitive disabilities. *Metaphilosophy*, 40, 3-4, pp. 331–351.
Nussbaum, M.C. and Glover, J., eds. 1995. *Women, Culture and Development*. Oxford: Clarendon Press.
O'Brien, T. 1998. The millennium curriculum: confronting the issues and proposing solutions. *Support for Learning*, 13, 4, pp. 147–152.
O'Brien, T. 2004. Social, emotional and behaviour difficulties. In A. Lewis and B. Norwich, eds., *Special pedagogy for special children? Pedagogies for inclusion*. Maidenhead: Open University Press, Ch. 13.
OECD 2000. *Special needs statistics and indicators*. Paris: OECD.
OECD 2003. *Diversity, inclusion and equity: insights from special needs provision*. Paris: OECD.
OECD 2007. *Students with disabilities, learning difficulties and disadvantages: policies, statistics and indicators*. Paris: OECD.
Ofsted 2000. *Evaluating educational inclusion: guidance for inspectors and schools*. London: Ofsted.
Ofsted 2010. *The special educational needs and disability review*. Reference 090221. London: Ofsted.

Oliver, M. (1999) Final accounts and the parasite people. In M. Corker and S. French, S., eds., *Disability discourse*. Maidenhead: Open University Press.

Oliver, M. 2004. The social model in action: if I had a hammer? In C. Barnes and G. Mercer, eds., *Implementing the social model of disability: theory and research*, Leeds: The Disability Press, pp. 18–32.

Open University 2006. *Making your teaching inclusive*. Online: www.open.ac.uk/inclusiveteaching/pages/understanding-and-awareness/models-of-disability.php (accessed 14.11.11).

Parsons, S., Lewis, A. and Ellins, J. 2009. The views and experiences of parents of children with autistic spectrum disorder about educational provision: comparisons with parents of children with other disabilities from an online survey. *European Journal of Special Needs Education*, 24, 1, pp. 37–58.

Peace, R. 2001. Social exclusion: a concept in need of definition? *Social Policy Journal of New Zealand*, 16, pp. 17–36.

Percey-Smith, B. and Thomas, N. 2001. *A handbook of children and young people's participation*. London: Routledge.

Peters, S.J. 2003. *Inclusive education: achieving education for all by inlcuding those with disabilities and special educational needs*. Report for Disability Group, Washington: World Bank.

Pihlström, S. 1997. *Pragmatists as transcendental philosophers, and Wittgenstein as a pragmatist*. Online: file:///Users/brahmnorwich/Documents/inclusion%20book/Pihlstrom%20Pragmatists%20as%20Transcendental%201997.webarchive (accessed 28.5.12).

Pinkus, S. 2005. Bridging the gap between policy and practice: adopting a strategic vision for partnership working in special education. *British Journal of Special Education* 32, 4, 1, pp. 84–87.

Pinney, A. 2004. *Reducing reliance on statements: an investigation into local authority practice and outcomes*. Research Report 508. London: DfES.

Pirrie, A. and Head, G. 2007. Martians in the playground: researching special educational needs. *Oxford Review of Education*, 33, 1, pp.19–31.

Plowden Report 1967. *Children and their primary schools: a report of the Central Advisory Council for Education (England)*. London: HMSO.

Pogge, T. 2004. Can the capability approach be justified? *Philosophical Topics*, 30, pp. 167–228.

Polat, F. and Farrell, P. 2002. What was it like for you? *Emotional and Behavioural Difficulties*, 7, 2, pp. 97–108.

Politics.ac.uk 2012. *Grammar schools*. Online: www.politics.co.uk/reference/grammar-schools (accessed 28.2.12).

Pollard, A. 2008. *Reflective teaching: evidence-informed professional practice*. Third edition. London: Continuum.

Popkewitz, T.S. 1984. *Paradigm and ideology in educational research: social functions of the intellectual*. London: Falmer Press.

Popper, K.R. 1972. *Objective knowledge, an evolutionary approach*. Oxford: Oxford University Press.

Porter, J., Daniels, H., Feiler, A. and Georgeson, J. 2011. Collecting disability data from parents. *Research Papers in Education*, 26, 4, pp. 427–443.

Power, A. and Wilson, W.J. 2000. *Social exclusion and the future of cities*. Centre for Analysis of Social Exclusion. CASE Paper 35. London: LSE.

Power, S. and Clark, A. 2000. The right to know: parents, school reports and parents' evenings. *Research Papers in Education*, 15, 1, pp. 25–48.

Preece, D. and Timmins. P. 2004, Consulting with students: evaluating a mainstream inclusion centre. *Support for Learning*, 19, 1, pp. 24–30.

Priestley, M. 2011. Whatever happened to curriculum theory? Critical realism and curriculum change. *Pedagogy, Culture and Society*, 19, 2, pp. 221–237.

Pugh, G., Aplin, G., De'Ath, E. and Moxon, M. 1987. *Partnership in action*. London: NCB.

Putnam, H. 1993. *The many faces of reality*. Illinois: Open Court Publishers.

Qualifications and Curriculum Agency (QCA) 2000. *The National Curriculum: handbook for primary teachers in England: Key Stages 1 and 2*. London: QCA.

Qualifications and Curriculum Agency (QCA) 2002 *Learning difficulties: planning, teaching and assessing the curriculum*. London: QCA.

Rae, A. 1996. *Survivors from the special school system. Action Research Centre for Inclusion*. Bolton: Institute of Higher Education. Online: www.inclusion-boltondata.org.uk/PdfData/Data%202.pdf (accessed 17.9.12.)

Rawls, J. 2001. *Justice as fairness: a restatement*. Cambridge, MA: Harvard University Press.

Ravet, J. 2011. Inclusive/exclusive: contradictory perspectives on autism and inclusion: the case for an integrative position. *International Journal of Inclusive Education*, 15, 6, pp. 667–682.

Reindal, S.M. 2009. Disability, capability and special education: towards a capability theory. *European Journal of Special Needs Education*, 24, 2, pp. 155–168.

Reiseer, R. 2012. *Implementing inclusive education. A commonwealth guide to implementing Article 24 of the UN Convention on the Rights of Persons with Disabilities*. London: Commonwealth Secretariat.

Reynolds, C.R., and Shaywitz, S.E. 2009. Response to intervention: prevention and remediation, perhaps. Diagnosis, no. *Child Development Perspectives*, 3, pp. 44–47.

Reynolds, J. 2010. Jacques Derrida. In *Internet Encyclopaedia of Philosophy*. Online: www.iep.utm.edu/derrida/ (accessed 12.11.12).

Riddick, B. 1996. *Living with dyslexia*. London: Routledge.

Rix, J. 2011. Repositioning of special schools within a specialist, personalised educational marketplace – the need for a representative principle. *International Journal of Inclusive Education*, 15, 2, pp. 263–279.

Rix, J., Hall, K., Nind, M., Sheehy, K. and Wearmouth, J. 2009. What pedagogical approaches can effectively include children with special educational needs in mainstream classrooms? A systematic literature review. *Support for Learning*. 24, 2, pp. 86–96.

Robeyns, I. 2003. *The capability approach: an inter-disciplinary introduction*. Online: www.capabilityapproach.com/pubs/323CAtraining20031209.pdf (accessed 18.5.12).

Rogers, C. 2007. *Parenting and inclusive education: discovering difference, experiencing difficulty*. Basingstoke: Palgrave Macmillan.

Rorty, R. 1989. *Contingency, irony and solidarity*. Cambridge: Cambridge University Press.

Rorty, R. 1999. Phony science wars. *Atlantic Monthly*, November. Online: www.theatlantic.com/past/docs/issues/99nov/9911sciencewars.htm (accessed 24.5.12).

Rose, N. 1985. *The psychology complex: psychology, politics and society in England 1869–1939*. London: Routledge, Kegan and Paul.

Rose, R. 1998. Including pupils: developing a partnership in learning. In C. Tilstone, L. Florian and R. Rose, eds., *Promoting inclusive practices*. London: Routledge, Ch. 7.

Rose, J. 2009. *Identifying and Teaching Children and Young People with Dyslexia and Literacy Difficulties*. London: DCSF.

Rose, R. and Shevlin, M. 2004. Encouraging voices: listening to young people who have been marginalized. *Support for learning*, 19, 4, pp. 155–161.

Roulstone, A. and Prideaux, S. 2008. More policies, greater inclusion? Explaining the contradictions of new labour inclusive education policy. *International Studies in Sociology of Education*, 18, 1, pp. 15–29.

Rouse, M. and Florian, L. 1996. Effective inclusive schools: a study in two countries. *Cambridge Journal of Education*, 26, 1, pp. 71–85.

Runswick-Cole, K. 2008. Between a rock and a hard place: parents' attitudes to the inclusion of children with special educational needs in mainstream and special schools. *British Journal of Special Education*, 35, 3, pp. 173–180.

Runswick-Cole, K. and Hodge, N. 2009. Needs or rights? A challenge to the discourse of special education. *British Journal of Special Education*, 36, 4, pp. 198–203.

Russell, B. 2004. *The history of western philosophy*. London: Routledge.

Russell, G. and Norwich, B. 2012. Dilemmas, diagnosis and de-stigmatization: parental perspectives on the diagnosis of autism spectrum disorders. *Clinical Child Psychology and Psychiatry* 17, 2, pp. 229–245.

Rutter, M. 2011. Research review: child psychiatric diagnosis and classification: concepts, findings, challenges and potential. *Journal of Child Psychology and Psychiatry*, 52, 6, pp. 647–660.

Rutter, M., Tizard, J., Yule, W., Graham, P. and Whitmore, K. 1976. Research report: Isle of Wight Studies, 1964–1974. *Psychological Medicine*, 6, 2, pp. 313–332.

Ryan, D. 2009. 'Inclusion is more than a place': exploring pupil views and voice in Belfast schools through visual narrative. *British Journal of Special Education*, 36, 2, pp. 77–84.

Sayed, Y. and Soudien, C. 2003. Reframing education exclusion and inclusion discourses. *IDS Bulletin*, 34, pp. 9–19.

Scott, D. 2007. Resolving the quantitative-qualitative dilemma: a critical realist approach. *International Journal of Research and Method in Education*, 30,1, pp. 3–17.

Searle, J. 1995. *The construction of social reality*. New York: The Free Press.

Sebba, J. and Sachdav, D. 1997. *What works in inclusive education? – Summary*. London: Barnardo's.

SEED 2003. *Moving forward! Additional support for learning*. Edinburgh: Scottish Executive Education Department. Online:http://scotland.gov.uk/Publications/2003/01/16161/16483 (accessed 20.11.12)

Sen, A. 1985. *Commodities and capabilities*. Amsterdam: Elsevier Science.

Sen, A. 1999. *Development as freedom*. Oxford: Oxford University Press.

SEN Regional Partnership 2004. *SEN regional partnerships and the voice of the child and young person. Case Study 8*. London: DfES.

Sennett, R. 1999. *Work and social inclusion*. Paper presented at Renner Institute, Vienna.

Sfard, A. 1998. On two metaphors for learning and the dangers of choosing just one. *Educational Researcher*, 27, 2, pp. 4–13.

Shakespeare, T. 2006. *Disability rights and wrongs*. London: Routledge.

Silver, H. 1994. *Social exclusion and social solidarity: three paradigms*. IILS Discussion Papers No 69. Geneva: ILO.

Simeonsson, R. 2009. ICF-CY: a universal tool for documentation of disability. *Journal of Policy and Practice in Intellectual disabilities*, 6, 2, pp. 70–72.

Singh, I. 2004. Doing their jobs: mothering with Ritalin in a culture of mother-blame. *Social Science and Medicine*, 59, 6, pp. 1193–1205.

Singleton, C.H. 2009. *Intervention for dyslexia*. Bracknall: The Dyslexia-Specific Learning Difficulties Trust. Online: www.thedyslexia-spldtrust.org.uk. (accessed 10.2.12).

Skelton, T. and Valentine, G. 2003. 'It feels like being deaf is normal': an exploration into the complexities of defining D/deafness and young D/deaf people's identities. *The Canadian Geographer*, 47, 4, pp. 451–466.

Skilbeck, M. 1984. *School-based curriculum development*. London: Harper Education Series.

Slee, R. 2008. Beyond special and regular schooling? An inclusive education reform agenda. *International Studies in Sociology of Education*, 18, 2, pp. 99–116.

Slee, R. 2010. *The irregular school: exclusion, schooling and inclusive education*. London: Routledge.

Slikwa, A. 2010. *From homogeneity to diversity in German education, in educating teachers for diversity – meeting the challenge*. Paris: OECD.

Soder, M. 1989. Disability as a social construct, the labelling approach revisited. *European Journal of Special Needs Education*, 4, 2, pp. 117–129.

Solity, J. 1991. Special needs: a discriminatory concept. *Educational Psychology in Practice*, 7, 1, pp. 12–19.

State of New Jersey 2010. *Choose the best possible education for your child*. State of New Jersey Department of Education. Online: www.state.nj.us/education/parents/special.htm (accessed 3.1.11).

Sternberg, R. 2005. Intelligence, competence and expertise. In A. Elliott and C. Dweck, eds., *Handbook of competence and motivation*. New York: Guilford Press.

Sutherland, G. 1984. *Ability, merit and measurement*. Oxford: Oxford University Press.

Swann Report 1985. *Education for All. Report of the Committee of Enquiry into the Education of Children from Ethnic Minority Groups*. London: HMSO.

Swanson, E.A. 2008. Observing reading instruction for students with learning disabilities. A synthesis. *Learning Disability Quarterly*, 31, pp. 115–133.
Szasz, T. 1974 *The myth of mental illness: foundations of a theory of personal conduct*. New York: Harper & Row.
Tanner, D. and Tanner, L.N. 1980. *Curriculum development*. New York: MacMillan.
TASH 2012. Statement about inclusive education. Online: http://tash.org/advocacy-issues/inclusive-education/ (accessed 10.11.12).
Taylor, S.J. 2001. The continuum and current controversies in the USA. *Journal of Intellectual and Developmental Disabilities*, 26, 1, pp. 15–33.
TDA 2009. *Inclusive teaching and learning for pupils with SEN and/or disabilities, the pillars of inclusion; training toolkit*. London: TDA.
Terzi, L. 2005. Beyond the dilemma of difference: the capability approach to disability and special educational needs. *Journal of Philosophy of Education*, 39, 3, pp. 443–459.
Terzi, L. 2010. *Justice and equality in education: a capability perspective on disability and special educational needs*. London: Continuum.
Thomas, C. 1999. *Female forms: experiencing and understanding disability*. Buckingham: Open University Press.
Thomas, C. 2004. How is disability understood? An examination of sociological approaches. *Disability and Society*, 19, 6, pp. 569–583.
Thomas, G. 1997. Inclusive schools for an inclusive society. *British Journal of Special Education*, 24, pp. 103–107.
Thomas, G. and Feiler, A., eds. 1988. *Planning for special needs: a whole school approach*. Oxford: Blackwell.
Thomas, G. and Loxley, A. 2001. *Deconstructing special education and constructing inclusion*. Buckingham: Open University Press.
Thomas, G. and Vaughn, M. 2004. *Inclusive education: a reader*. Maidenhead: Open University Press.
Thomas, G., Walker, D. and Webb, J. 1998. *Making of the inclusive school*. London: Routledge.
Thurlow, M. 2002. Positive educational results for all students. *Remedial and Special Education*, 23, 4, pp. 195–202.
Tomlinson, S. 1982. *A sociology of special education*. London: Routledge, Kegan and Paul.
Tomlinson, S. 1985. The expansion of special education. *Oxford Review of Education*, 11, 2, pp. 157–165.
Torgeson, J.K., Wagner, R.K., Rashotte, C.A., Rose, E., Lindamood, P. Conway, T. et al. 1999. Preventing reading failure in young children with phonological processing disabilities; group and individual responses to instruction. *Journal of Educational Psychology*, 91, pp. 579–593.
Truss, C. 2008. Peter's story: reconceptualising the UK SEN system. *European Journal of Special Needs Education* 23, 4, pp. 365–377.
UNESCO 1994. *The Salamanca statement and framework for action on special needs education*. Paris: UNESCO.
UNESCO 2001. *Open file on inclusive education: support materials for managers and administrators*. Paris: UNESCO.
UNESCO 2004. *Embracing diversity: toolkit for creating inclusive, learning-friendly environments*. Bangkok: UNESCO.
UNESCO 2005. *Guidelines for inclusion: ensuring access to education for all*. Paris: UNESCO.
UNESCO 2009. *Policy guidelines on inclusion in education*. Paris: UNESCO.
UNICEF 1989. *Convention on the Rights of the Child*. Online: www2.ohchr.org/english/law/crc.htm (accessed 3.7.12).
UNICEF 2009. *Thinking rights. Secondary school resource pack*. London: UNICEF.
United Nations 2006. *Convention on the Rights of Persons with Disabilities and Optional Protocol*. Online: www.un.org/disabilities/documents/convention/convoptprot-e.pdf (accessed 20.11.12).
Unterhalter, E., Vaughn, R. and Walker, M. 2007. *The capability approach and education*. Online: www.capabilityapproach.com/ (accessed 25.10.12).

Vaughn, S. and Fuchs, L.S. 2003. Redefining learning disabilities as inadequate response to instruction: the promise and potential problems. *Learning Disability Research and Practice*, 18, 3, pp. 137–146.

Vaughn, S. and Linan-Thompson, S. 2003. What is special and special education for students with learning disabilities? *The Journal of Special Education*, 37, 3, pp. 140–149.

Vaughn, S. and Schumm, J.S. 1995. Responsible inclusion for students with learning disabilities. *Journal of Learning Disabilities*, 28, 5, pp. 264–270.

Vernon, J. 1999. *Parent partnership: perspectives on developing practice*. Research Report RR162. London: NCB/DfEE.

Ware, J. 2004a. Profound and multiple learning difficulties. In A. Lewis and B. Norwich, eds., *Special teaching for special children? Pedagogies for inclusion*. Maidenhead: Open University Press, Ch. 6.

Ware, J. 2004b. Ascertaining the views of people with profound and multiple learning disabilities. *British Journal of Learning Disabilities*, 32, pp. 175–179.

Warnock, M. 2005. *Special educational needs: a new look*. Impact Series No.11. London: Philosophy of Education Society of Great Britain.

Warnock, M. and Norwich, B. 2010. *Special educational needs: a new look*. L. Terzi, ed. London: Continuum.

Weare, K. 2004. *Developing the emotionally literate school*. London: Sage.

Wedell, K. 1993. *Special education: the next 25 years*. National Commission on Education Briefing No. 14. London: National Commission on Education.

Wedell, K. 2005. Dilemmas in the quest for inclusion. *British Journal of Special Education*, 32, 1, pp. 3–11.

Weiner, B. 1985. An attributional theory of achievement motivation and emotion. *Psychological Review*, 92, 4, pp. 548–573.

Westling-Allodi, M. 2007. Children with cognitive disabilities in a Swedish educational context: reflections from a case study. *Disability and Society*, 22, 6, pp. 639–653.

Wheelahan, L. 2010. *Why knowledge matters in curriculum: a social realist argument*. London: Routledge.

Whitaker, P. 2007. Provision for youngsters with autistic spectrum disorders in mainstream schools: what parents say – and what parents want. *British Journal of Special Education*, 34, 3, pp. 170–178.

White, J. and Barber, M., eds. 1997. *Perspectives on school effectiveness and school improvement*. London: Bedford Way Papers, Institute of Education, London University.

WHO 1980. *International classification of impairments, disabilities and handicaps*. Geneva: WHO.

WHO 2002. *International classification of functioning, disability and health: towards a common language for functioning, disability and health*. Geneva: WHO.

WHO 2007. *International classification of functioning, disability and health*. Geneva: World Health Organisation.

Wiggins, D. 1985. Claims of need. In T. Honderich, ed., *Morality and objectivity*. London: Routledge, Kegan and Paul.

Wilkins, L. 2008. *Learning the hard way: a strategy for special educational needs*. London: Policy Exchange.

Williams, S. J. 1999. Is anybody there? Critical realism, chronic illness and the disability debate. *Sociology of Health and Illness*, 21, 6, pp. 797–819.

Wolfendale, S. 1983. *Parental participation in children's development and education*. London: Taylor and Francis.

Wolff, J. 2009a. Cognitive disability in a society of equals. *Metaphilosophy*, 40, 3–4, pp. 402–415.

Wolff, J. 2009b. Disability, status enhancement, personal enhancement and resource allocation. *Economics and Philosophy*, 25, pp. 49–68.

Wooldridge, A. (1994) *Measuring the mind: education and psychology in England, 1860–1990*. Cambridge: Cambridge University Press.

Worrell, J. and Taber, M. 2009. Special education practices in China and the United States: What is to come next? *International Journal of Special Education*, 24, 3, pp. 132–142.

Wright, K. 2008. Researching the views of pupils with multiple and complex needs; is it worth doing and whose interests are served by it? *Support for Learning*, 23, 1, pp. 32–40.

Wrigley, T. 2003. *Schools of hope: a new agenda for school improvement.* Stoke-on-Trent: Trentham Books Ltd.

Ylonen, A. and Norwich, B. 2012. Using lesson study to develop teaching approaches for secondary school pupils with Moderate Learning Difficulties: teachers' concepts, attitudes and pedagogic strategies. *European Journal of Special Needs Education,* 27, 3, pp. 301–317.

Young, M.F.D. 2007. *Bringing knowledge back in: from social constructionism to social realism in the sociology of education.* Abingdon: Routledge.

Zachar, P. 2000. Psychiatric disorders are not natural kinds. *Philosophy, Psychiatry and Psychology*, 7, pp. 167–194.

Zigmond, N. and Baker, J.M. 1996. Full inclusion for students with learning disabilities: too much of a good thing? *Theory for Practice*, 3, 1, pp. 26–34.

Zigmond, N., Kloo, A. and Volonino, V. 2009. What, where, and how: special education in the climate of full inclusion. *Exceptionality,* 17, 4, pp. 189–204.

Zirkel, P.A., and Thomas, L. B. 2010. State laws and guidelines for implementing RTI. *Teaching Exceptional Children*, 43, 1, pp. 60–73.

INDEX

Abberley, P. 26
ability 81; fixed limits 81
additional needs 39, 138
additional support needs 40, 11, 138
Adelman, H.S. 14
Adelman, H.S. and Taylor, L. 49
ADHD (attention deficit hyperactivity disorder) 37, 45, 46, 88
Ainscow, M. 82, 110
Ainscow, M. and Muncey, J. 18
Ainscow, M. et al. 1, 3, 99, 108
Alexander, H.A. 151
Alexander, R.J. 60, 65, 73, 77, 158
Allan, J. 6, 8, 9, 87, 111, 131, 138, 147
Allan, J. and Slee, R. 5
Alliance for Inclusive Education 136
Altman, B.M. 142
Ameson, A. et al. 2
APA (American Psychological Association) 37
aporias 8
Archer, M. 29
Armstrong, D. 111
Armstrong, D. et al. 5, 92
Arnstein, S.R. 121
Artiles, A.J. 7
Artiles, A.J. et al. 50, 103

ASD (autistic spectrum disorder/autism) 37, 46, 78, 85, 88
Asperger's syndrome 43
assimilation 95
assistive technology 71
attribution theory 5
autistic spectrum condition (ASC) 48
Avramidis, E. et al. 64

Badley, E.M. 53
Ball, S. 126
Barnes, C. and Sheldon, A. 43
Baron-Cohen, S. et al. 48
barrier 21; barrier removing 5; to learning and participation 20
Barton, L. 2, 3, 4, 26
Barton, L. and Tomlinson, S. 18
Bastiani, J. 121
Bauman, Z. 102
behaviour, emotional and social development needs 37
benevolent humanitarianism 18
Berlak, A. and Berlak, H. 62–63, 66
Berlin, I. 6, 9–10, 66, 154
Bernstein, B. 96
Berry, J. 95
Bhaskar, R. 29, 151

bi-culturalism 96
Billig, M. et al. 62, 66–67
bio–psycho–social model 49
Blamires, M. 71
Booth T. 19, 147, 161
Booth T. and Ainscow, M. 5, 20, 22, 38, 44, 54, 55, 113
Booth, T. and Potts, P. 94
Booth, T. et al. 20
Bourdieu, P. 8
Brantlinger, E. 125, 147
Brighouse, H. 126–127
Brighouse, H. and Swift, 126–127
Brogan, C.A. and Knussen, C. 42
Brown, C. 137, 144
Burnett, N.B. 152
Burt, C. 14
Bury, M. 27

CAF (Common Assessment Framework) 39
Capability approach 12, 139–143; as principled approach 141; adequacy versus equality 144
Carroll, J.B. 81
categories: allocating additional resources 47; as diagnostic 42; distinctive characteristics 46; for communication 46; positive social identity 47;
categories, purposes of: practical kinds 46, 43; real or socially constructed 43; useful for teaching 47
causal modelling framework 50
choice–equity dilemma 125–128
Cigman, R. 3, 48, 76, 130, 132–133, 135, 158–159
Clarke, C. et al. 3
Clarke, J. 128
Clough, P. 145
cognition and learning needs 36
collective consumerism 128
commonality stance 47
communication and interaction needs 37

complex needs 39
compromise 8–9
continuum: concept 15; of curriculum approaches 70; of teaching strategies 80, 88–89
Cook, B.G. and Shirmer, B.R. 73, 74, 87
Cooper, P. 70
Cooper, P. and Jacobs, B. 109
Corbett, J. 18, 38, 42, 137
Corker, M. and French, S. 26, 28
creative teaching 80
Critchley, S. 9
critical realism 29, 151
Crotty, M. 149
Crow, L. 27
CSIE (Centre for the Study of Inclusive Education) 99, 106, 135
curriculum: common, 54; commonality – differentiation 11, 54, 62, 63; as chart of culture 57; as classical humanism 56; competency based 59; epistemological dilemmas 61; general skills 60; global rights based 55; inclusive curriculum 54; as learning technology 57; as pattern of learning activity 57; as progressive ideology 56; as structure of form and fields of knowledge 56;

Dahl, R.A. 6, 7, 155
Dart, G. 35
Davis, P. and Florian, L. 73–74, 85
Davis, A. 46
De Boer, A. et al. 123
De Hann, A.D. 94
decent society 132
deconstruction 8
deficit thinking 82
denial of reality 43
Denzin, N.K. and Lincoln, Y.S. 146
Derrida, J. 8–9
Dessent, T. 111
diagnosis as distressing 42

dichotomies 130; integration versus inclusion 2; medical versus social model 120; personal tragedy versus social oppression 29; social versus individual 20; transformational versus conservative 112
differentiation stance 47
difficulties and disabilities 17; high incidence 70
dilemmas: experiencing 15; resolve 18; ideological 62
dilemma of: autonomy–control 62, 155; equal versus additional resource allocation 62; identification 46; common versus diverse school curriculum 61; educational research 146; participation–protection 155; pursuit of knowledge versus social improvement 147; realism–relativism 155; management versus autonomy 62; plural democracy 7, 155; utility–culture 61
dilemmas of difference 6, 8, 47, 115, 153, 155
disabilism 27
disability: as disadvantage 27; discrimination legislation 40; movement 21; people first usage 26; restrictions on activity versus restricted activity 27; as socially disadvantaged–oppressed 30; as social relations concept 27: as ontologically intersubjective 152; studies 21
diversity: homogenising tendency 130
Docx, E. 149
Douglas, M. and McLinden, M. 70
Doyal, L. and Gough, I. 139–141
DSM (Diagnostic Statistics Manual) 37
Dumit, J. 42
dyslexia 43, 45, 46, 51, 70
Dyson, A. and Howes, A. 146, 152
Dyson, A. 3, 19, 20
Dyson, A. et al. 106
dyspraxia 70

EADSEN (European Agency for the Development of Special Educational Needs) 2, 85, 105, 117–118,
EAL (English as additional language) 16, 40, 85, 138
Ecclestone, K. 58
ECM (Every Child Matters) 39
Education for All (EFA) 130, 136
educational sub-normality 17
Edwards, D. and Mercer, N.M. 66
Edyburn, D.L. 71
Egan, K. 56, 65
Elkins, L. et al. 123
emancipatory versus investigatory approach 25
epistemic fallacy 29
Eraut, M. 24
Evans J. and Lunt, I. 6
evidence-based approaches 147

Fagan, A. 2, 135
Farrell, M. 109
Farrell, P. 3
Farrugia, D. 42
Fenstermacher, G. 151
Fielding, M. 118
Fletcher, J.M. and Vaughn, S. 50
Florian, L. 4, 8, 24, 75, 69, 78, 79, 106, 159
Florian, L. and Black Hawkins, K. 75–76, 80
Florian, L. et al. 145
Florian, L. and Kerschner, R. 75
Florian, L. and McClaughlin, M. 52
Frederickson, N. and Cline, T. 17, 51
Freeman, M. 114
Frith, U. 50
Fuchs D. and Fuchs, L.S. 147–148
Fuchs, D. et al. 69
Furedi, F. 58

Gallagher, D.J.148
Gardner, H. 58
general and specialised teaching 89

general differences model 85–86
Gibbs, S. J. and Elliott, J.G. 47, 90
gifted and talented 41
Goacher, B. et al. 14, 17
Goodley, D. 75
Gorard, S. 150
Gore, C. 145
Gough, I. 141
grammar schools 97, 103
Gray, J. 139
Gray, P. 128
Gregory, S. 70
Grove, N. 64
Gulliford, R. 13

Habermas, J. 149, 152
Hacking, I. 43, 134, 143, 148–149, 158
Hammersley, M. 146, 149, 152
Hansen, D.L. and Hansen, E.B. 124
Harding, E. 119
Hardman, M.I. and Dawson, S. 63, 89
Hargreaves, D. 66
Harris, R. and Burns, K. 60
Hart, S. 81, 114
Hart, S. et al. 24, 79
Haslam, N. 45
Hastings, R. and Remington, B. 42
Hastings, R. et al. 17, 42
Hatcher, P.J. et al. 69
Healy, K. 120
Hedegaard, M. 76
hedgehog and fox 9, 154–155
Hegarty, S. 146
Hill, M. 145
Hodgson, A. and Spours, K. 63
Hodkinson, A. 6
Hollenweger, J. 52, 143, 158
Honneth, A. 95
Hornby, G. and Witte, C. 115
House of Commons Select Committee report (2006) 40, 122
Howe, K.P. and Weiner, K.G. 63
Hughes, J. 96, 141

ICF (International Classification of Functioning) 30, 51, 143, 158; compatible with RTI 52
ICIDH (International Classification of Impairments, Disabilities and Handicaps) 51
IDEA (Individuals with Disability in Education Act) 16, 35, 83
ideological purity–impurity 9, 154
impairment–disability duality 26, 28
Imre, R. 53
inclusion: 'all children under same roof' 109; full/radical 83, 101, 131–133, 156; Inclusion Index 55, 98; learning concept 109; moderate 76, 131; multi-dimensional and multi-level 108, 157; never-ending process 20; passionate intuition 1, 102; protect purity 101, 110; radical provocation 110; responsible 131; self-insulating concept 101; universal 76; universal versus moderate 132
inclusive education as ethical provocation 9
inclusive learning friendly classrooms 74
inclusive pedagogy 11, 73, 160; practical issues 82; usefulness 79; versus individualised inclusion 85
inclusive schooling 11, 92; as impairment friendly 111
incommensurability of paradigms 150
individual differences model 85–86
integration 93
intellectual disabilities 43
intelligence 81
intensification 89; personalised 91
intensifying teaching strategies 80
interactionist model 21
interventions: specialist–generalist 69

Jahnukainen, M. 115
Jeffrey, B. 80
Johnson, R. and Onwuegbuzie, A. 150

Jordan, R. 70
Jordan, R. et al. 120
Judge, H. 61, 63, 65, 159
justice as fairness 144
Jutel, A. 42, 82

Kauffman, J.M. and Hallahan, D.P. 147
Kauffman, J.M. and Sasso, G.M. 148
Kavale, K.A. and Mostert, M.P. 69
Kay, J. 125
kinds of things: indifferent–interactive kinds 44; natural or indifferent kinds 46
King-Sears, M. 71
Knight, J. 89
Knowledge: relative–realist options 61
Koch, T. 25
Kraus, K. 8
Kritzer, J.B. 35
Kyriazopoulou, M. and Weber, H. 122

labelling 41; cycle 42
Ladder of Participation 114, 121
Lake, J. and Billingsley, B. 122
Lamb, B. 120, 122
Landsman, G. 124
Laughlin, F. and Boyle C. 42
Lave, J. and Wenger, E. 23
Lawson, H. et al. 64
Lawton, D. 56
learning: as individual and social process 23; participative model 75; socio-cultural theories 75
learning abilities 81
learning difficulty 17; as difficulties in learning 35; versus learning difference 48
Lewis, A. 114
Lewis A. and Norwich, B. 66–67, 70, 80, 87, 160
Lewis, A. et al. 116–119
Lindsay, G. 146–147
Low, C. 101, 110, 131

Lundy, L. 114
Luttrell, W. 150

MacBeath, J. et al. 83
Mace, R. 71, 72
McClaughlin, M. and Florian, L. 15
McClaughlin, M. et al. 64, 124
McDonnell, L.M. et al. 63
McGuire, J.M. et al 71, 72
MacMillan, D.L. et al. 147
'many kinds' argument 85–87, 159
Margalit, A. 132
markets 11; market approach – neo-liberal 6, 125; 'free markets' 125
Marks, J. 38
Marx, K. 146
Marxian approach 44
Masschelein, J. and Simons, M. 75
May, H. 118
Mead, G.H. 62
medical versus social model 21, 26, 44; medical model as individual deficit model 23
Mental Capacity Act (2005) 119
mental disorders: functional impairments 45
mental sub-normality 42
Mercer, C.D. et al. 88
Messinger-Willman, J. and Marion, M.T. 71
Midgley, M. 139
Miles, S. and Singal, N 4, 130
Minow, M. 5, 6, 47, 143
Mitra, S. 141–142
Mittler, P. 3
mixed methodology 150
MLD (moderate learning difficulties) 17, 37, 46, 116
Molloy, H. and Vasil, L. 82
Moore, D. et al. 73
Morris, J. 27
Morton, J. and Frith, U. 50
Muir, R. 128
Myers, J.A. et al. 96

National Curriculum 59, 63, 67; Inclusive Statement 67
National Literacy Strategy (NLS) 49
needs: intermediate 139; sensory and/or physical 37
neuro-diversity 48
neuro-science 46
No Child Left Behind 59, 64
Nordenfelt, L. 52
Norwich, B. 5, 6, 9, 17–18, 42, 47, 49, 64, 66, 97, 109, 143,
Norwich, B. and Kelly, N. 116, 118, 120
Norwich, B. and Lewis, A. 69, 73, 77
Norwich, B. et al. 122
Nussbaum, M.C. 120, 141, 144
Nussbaum, M.C. and Glover, J. 141

O'Brien, T. 64, 70
OECD (Organisation for Economic and Cooperation and Development) 16, 31
Ofsted (Office for standards in education) 39, 83, 98
Oliver, M. 21, 146
ontology 134

paradigms: three-way classification 152
parent partnership 122
Parsons, S. et al. 122
participation 113; in practice 118
partnership 113
Peace, R. 94
Percey-Smith, B. and Thomas, N. 120
personalisation 90
Peters, M. 35
Pihlstrom, S. 152
Pinkus, S. 122
Pinney, A. 34
Pirrie, A. and Head, G. 1, 101, 134
Plowden Report (1967) 121
PMLD (Profound and Multiple Learning Difficulties) 119
Pogge, T. 142–144
Polat, F. and Farrell, P. 115

Pollard, A. 79–80
Popper, K. 61, 149
Porter, J. et al. 40
post-modern approaches 147–148; social constructionism 29
post-structural discursive turn 28
Power, A. and Wilson, W. 94
Power, S. and Clark, A. 121
pragmatism 150–151; transcendental pragmatism 151; transcendental argument 151
Preece, D. and Timmins, P. 109
Priestley, M. 60
Pugh, G. et al. 121
Puttnam H. 173

Rae, A. 116
randomised control trials (RCT) 151
Ravet, J. 85–87, 91
Rawls, J. 142, 144
realism 149
reflective teaching 80
Reindal, S.M. 145
Reiser, R. 135
Response to Instruction (RTI) 49
Reynolds, J. 9
Reynolds, C.R. and Shaywitz S.E. 50
rhizomatic pedagogy 75
Riddick, B. 121
right to inclusion 134
rights: universality 135; and needs 12; respecting teaching 80
Rix, J. 102, 105
Rix, J. et al. 73
Robeyns, I. 144–145
Rogers, C. 4, 122, 124, 130
Rorty, R. 148–149
Rose, J. 90
Rose, N. 14
Rose, R. 119
Rose, R. and Shevlin, M. 125
Roulstone, A. and Prideaux, S. 101, 111–112
Rouse, L.M. and Florian, L. 3

RTI (Response to Instruction) *see* Response to Instruction (RTI)
Runswick-Cole, K. 123
Runswick-Cole, K. and Hodge, N. 42, 135, 137
Russell, G. and Norwich, B. 124
Rutter, M. 42
Rutter, M. et al. 15, 17
Ryan, D. 116

Sayed, Y. and Soutien, C. 96
science wars 148
Scott, D. 150–151
Searle, J. 152
Sebba, J. and Sachdav, D. 3
SEN: ambiguous 157; arguments against 37; Categories A, B and C 32;
Code of Practice 34, 118; devaluing label 18; disabilities, difficulties and disadvantages 32; fit with disability legislation 40; Green Paper (2011) 40; ideological rationalisation 19; not about difficulties and disabilities 37; pedagogy 74; perpetuating negative labelling 38; poorly defined super-category 39; resource focus 37, 41; separatist industry 38
Sen, A. 139–144
Sennett, R. 94
Sfard, A. 23, 75
Shakespeare, T. 3, 24, 50, 72, 110, 159
Silver, H. 94
Simeonsson, R. 51
Singh, I. 42
Singleton, C.H. 90
Skelton, T. and Valentine, G. 117
Skilbeck, M. 56
SLD (severe learning difficulties) 37
Slee, R. 3, 4, 8–9, 46, 110, 112, 130–131
social and emotional literacy 59
social construction 152; social constructionism 4, 134
social exclusion 94–95

social inclusion 54, 94; social integration 94
social realism 61, 159
social recognition 95
Soder, M. 36
solidarity 94
Solity, J. 18, 38, 42
special schools: co-located 161; reverse integration 161
specialisation 4; specialisation of schools 103
specialised programmes 68–69, 72; accept–circumvent 69; address–remediate 69
specialised teaching 77
specialist teacher 77
SpLD (specific learning difficulties) 46
standards accountability 6
Sternberg, R. 81
Sutherland, G. 15
Swann Report 1985 63
Swanson, E.A. 83
systems limitation perspective 20
Szaz, T. 15

Tanner, D. and Tanner, L.N. 56
Taylor, S.J. 161
tensions 9, 65, 153; autonomy–control 11; choice–equity 7; dimensions and categories 37; generic–specialist 7; healthy to recognise 65; in parental perspectives 123; realism–relativism 7, 139; knowledge as investigation–emancipation 7; parental choice–equity of provision 115; participation–protection 7, 115, 119–120, 121; resolved 65
Terzi, L. 141–145
Thomas, C. 27, 30
Thomas, G. and Feiler, A. 93
Thomas, G. and Loxley, A. 4, 23, 69
Thomas, G. and Vaughn, M. 19, 22, 93, 96, 106
Thomas, G. et al. 93

three dimensions model of needs 48, 158
three-tiered model 49
Thurlow, M. 63
Tomlinson, S. 18–19, 38, 44, 137
Torgesen, J.K. et al. 69
Truss, C. 122

UDHR (Universal Declaration of Human Rights) 134
UNCRC (United Nations Convention of the Rights of the Child) 114, 135
UNCRPD (United Nations Convention on the Rights of Persons with Disabilities) 136; Article 24 2
UNESCO 1–3, 54, 74, 92, 130, 135–136; Salamanca Statement 93, 137
UNICEF 80
universal design 11, 70–72
universal inclusive pedagogy 82, 159
universal regulated voucher model 127
Unterhalter, E. et al. 142
utopian 101

value tensions 65; plural values 156
Vaughn, S. and Fuchs, L.S. 49–50
Vaughn, S. and Schumm, J.S. 131
Vernon, J. 120, 128

'wait to fail' model 50
Ware, J. 70, 119
Warnock, M. 17, 109, 122
Warnock, M. and Norwich, B. 110
Warnock Committee Report 11, 13
'Wave' model 49
Weare, K. 58
Wedell, K. 13–14
Weiner, B. 6
Westling-Allodi, M. 123
Wheelan, L. 60
Whitaker, P. 122
White, J. and Barber, M. 66
WHO 143; ICIDH 25
Wiggins, D. 139–141
Wilkins, L. 38
Williams, M. 29, 152
Wolfendale, S. 121
Wolff, J. 6, 125, 157
Wooldridge, A. 15
World Health Organization (WHO) 51
Worrell, J. and Taber, M. 35
Wright, K. 119
Wrigley, T. 154

Ylonen, A. and Norwich, B. 102
Young, M.F.D. 60, 61, 159

Zacher, P. 45
Zigmond, N. et al. 83
Zirkel, P.A. and Thomas, L.B. 50